The Religious Sublime

South Atlantic Modern Language Association Award Study

David B. Morris

The Religious Sublime

Christian Poetry
and Critical Tradition
in 18th-Century England

The University Press of Kentucky

Frontispiece:
Altarpiece formerly at Magdalen College, Oxford,
painted by Isaac Fuller (frontispiece to the fourth edition
of Joseph Addison's poem *The Resurrection*)

ISBN: 0–8131–1270–2

Library of Congress Catalog Card Number: 70–190534

Copyright © 1972 by The University Press of Kentucky

A statewide cooperative scholarly publishing agency
serving Berea College, Centre College of Kentucky,
Eastern Kentucky University, Kentucky Historical Society,
Kentucky State College, Morehead State University, Murray
State University, University of Kentucky, University of
Louisville, and Western Kentucky University

Editorial and Sales Offices: Lexington, Kentucky 40506

To Dee

Contents

Acknowledgments

To my teacher and friend Samuel Holt Monk I owe much more than thanks. He first helped me approach this subject in a doctoral dissertation and has stood by unfailingly during my subsequent revisions. Praise, like thanks, is equally unnecessary to a scholar who perfectly resembles Pope's description: "Still pleas'd to teach, and yet not proud to know." My affection and esteem, then, are all that I can possibly convey in wishing that this book could be worthy of the man.

Another debt of thanks is a great pleasure to mention here. Martin Battestin and Ralph Cohen have in different but important ways helped me to understand the possibilities of my subject. Credit for such ponderous assistance would no doubt alarm them: to a large extent, they did not provide direct advice but a more subtle and exemplary direction. By trying to understand their work I gradually came to know more of my own.

For their comments on particular parts of the manuscript, I would like especially to thank Paul K. Alkon, Walter John Hipple, Jr., and my friend the late Robert D. Saltz. I am also grateful to the University of Virginia for timely and generous fellowship aid. Robert D. Hume graciously assisted me in reading proof. Whatever errors remain are, I regret to say, my own.

My wife, Dee, assisted unsparingly. Of her profounder help, Longinus has taught me that silence is the only true expression.

Introduction

The *sublime* arises from the nobleness
of thoughts, the magnificence of the
words, or the harmonious and lively
turn of the phrase; the perfect *sublime*
arises from all three together (Jo-
seph Addison, quoted in Johnson's
Dictionary).

The discovery of the sublime was one of the great adventures
of eighteenth-century England: accompanying the establishment
of a commercial empire, the growth of industrialism, the inven-
tion of the common reader, and the rise of the waltz, a taste de-
veloped among almost all classes of society for the qualities of
wildness, grandeur, and overwhelming power which, in a flash
of intensity, could ravish the soul with a sudden transport of
thought or feeling. In an age conscious of man's limited middle
state, sublimity lifted men above the daily world of prudence; in
an age of reason, it temporarily teased men out of thought-
constricting systems of belief. Sublimity liberated the eighteenth-
century imagination from all that was little, pretty, rational,
regular, and safe—although only for as long as the moment of
intensity could be sustained. It spans the chasm separating Pope's
"Messiah" from Blake's prophetic books, and it is one of the few
literary topics on which Addison and Wordsworth would find
much to agree. The history of taste provides no better example
of an aesthetic idea which, emerging with apparent suddenness,
virtually dominated the imagination of an entire century.

The study of sublimity in the eighteenth century has attracted
some of the best scholars of our day. Samuel Monk in 1935 initi-
ated modern interest with his valuable book *The Sublime: A
Study of Critical Theories in XVIII-Century England* (rpt.

Ann Arbor, Mich., 1960). Subsequently, both Ernest Tuveson[1] and Marjorie Nicolson[2] have clarified the scientific and philosophical implications of the taste for sublimity in nature, while Josephine Miles[3] and Martin Price[4] have attempted, using different strategies, to define the special eighteenth-century mode of the "sublime poem." It seems entirely appropriate that the sublime should comprise a subject too vast for a single scholar to discuss fully and that much work still remains to be done. My own study, then, is meant to supplement—not, by any means, to supersede—the investigations of those who have written already on the sublime. Its aim is to treat an aspect of the subject which deserves to be rescued from neglect: that is, the close association between sublimity and religious poetry in eighteenth-century England.

The general relationship between sublimity and religion has been attributed in the past to three main causes: the impact of Newtonian science, the influence of physico-theological thought, and the implications of Lockean epistemology. Newton in effect deified the concept of immensity by calling space the vast sensorium of God. The empty interstellar reaches, which had terrified Pascal with thoughts of nothingness, could be comfortingly addressed by Addison as evidence of God's stupendous handiwork, and the notion of the universe as a sublime but explicable artifact blended easily with the physico-theological doctrine of fitness: from the wheeling of the planets to the operation of the bladder—the last being Cotton Mather's solemn contribution to the encyclopedia of physico-theological lore—the created universe was held to show a world instinct with purpose. Thus, even the wildest and apparently most irregular aspects of nature, which earlier ages had shunned, could be explained as part of the divine economy and appreciated as revelations of God's power and wisdom. Certainly the new enthusiasm for scientific and rationalistic explanations of the natural world helped to support the doctrine of fitness, but perhaps an additional reason for its popularity was its usefulness in filling the void created by Locke's rejection of innate ideas. Unable to argue that man is born with a knowledge of God, eighteenth-century thinkers increasingly sought to derive assurances of God's existence from human experience. Mountains, seas, and other sublime objects of immensity became for many, as Tuveson explains, "images of God's being constantly before human eyes."[5] Such general explanations of the relationship between sublimity and religion are thoroughly sound. But, in stressing only science, theology, and epistemology, they necessarily limit our understanding of a complex phenomenon. Particularly, they ignore the long and influential literary tradition of the religious sublime.

During the early years of the century, while men were just awakening to the lure of wild and vast scenes of nature, English poets and critics were establishing a similarly close relationship between sublimity and religion. Their interest was at first primarily literary, and they took as their exemplars not Newton and Locke but Longinus, Milton, and the Bible. Their subject was as often the supernatural world of Christian mystery as the explicable, if awesome, world of nature. In fact, to a number of poets and critics, the literary tradition of the religious sublime seemed to promise breakthroughs as exciting as those achieved by the advancement of science: a way had been found at last, some claimed, to surpass the triumphs of Greek and Roman literature. Its adherents never comprised a formal school or movement, but their agreement about a new direction for modern poetry created a significant opposition to the general course of neoclassical aesthetics. Often, it is true, they disagreed mainly with the subjects and styles of their orthodox contemporaries, not with the basic assumptions about man's relationship to nature, to human history, and to God which unite many apparently heterodox eighteenth-century works. At their boldest, however, like the Imagists in the early twentieth century, they wished to revive an older theory of poetry and to update it by exploring a specific range of new subjects and techniques; like the Imagists, they were conscious revolutionaries in poetry, challenging their age to alter the expectations which readers bring to verse. Their attempt never succeeded in overturning the established patterns of eighteenth-century literary thought, but they did manage to sustain a consistent pressure for change which probably helped to alter, rather than to reverse, the nature of poetic expectations during the century. Their influence, like that of third parties in American politics, was oblique, unacknowledged, and difficult to document. The reader must judge the degree of influence for himself. But, to move beyond the always knotty problem of calculating causal relationships in literary matters, the proponents of the religious sublime created a valuable body of writing which deserves study for several reasons: it sets in relief the work of major writers who resisted its claims, it possesses a coherence which argues its relevance to its own time (and, hence, to our understanding of the age), and, most importantly, it offers a clear instance of literary conflict and transition in a period too often pictured as monolithic.

The religious sublime has multiple origins: scientific, physico-theological, epistemological, and literary; and, as such a background suggests, the work of individual writers often reveals the shared traits of various traditions. Nevertheless, in attempting to achieve a sense of historical perspective which justifies viewing individual works as part of a larger pattern of consistency, it seems proper to analyze the religious sublime by considering its separable (but not wholly separate) literary and scientific aspects. Further, since Marjorie Nicolson and Ernest Tuveson have already discussed at length the Newtonian and Lockean contributions to the sublime, there is no need for me to review their evidence at length or to confirm findings which have been widely accepted. In choosing to discuss the literary tradition of the religious sublime, then, I have been guided mainly by a desire to explore new ground. The artificial separation of literary and scientific aspects—however convenient and valid for purposes of analysis—does not imply a corresponding split in the minds of eighteenth-century Englishmen, whose curiosity spanned the divisions of modern consciousness. Thus, before proceeding further, I should like to discuss one recent trend in scholarly treatments of the sublime which seems to me quite misleading; that is, the implication that sublimity in nature and sublimity in literature are essentially unrelated phenomena, developing along disconnected, if parallel, lines.

This implication, which underlies Marjorie Nicolson's *Mountain Gloom and Mountain Glory*, probably derives from Ronald Crane's review of Monk's *The Sublime* (*Philological Quarterly* 15 [1936]: 165–67) where Crane rightly distinguished between two different approaches to the sublime. He proposed the term *rhetorical sublime* to describe the general interests of poets and critics, for whom sublimity meant the exploration of certain literary effects. Around mid-century, however, a new class of writers appeared. These men, usually called "aestheticians" by modern scholars, studied the sublime as part of a broader analysis of human responses to varieties of aesthetic experience: "their characteristic subject-matter," Crane wrote, "was not compositions and authors but 'the pleasures of the imagination'—the varied responses of men's feelings to stimuli from the outer world." [6] This approach Crane called the *natural sublime*. Unfortunately, the terms which he chose to characterize this useful and valid distinction have created serious dangers of misinterpretation.

The term *rhetorical sublime* is unsatisfactory because it implies that sublimity in literature is mainly a matter of stylistics, a view which conflicts with Boileau's assertion that by sublimity Longinus did not mean "what orators call the sublime style." [7] It is true, of course, that critical discussions of sublimity often touch upon style, but few eighteenth-century writers believed that style alone created the sublime. Their concern with style is oblique: they warn against verbal faults which can degrade sublimity to bathos, and they praise judicious expression—often language so simple and concrete as to constitute almost a nonstyle, an approach toward the radical equation of words and things. Sublimity, most agree, achieves its intensest power through language which implies the transcendence of language, when, as one eighteenth-century critic put it, "we are made to understand, that there is in the mind something too great for utterance." The essence of sublimity is soaring nobility of thought and the force of emotional transport. Where these are absent, the age believed, no amount of rhetoric can produce the sublime. Indeed, since most readers today do not share Crane's comprehensive notion of rhetoric—but, like Yeats, use the term as a synonym for inherently unpoetic public eloquence—we would be wise to avoid a label which suggests that eighteenth-century poets and critics invariably confused the sublime with hollow forms of oratorical pretentiousness.

The term *natural sublime* also poses confusions. It is used today not, as Crane intended, to identify the aesthetic analysis which commences in the second half of the century but to mean "sublimity in nature"—so that any description of a chaotic sea or threatening precipice is freely associated with Crane's restrictive term. Further, the term itself is misleading even when applied solely to the work of eighteenth-century aestheticians: while such writers do investigate human responses "to stimuli *from the outer world*," they by no means restrict their analysis to responses elicited by natural scenes. Many find literature an equally rich storehouse of data. But the worst offense of the term *natural sublime* is its implication that sublimity in nature and sublimity in literature are basically unrelated. "Longinus did little else for the 'natural Sublime,' " writes Marjorie Nicolson, "than to offer some assistance in vocabulary."[8] She traces the origin of the "natural sublime"—by which she means the appreciation of grandeur in nature—to the expanded universe revealed by science and argues that this tradition develops parallel to, but apart from, the tradition of the "rhetorical sublime." My main objection to such a view is that it projects upon the past our modern split into two cultures. To the integrated vision of many eighteenth-century Englishmen, nature and art did not occupy separate realms but often appeared as aspects of a single object of consciousness. "As I have made several Voyages upon the Sea," wrote Addison, "I have often been tossed in Storms, and on that occasion have frequently reflected on the Descriptions of them in ancient Poets. I remember *Longinus* highly recommends one in *Homer*."[9] To apply Pope's famous words, "*Nature* and *Homer* were, he found, the same."

I do not wish to overstate my objections. Valid reasons exist for distinguishing the experience of gazing at a mountain from that of reading a poem and for contrasting the taste for sublimity in nature, which has lasted to our own day,[10] with the less enduring taste for sublime poems: for such purposes, the term *natural sublime* proves convenient. But when the term *natural sublime* is used to imply that literature and nature in the eighteenth century belong to essentially isolated realms, then its usefulness vanishes. Whether meditating by the sea, contemplating the night sky, or crossing the Alps, eighteenth-century enthusiasts for nature rarely forgot their reading: the classics were Addison's guidebook to Italy, while Joseph Warton's vision of unspoiled nature comes straight from Lucretius and Shaftesbury. Nor in their reading did men suddenly enter a region of pure thought, remote from the world of nature. Pope's primary rule for modern poets was "First follow Nature," and his direction applies to the amusing story about James Thomson's contempt for a nameless urban poet. "He write an Epick poem!" Thomson scoffed. "It is impossible: he never saw a mountain in his life." [11] Even if apocryphal, the story seriously implies that viewing a mountain and writing a poem could be considered complementary and inseparable because both are imaginative activities which involve the experience of sublimity.

One final reason for abandoning Crane's terms—as I have done in this study—is that the distinction between sublimity in nature and sublimity in literature dissolves completely when one considers the religious sublime. To an age which habitually spoke of nature as a "book," the landscape appeared vitally suffused with religious ideas and literary values. Thomas Gray, for example, saw in the sublime terrain around the Grande Chartreuse something more than rocks and stones and trees: "Not a precipice, not a torrent, not a cliff," he reported to Richard West, "but is pregnant with religion and poetry." [12] Reading, of course, was itself the century's most popular form of travel, and sitting in his study Gray would have recognized a similar mingling of the natural, the literary, and the religious in almost any passage of sublime description from Thomson's *The Seasons* or from his own prophetic poem *The Bard*, which Joseph Warton in 1782 cited as a model of sublime verse. The poetry of natural description, exemplified by *The Seasons*, comprises a special class of eighteenth-century verse, and its uniqueness derives in part (as I shall argue later) from a distinctive use of the sublime. But it is easy to exaggerate the apparent differences between the poetry of natural description and other sublime religious verse.[13] Indeed, Thomson's awesome landscapes—described in language rich with allusions to Virgil, Milton, and the Bible—reappear with little modification in such explicitly religious, literary, and rhetorical works as Christopher Smart's Seatonian poems. Eighteenth-century man experienced the sublime in two main contexts—literature and nature—but while the context changed, the experience remained much the same. And perhaps the single most important point of continuity is the basic association between sublimity and religion. This association may be traced with some confidence to various separable origins. But when eighteenth-century Englishmen enjoyed the religious sublime, they experienced an aesthetic pleasure which transcended the often uncertain boundaries of nature and of art. This study of the literary tradition of the religious sublime, then, presents a neglected aspect of a subject which should not be oversimplified or rigidly schematized. By balancing it with other approaches to sublimity already published, the modern reader can to some degree recreate the complex vision which eighteenth-century writers took for granted.

The very multifariousness of the concept of sublimity has forced me to adopt in this study four principles of procedure about which the reader ought to be warned. The first is a principle of exclusion. The association between sublimity and religion runs through all the arts, but I have chosen to concentrate only upon poetry and criticism. Thus, Handel, Raphael, and Michelangelo—to name the most obvious figures—will not be discussed; nor will I treat the lowlier but scarcely less popular authors of Gothic fiction and of other prose narratives, although many are pertinent to my subject. The exclusion of prose fiction, sculpture, painting, and music, however, permits an intensification of analysis by avoiding an almost limitless expansion of scope; indeed, much that is said here concerning poetry and criticism can be applied, with reasonable caution, to other arts. When an entire book ought to be devoted solely to Blake's use of the graphic traditions of the religious sublime, it seemed best to restrict attention to a single subject which could be treated in detail. Perhaps a comprehensive study of its importance to the limited fields of poetry and criticism may be the best means of persuading qualified scholars that the religious sublime deserves to be fully explored as it affects the development of all the arts in eighteenth-century England.

The second principle involves an acceptance of limited confusion. "Sublimity," wrote Joseph Priestley in the last quarter of the eighteenth century, "hath been used in a more vague sense than almost any other term in criticism." [14] His assessment is dishearteningly accurate, although vagueness results partly because no critical term had been used so often. Further, much of the confusion was not due to intentional or unintentional evasion but to the multiplicity of competing definitions. Almost no critic could resist explaining what Longinus had meant by the sublime, and Priestly added a chapter of his own to the voluminous literature of definition and illustration. But, finally, although disagreement about matters of taste is proverbial, eighteenth-century writers are remarkably consistent in the practical application of the adjective *sublime*, and it seems sensible to interpret some critical scuffling about precise definition as a sign of vitality. The vagueness of the term *sublimity* exists within a surprisingly narrow boundary of agreement. To a reader who will suspend temporarily an irritable reaching after exact clarity, what is vague in one context often becomes distinct through an accumulation of specific examples.

If the term *sublime* necessarily admits a degree of imprecision, few men of good will can agree on a definition of religious literature. To appeal to the period itself is useless. Johnson's two definitions of *religious* which might describe a class of literary works—1) "Pious, disposed to the duties of religion," and 2) "Teaching religion"—hardly apply to the poetry discussed in this study. Poetry of the religious sublime generally ignores the ethical aspect of worship which concerns duties, and didacticism is equally foreign to its nature. In fact, the religious sublime exists mainly outside the rigorously moral and systematically theological realm of Johnsonian piety, and in this sense it probably reflects the dilution of orthodox belief during the century. My specific interest in the religious sublime is limited generally to the use of Christian supernaturalism. Thus I can agree with Helen Gardner that "to define religious poetry as poetry that treats of revelation and of man's response to revelation does not equate religious poetry with Christian poetry; but the great majority of English religious poems on this definition will be found to be Christian poems in some sense."[15] At times, I will surely seem to wander outside the pale of my subject or to ignore works (even such popular works as Robert Blair's *The Grave*) which clearly fall within it. Fortunately, literature is not written to fit the convenient pigeonholes of criticism, nor can criticism be useful if it attempts, like the goddess of Pope's *Dunciad*, to lick up everything in its way. The greatest critic and lexicographer of the eighteenth century offers shrewd advice to modern students of the period:

> Definitions [wrote Samuel Johnson] have been no less difficult or uncertain in criticism than in law. Imagination, a licentious and vagrant faculty, unsusceptible of limitations, and impatient of restraint, has always endeavoured to baffle the logician, to perplex the confines of distinction, and burst the inclosures of regularity. There is therefore scarcely any species of writing, of which we can tell what is its essence, and what are its constituents; every new genius produces some innovation, which, when invented and approved, subverts the rules which the practice of foregoing authors had established.[16]

What Johnson wrote with reference to comedy also holds true for religious poetry. My own interest in Christian supernaturalism is not offered as a choice which denies the existence of other forms of religious verse. Rather, within the latitude provided by the principle of limited confusion, it seeks to provide rational bounds to a subject, like the imagination itself, almost unsusceptible of limitations.

The third principle, less widely accepted than one might suspect, is that a close and fruitful relationship exists between eighteenth-century poetry and criticism. Like Addison, Dennis, the Wartons, and Dr. Johnson, many eighteenth-century critics were also practicing poets. They read the same treatises on poetry, shared a generally homogeneous literary milieu, and agreed that literature was a civilized art which requires a knowledge of critical doctrine and the good taste to apply it flexibly. Modern studies of Milton have shown that the comments of eighteenth-century critics can illuminate works closer to their own age than to ours; and I believe that one of the best ways to understand the nature of eighteenth-century poetry is to understand the principles and insights of contemporary critics. Except for the work of Addison, Pope, and Johnson, the criticism of the age is sadly neglected; and when treated at all, it is most often discussed in isolation, without more than passing mention of its application to the practice of various writers. I hope the present study will help to demonstrate the intricate relationship between critical precept and poetic practice in the eighteenth century.

The fourth principle of procedure concerns general aims and methods. In this case, the method has evolved from the nature of the subject: I have not attempted to fit the study of the religious sublime to a preconceived methodology. My main aim is to provide an analytical and descriptive view of literary change. In confronting a subject both huge and untidy, which sprawls over traditional categories of idea, genre, theory, mode, and effect, I have attempted a twofold approach. First, I have tried to give a sense of historical origin and development. While working within a general historical framework, however, I have not meant to commit myself or the reader to an implicit theory of evolutionary growth or (except where the evidence is compelling) of direct causal influences.[17] The first chapter discusses a series of forces which help to explain why a theory of the religious sublime should appear in the first decade of the eighteenth century, although it cannot pretend to explain precisely how these forces interacted. The second chapter studies in detail the critical thought of John Dennis, England's first theorist of the religious sublime, and attempts to explain how he developed the idea and what importance it held in his general system of poetry. It does not, however, undertake to prove direct influences: Dennis's reliance upon Dryden or Thomson's reliance upon Dennis must remain matters for speculation. My consistent goal, as in the final chapters, has been to indicate the importance of the religious sublime to the work of various eighteenth-century writers and to offer, from the unifying perspective of a single concept, a view of literary change. In E. M. Forster's terms, I am offering a "story" rather than a "plot," because I am more interested in continuity (and discontinuity) than in causation. And, insofar as it is a truism that no idea exists outside of the consciousness of individuals, I am offering what Louis O. Mink calls a story "not of 'ideas,' but of men thinking and feeling." [18] Such a narrative of change can, I trust, provide genuine interest for readers concerned with understanding the literature of eighteenth-century England.

In addition to working within a chronological framework of change, I have tried to emphasize general patterns which underlie the poetry and criticism of the religious sublime. Thus, Chapter Three treats the patterns of critical thought which support and clarify the poetry of the religious sublime, while Chapters Four and Five analyze the main varieties of sublime religious verse. Some readers may be alarmed that I mix categories of analysis. My explanation is that only a mixed classification—including subject, mode, concept, and author—can encompass the diversity of the subject: to approach the religious sublime from a single perspective would be like attacking Proteus with a hammer. The description of literary patterns, of course, can be an exceedingly sterile process when pursued as an end in itself. The naturalist's use for categories finds no exact parallel in the work of literary critics. But such patterns as this book discovers in the religious poetry and criticism of eighteenth-century England can be a useful means of enlarging our knowledge of how periods differ. The religious poetry of the eighteenth century, with the exception of the hymn, finds few admirers today, especially when our historical vision extends to the brilliant religious verse of the ages immediately preceding and following. The religious sublime is a useful subject for study, however, especially because it represents the beginning and end of a tradition located fundamentally within a single century. In speculating upon its peculiar relevance to the eighteenth-century mind, one also invites speculation about the nature of the changes which rendered useless the examples of Donne or of Herbert and which reinvigorated religious poetry in the Romantic era. The life and death of literary forms, as Alastair Fowler has insisted, is a phenomenon which poses serious questions for the modern scholar.[19] Whatever its limitations, this study is an attempt to respect the seriousness of the questions which need to be asked about the nature of eighteenth-century literary change.

Chapter One

The Literary Origins of Religious Sublimity

Developing the argument of his *Grounds of Criticism in Poetry*, John Dennis announced in 1704, "I now come to the Precepts of *Longinus*, and pretend to shew from them, that the greatest Sublimity is to be deriv'd from Religious Ideas."[1] This particular step in his argument required some ingenuity because Longinus had discovered no explicit relationship between sublimity and religious ideas. Dennis's strained effort to explain the silence of Longinus on this crucial point suggests that Longinus is not the direct source of English theories of the religious sublime. The origin, rather, is to be found in an accumulating body of opinion concerning the grand style, the poetry of the Bible, and the nature of poetry itself. This body of opinion assumed new significance with the appearance of Boileau's translation of Longinus in 1674. Thus, while Longinus did not formulate a theory of religious sublimity, the reappearance of the *Peri Hupsous* in the late seventeenth century suddenly clarified a number of previously vague or unconnected ideas concerning the nature of great writing. An understanding of these origins will help to explain why a theory of the religious sublime should emerge in the first decades of the eighteenth century and why, when it did emerge, its fundamental arguments should find such general support.

EARLY RHETORIC AND CRITICISM

The English word *sublime* when used by literary critics has not always evoked the authority of Longinus. Longinus, who fathered virtually all modern discussions of sublimity, had no significant influence upon English poetry and criticism before Boileau's French translation of the *Peri Hupsous* appeared in 1674. The date of composition of the *Peri Hupsous* is uncertain; estimates range from the first to the third centuries A.D. The treatise seems to have been unknown during the Middle Ages; and although editions were available in the Renaissance,[2] such a knowledgeable English humanist as Milton makes only one passing reference to Longinus. For over a millennium, the sublime (*sublimis*=lofty) was simply a synonym for the high or grand style. It might be defined much as Ben Jonson defined the grand style in *Timber* (1641): "the words are chosen, their sound ample, the composition full, the absolution plenteous, and powr'd out, all grave, sinnewye, and strong."[3] Until the late seventeenth century, sublimity always referred to style and diction. Of course, decorum required that the sublime style be reserved for appropriately great subjects or occasions. But only when the discussion of sublimity emphasized matter as well as words would critics liberate the sublime from a purely stylistic context. Nevertheless, the discussion of sublime style indirectly provided a basis for critical developments by its stress upon the particular function of the grand style in moving great emotion.

Quintilian, typical of classical rhetoricians in general, insisted that style is closely related to intention. According to Quintilian, the plain style instructs, the middle style charms or conciliates, and the grand style transports the audience with irresistible persuasive force.[4] By adding the function of *movere* to the Horatian formula of delight and instruction, classical rhetoric emphasized the single quality indispensable to later theories of sublimity; as Samuel Monk notes, "The presence of emotion in art is the point of departure for the eighteenth-century sublime."[5] The relationship between the moving power of the grand style and later theories of the sublime is foreshadowed by the metaphor which both Quintilian and Longinus use to suggest the emotional effect of great rhetoric. "It is this force and impetuosity," Quintilian writes of the grand style, ". . . that Aristophanes compares to the thunderbolt."[6] The thunderbolt is also Longinus's recurrent image for the astonishing force of sublimity. The image for both Quintilian and Longinus associates great rhetoric with god-like energy. The great orator awes his audience as if Jove himself were hurling thunderbolts from Olympus. Yet their use of a similar image belies fundamental differences in approach between Quintilian and Longinus. Quintilian, unlike Longinus, considers grandeur largely a matter of style. So long as the *Peri Hupsous* lay neglected through the Middle Ages and Renaissance, stylistic approaches dominated discussion of the nature of great writing.

The major contribution of medieval and Renaissance rhetoricians to the future development of the religious sublime was their use of the Bible in discussions of rhetoric. The parables of Jesus, the letters of Saint Paul, and passages from Old Testament poets and prophets became standard sources for the illustration of different rhetorical tropes and figures. The medieval interest in the rhetoric of the Bible, however, had little direct influence upon the work of eighteenth-century poets and critics, who, until the second half of the century, too often viewed the Middle Ages as a period of superstition, barbarism, and ignorance. Yet eighteenth-century poets and critics were close readers of the great English and continental writers of the Renaissance. These Renaissance writers, often moving comfortably between the classical and Christian literary realms, made recognition of the sublime style of the Bible a commonplace of English critical theory.

English writers of the sixteenth and seventeenth centuries frequently looked to the Bible for "flowers" of rhetoric. A number of rhetorical handbooks illustrated particular devices of style with biblical examples, and several rhetorics specialized particularly in analysis of biblical eloquence.[7] Such treatments, of course, discussed many aspects of biblical rhetoric, and the sublime style was only one of these aspects. But because they viewed the Bible as the language of God adapted to human capacities, Christian rhetoricians often insisted that the Bible inevitably contained the noblest examples of every variety of human speech, including the sublime. John Smith's *Mysterie of Rhetorique Un-vail'd* (1657) is characteristic of earlier works in declaring that the Bible "abounds with tropes and figures of all sorts, as containing the most excellent and sublimest eloquence."[8] Smith's use of the superlative degree is deliberate. Sublime rhetoric fills the works of Cicero and Demosthenes. But the sublimest eloquence is that of the Bible.

Renaissance critics significantly aided later analysts of biblical sublimity by extending the discussion of scriptural eloquence from rhetoric to poetry. The close association between rhetoric and poetry in the Renaissance made such an extension perhaps inevitable and certainly easy. But Renaissance emphasis upon the poetry of the Bible did not result simply from a blurring of the boundaries between poetry and rhetoric. Two related ideas supported the new interest in the poetry of the Bible. First, Renaissance critics often emphasized that poetry originated with God. Poetry, wrote Ben Jonson, is "the Queene of Arts, which had her Originall from heaven, received thence from the *'Ebrewes*, and had in prime estimation with the *Greeks*, transmitted to the *Latines* and all Nations that profess'd Civility."[9] The progress of poetry, for Jonson, begins with the Old Testament bards inspired directly by God. The poet who wishes to drink from the fountainhead must look to the Bible.

Renaissance discussions of biblical poetry also stressed a point which at first seems purest tautology: that parts of the Bible were written in Hebrew meter. The apparent tautology vanishes when one recalls that Sidney, typical of many Renaissance writers, considered verse merely an accidental property of poetry. Poetry involved the creation of idealized fictions which might persuade man to love virtue and hate vice; whether such creations were conveyed in verse or prose did not affect their status as poetic truth. Although the truth of the Bible was never in question, it nevertheless delighted the Renaissance taste for copious proof and illustrious pedigree to observe that the Bible contained not only poetry but verse. No one, unfortunately, understood the technical nature of Hebrew versification. Still, its existence was widely recognized, as in the Tremelius-Junius Latin Bible (1580) which Sidney quoted in order to laud "the poeticall part of the Scripture,"[10] and the general interest in biblical poetry

and versification undoubtedly grew in part because it suggested
an argument against those who attacked the validity of modern
verse. Sidney, for example, who must apologize for poetry before
he can begin to explain it, strengthens his defense of poetry with
the argument that "the chiefe [poets] both in antiquitie and
excellencie were they that did imitate the inconceiuable excel-
lencies of GOD. Such were *Dauid* in his Psalmes, *Salomon* in his
song of Songs, in his Ecclesiastes, and Prouerbs, *Moses* and
Debora in theyr Hymnes, and the writer of *Iob.*" [11] The implica-
tion is clear: if God found poetry a suitable medium for his
prophets and holy men, surely mortals cannot object to the art.

   Most critics and poets of the English Renaissance agreed with
Sidney that the Bible contains the oldest and best poetry known
to man. Such a view, however, was not likely to become an active
stimulus for modern poets until certain difficulties were over-
come. One main difficulty involved the neoclassical belief that
poetry is the art of imitating nature. "*Poetry* and *Picture* are
Arts of a like nature," wrote Ben Jonson, "and both are busie
about imitation." [12] The alliance between poetry and pictorialism
is necessarily close for Jonson because the neoclassical doctrine
of imitation implies that the poet will have a clear conception of
the objects or qualities to be imitated. Indeed, the definiteness
of much classical art derives in part from this emphasis upon
pictorial imitation as the standard of creative judgment. But
when Sidney praised the biblical poets, he praised them for
imitating the "inconceiuable" excellencies of God. Thus a
poet attempting to emulate biblical grandeur would face the
paradox of having to imitate what he could not conceive. Isaiah's
question "To whom then will ye liken God? or what likeness
will ye compare unto him?" (40:18) raises a serious question for
the neoclassical religious poet. The dilemma troubled several
generations of poets who sought to reconcile inconceivable sub-
jects and ideas to the imitative medium of poetry.

   There were several recourses for poets who wished to follow
the example of the biblical poets and prophets. First, instead of
attempting directly to imitate the inconceivable, the modern
poet might simply paraphrase either the Bible itself or existing

and successful imitations of the Bible. The appearance of the King James authorized version seems to have freed a vast energy among English writers, and the Bible quickly became the subject of innumerable poetic paraphrases. Sidney himself chose this alternative, translating not only the thoughts and images of David but also frequently imitating the intricate meters of David's French translator, Clément Marot. Paraphrase of scripture became a recognized and praiseworthy kind of poetic creation,[13] especially because the Sternhold-Hopkins version of the Psalms offended the literary taste of many. In fact, the paraphrase of scripture in the sixteenth and seventeenth centuries rivaled the writing of pastorals as an exercise for callow poets. Not every biblical paraphrase, of course, emphasized passages recognized for their grandeur. The Bible contains many moods and styles. But poets often chose for paraphrase passages which later were considered prime examples of sublimity. Psalm 18, for instance, became a favorite illustration of sublimity in the eighteenth century, but no later critic ever surpassed George Wyther's rapturous account, written long before the popularity of Longinus. "Tell me," asked Wyther, "where haue you found in any Poet more liuely or Heroicall descriptions? Where can you read more stately expressions? Or how were it possible better to insinuate, into the vnderstanding, the apprehension of the incomprehensible, and inexpressible Maiestie of GOD?"[14] Wyther, like Sidney, discovers in the Psalms a poetry of the incomprehensible and the inexpressible; like Sidney, his way of imitating such greatness was through paraphrase.

A second way to imitate biblical greatness was to create an original poem (rather than a paraphrase) which borrowed its subject or style from the Bible. As Abraham Cowley noted, "All the *Books* of the *Bible* are either already most admirable and exalted pieces of Poesie, or are the best *Materials* in the world for it."[15] Especially in France, where the biblical epic became a fashion, poets throughout the seventeenth century thought of the Bible as a mine of poetic materials. Cowley himself claimed to have imported the biblical epic to England with his *Davideis* (1656), and he proved that a scriptural subject and spirit could sustain works of shorter length by publishing his influential Pindaric odes. One of the English Pindarics was a direct paraphrase of scripture, while three were original religious poems based on scriptural themes. Cowley's example, associating the style of Pindar with that of the Hebrew prophets, almost single-handedly created the new genre of the "sacred ode," a genre which was particularly popular in the late seventeenth and early eighteenth centuries. And one important aspect of the popularity of the sacred ode was its close association with the concept of sublimity.[16] According to Norman Maclean, "The popularity of Longinus merged quickly with that of the Cowleyan ode; and, almost as soon as the concept of sublimity became well known in England, it was regarded as peculiarly exemplified by the Great Ode."[17] Cowley himself, however, was never satisfied with his emulation of biblical sublimity. Describing his effort to write divine poetry, he modestly admitted, "I am farre from assuming to my self to have fulfilled the duty of this weighty undertaking: But sure I am that there is nothing yet in our *Language* (nor perhaps in *any*) that is in any degree answerable to the *Idea* that I conceive of it."[18] Before the publication of *Paradise Lost*, there was a good deal of truth in Cowley's observation: nonlyric religious poetry had failed to capture the Hebrew poetic spirit.

Critics, too, faced difficulties in reconciling their admiration for biblical poetry with a neoclassical theory of imitation. Yet most critics seem to have conceded cheerfully that the principle of imitation could not wholly account for the mystery of great writing. Even the strictest French classicists recognized fugitive qualities in art which defy analysis. The inability of criticism to account for these mysterious beauties was simply codified as part of the critical system. Whatever could not be explained in great art, the French declared, was an example of the unexplainable. The *je ne sais quoi*, thus, replaced earlier ideas of poetic "grace"[19] which had always, indirectly, suggested both the flexibility and shortcomings of the doctrine of imitation. And never perhaps did the doctrine of imitation seem less adequate than in explaining the poetry of the Bible, as George Wyther illustrates in his almost mystical encounter with the limits of criticism:

Nay I could shew you Straines of *Poesie*, and such flowers of Rhetoricke, as among them could neuer yet be found. But some there be that are not expressible, and I may resemble them to the purest sort of Lightning. For, as that passeth through a purse . . . and there melts the Coyne, without leauing any impression or signe vpon the leather: So, there be certaine Rhetoricall passages in these *Psalmes*, so pure from sensibilitie, that they can and doe conuey things through the senses, vnperceiued; and yet melt the heart, and worke strange operations in the soule, such as no man can imagine, but he that hath felt them.[20]

For Wyther, emotional reactions in a reader or listener should be traceable to specific rhetorical devices, but in the Bible he found hidden sources of emotion which defied rational analysis. His description here is not an account of rhetorical techniques; it records his inexplicable reactions to certain mysteriously moving passages. He knows he has been moved, but he does not know how. His perplexity, in retrospect, reflects the historical dilemma of early English criticism. Confronted by the poetry of the Bible, analytic criticism had to be abandoned. The Bible was understood to be the inspired word of God and therefore must inevitably transcend the human techniques of literary analysis. Until the eighteenth century, this hesitancy to analyze things divine by the dim light of human reason characterized most critical reactions to the poetry of the Bible.

Throughout most of the seventeenth century, the poetry of the Bible inspired enthusiastic rapture but very little acute literary analysis. In 1622 Henry Peacham offered his readers the following series of observations: "What are the Psalmes of *Dauid* . . . but a Diuine Poeme, going sometime in one measure, sometime in another? What liuely descriptions are there of the Maiestie of God. . . . What liuely similitudes & comparisons. . . . What excellent Allegories . . . what *Epiphonema's*, *prosopopoea's*, and whatsoeuer else may be required to the texture of so rich and glorious a peece!"[21] Peacham's appreciation of biblical greatness makes him perhaps the father of exclamatory criticism, but his helpless "whatsoeuer else" demonstrates not only a failure of vocabulary but also, and more importantly, a failure of critical approach. Thirty years later, Edward Benlowes was equally assertive and equally vague. "Divine Poesy," he wrote, "is the internal triumph of the mind, rapt with St. Paul into the third heaven, where she contemplates ineffables."[22] Benlowes's vision of the mind contemplating ineffables yields to his aphoristic summary of the necessary attributes of the poet: "Sublime poets are by Nature strengthened, by the power of mind inflamed, and by divine rapture inspired."[23] Nature, mind, and God somehow cooperate to create sublime poetry, but the alchemy remains obscure. Increasingly, however, English critics began to demand more precise explanations; and, as the doctrine of imitation failed to explain the most moving and mysterious parts of poetry, criticism sought supplementary accounts of the nature of great writing. Critics began to extend their ken from the poetic product to the poetic process. This critical extension, by supplementing the doctrine of imitation with a rudimentary psychology of the creative mind, helped to prepare a fertile ground for the reception of Boileau's translation of Longinus. As the seventeenth century proceeded, literary criticism drew increasingly serious study from men of various backgrounds and stations. Among such men, none did more to clarify alternative theories of the nature of great writing than John Milton and Thomas Hobbes.

MILTON AND HOBBES

Milton described poetry as the inspired gift of God. This conception of poetry is not borrowed from Hesiod or Ovid but from nonclassical sources: from the Renaissance tradition of the Christian muse and from his own reading of the Bible. The tradition of the Christian muse was popularized in England particularly through the "Urania" of Du Bartas, published in Joshua Sylvester's English translation (1605). Du Bartas was a favorite of King James, and his influence upon later English poetry is well known. In opposition to Sidney, who defined the poet as a maker or craftsman, Du Bartas argued that poetry requires more than skill. "Each *Art* is learn'd by *Art*," he declared, "but Poesie/ Is a meere

Heauenly gift"[24]—a statement implying the folly of analyzing by human art something which transcends both artifice and humanity. In fact, Du Bartas fails to mention art at all. His main advice is that poets must seek the proper supernatural assistance.

> Let Christ (as Man-God) be your double Mountaine
> Whereon to Muse; and, for the winged hooue
> Of Pegasus, to digge th' Immortall Fountaine,
> Take th' Holy-Ghost, type't in a Siluer Doue.[25]

The passage develops a running parallel between Christian and classical theories of poetic inspiration. Both theories ally poetry with a source of energy located outside man. Directing Du Bartas's development of the parallel, however, is the unspoken assumption—central to Milton's poetics—that the classical account is an erring fable. Just as the false religion of the pagans falls before Christian Revelation, so the pagan account of the poetic process as a form of divine madness yields to a theory which it imperfectly shadows forth: the theory of prophetic truth.

The doctrine of inspiration which Du Bartas espoused would have seemed especially plausible to Milton because it was sanctioned by the authority of scripture. Isaiah, who had prophesied after his lips were touched by a glowing coal from Jehovah's secret altar, became for Milton the prototype of the poet. In *The Reason of Church Government* (1641), Milton rejected various false means of poetic inspiration, such as wine and frenzy, and insisted that his own poetry would eschew the classical invocations of "Dame Memory and her Siren daughters." Instead, he would proceed only "by devout prayer to that eternall Spirit who can enrich with all utterance and knowledge, and sends out his Seraphim with the hallow'd fire of his Altar to touch and purify the lips of whom he pleases."[26] Milton's clear allusion to Isaiah (6:6) identifies the Old Testament origin of his poetics. Of course, Milton never slighted human sources of poetic knowledge and experience; he was, to understate, immensely learned. But, although the poet must master both the craft of verse and a variety of learning, Christian and non-Christian, Milton insisted that the final vivifying source of great writing must be God. Thus, whenever Milton describes the poetic process, he locates the ultimate source of great writing outside man, beyond the powers of art alone.

Hobbes located the poetic process within the human mind, devising a natural explanation for the process which Milton had explained supernaturally. In "The Answer of Mr. Hobbes to Sr Will. D'Avenant's *Preface* Before *Gondibert*" (1650), Hobbes offers his version of the creative process: "Time and Education begets experience; Experience begets memory; Memory begets Judgement and Fancy: Judgment begets the strength and structure, and Fancy begets the ornaments of a Poem." [27] Perhaps parodying those, like Milton, who based their theory of poetic inspiration upon the Bible, Hobbes borrows the most prosaic of all biblical devices, the begat formula, to frame his description of the poetic process. Sarcasm and parody in Hobbes usually point to areas of intense intellectual conflict, and his most substantial objection to the aesthetics of Milton concerns the role of memory in the creation of poetry. For Hobbes, memory is the necessary link between mind and matter since it begets Fancy and Judgment, the two faculties directly responsible for the creation of poetry. "The Ancients therefore fabled not absurdly," he argued, "in making memory the Mother of the Muses." [28] The sentence reads like a direct rebuttal of Milton's banishment of Dame Memory and her Siren daughters. Further, Hobbes considered Du Bartas's view that poetry is written "as in a holy Trance" [29] to be a superstitious and willful delusion. "I can imagin no cause but a reasonless imitation of Custom, of a foolish custome," declared Hobbes, "by which a man, enabled to speak wisely from the principles of nature and his own meditation, loves rather to be thought to speak by inspiration, like a Bagpipe." [30] Again, the sarcasm of Hobbes's reductive simile betrays an intense commitment to a rationalistic psychology of the creative process. In fact, it was partly the Hobbesian scorn of inspiration which forced eighteenth-century critics to found their admiration for biblical poetry upon rational literary analysis— an analysis basic to the religious sublime.

Milton and Hobbes both supplemented the theory of imitation with forcefully expressed alternatives, but (as one might expect) neither writer wholly won over his contemporaries. Milton's defense of inspiration had two evident defects. First, it was vulnerable to the growing mistrust of individual enthusiasm after the Civil Wars. Roscommon's caution to poets conceals the weight of firsthand experience of the terror of recent political and religious violence:

> Beware what Spirit rages in your breast;
> For ten inspir'd ten thousand are Possest.[31]

It is the health of the nation, not simply the psychic stability of the poet, which Roscommon has in mind. Of course, most Restoration critics—of whom Pope thought Roscommon foremost—admired a poetry of spirit. Genius had always provided the essential spark in even the most rational and correct compositions. But, while genius (like talent) is not equally apparent in all men, it can be explained as a human potential which is especially well developed in certain lucky individuals. This explanation does not necessarily rob poetry of its grandeur; but it does divest it of a supernaturalism which, as in the case of Cowley, was too obviously affected; and the divestiture began to seem particularly necessary if readers, in their disgust with imposters, were not to turn from poetry altogether. Giles Jacob certainly spoke for many of his better known contemporaries when, after stating that poetry is descended from a religious origin, he asserted that "this Divine Art . . . has lately so much suffer'd in its Reputation, by the Performances of some who have thought themselves inspir'd, and whose Readers too have many of them thought the same, that the best Judges come strongly prejudic'd against any thing of this kind, as generally expecting nothing but Froth and Emptiness."[32] When poetry loses the sympathy of those equipped to be its "best Judges," the cultural night of Pope's *Dunciad* is not far off. Nor does Jacob permit us to ignore his indictment by arguing whether Wordsworth's common man or Hume's elite of taste is the proper judge of poetry. The imposture which Jacob attacks is apparently unknown only to the deluded: any man of sense, he implies, can see through the emperor's new clothes.

The second major defect of Milton's poetics was equally debilitating. In an age as wary of absolutism as of uncontrolled dissent, the doctrine of inspiration seemed to foreclose further discussion of the nature of great writing. Although Milton himself insisted that decorum was the "great masterpiece" to be observed in poetry—a view which requires the affirmation of rational control in the poet—the theory of inspiration implies that violations of accepted decorum can be absolved simply by appeal to the Holy Spirit. In effect, the doctrine of inspiration is potentially as restrictive as the dramatic Rules of Aristotle, and Restoration critics (like their counterparts in the Royal Society) demanded the right to test received authority by the evidence of their own peculiarly English and modern experience. The weakness of a poetics of inspiration lies in its appeal to singular experience and its necessity of supra-rational justification, and these weaknesses were constantly paraded by those who wished to expose them. But such exposures resembled an oratory of display more than genuine argument. In the Restoration, the irrelevance of the doctrine of inspiration was almost a premise or assumption of critical thought and not a carefully reasoned deduction. Poetry had quietly but thoroughly been assimilated to the realm of second causes; its nature, thus, could be understood by exploration of the laws of human behavior. The developing interest in rational literary analysis required the exclusion—as an assumption upon which any accurate knowledge could be based—of an essentially mystical theory of great writing.

Hobbes's view of the poetic process, while more acceptable to most seventeenth-century readers, also had limitations. It too greatly mechanized a process which most poets and critics recognized was not wholly mechanical. The operation of Fancy and Judgment upon the materials stored in the memory reduced the mystery of great writing to a methodical clarity. One measure of the loss which sometimes accompanies gains in clarity appears in the work of writers who, through early ineptitude or abiding dullness, seize any psychological principle as a full explanation

of the poetic process. (Future critics will doubtless show how our
belief in Freudian hypotheses shaped the kinds of poetry we
imagined possible.) Thus Mark Van Doren in *The Poetry of
John Dryden* (New York, 1920) argues convincingly that Dry-
den's worst early verse illustrates a mechanical application of
Hobbesian Judgment and Fancy: two lines of statement fol-
lowed by two lines of ornament. Like the earlier theory of the
bodily humours, which profoundly affected seventeenth-century
drama, the theory of Fancy and Judgment accounted for man
as a physical but not as a spiritual being. The Earl of Mulgrave,
for example, who accepted the notion that Fancy and Judgment
are partners in the creation of poetry, recognized an additional
force which is required of the successful poet:

> *A Spirit which inspires the work throughout,*
> *As that of Nature moves this World about:*
> *A heat that glows in every word that's writ,*
> *That's something of Divine, and more than Wit;*
> *It self unseen, yet all things by it shown*
> *Describing all men, but describ'd by none:*
> *Where dost thou dwell? what caverns of the Brain*
> *Can such a vast and mighty thing contain?* [33]

Mulgrave associates great poetry with a force that is either hid-
den deep within the mind itself or originates outside man. Like
others of his age, he recognizes that great poetry cannot be ex-
plained merely through analysis of the poetic process and that
the "caverns of the Brain" contain wonders undreamed-of by
Hobbes's philosophy.

After 1674 another phenomenon left the Miltonic doctrine
of inspiration and the Hobbesian doctrine of Fancy and Judg-
ment seeming equally inadequate explanations of the nature of
great writing. With the publication of Boileau's translation of
Longinus, critics began to discover both a new vocabulary and
a new method of literary analysis. The change was not in-
stantaneous, but it was thorough. Critics, even if they rejected
Longinus (and few did), at least had to consider seriously the
implications of his treatise. In addition, the relationship between

great poetry and religious ideas suddenly appeared in sharper focus. The time was approaching when John Dennis, a critic schooled in the Restoration, would create a fully developed theory of the religious sublime.

BOILEAU'S LONGINUS

The perplexity of poets and critics concerning the nature of great writing helps to explain the popularity of Boileau's translation of the *Peri Hupsous*, which appeared in 1674. Addison's reaction is probably typical. After noting that an acquaintance with ancient and modern criticism is necessary for anyone who wishes to acquire a fine "taste," he adds that he does not refer simply to learning the "Mechanical Rules" of poetry. There is, he says, "something more essential, to the Art, something that elevates and astonishes the Fancy, and gives a Greatness of Mind to the Reader, which few of the Criticks besides *Longinus* have consider'd" (*Spec.* 409). It is likely that Addison read Longinus in Boileau's translation, as did most English readers early in the century. In fact, the word *sublime*, which Dr. Johnson described as "a Gallicism, but now naturalized,"[34] owes its currency to Boileau's transformation of the Greek title into *Traité du Sublime*. Almost at once, Longinus became an accepted authority, rivaling the fame of his translator. Dryden praised him as "undoubtedly, after Aristotle, the greatest critic amongst the Greeks,"[35] and later critics might have omitted the qualification. The swift acceptance of Longinus might helpfully be compared to the modern discovery of the Metaphysical poets, for neglected works are not revived through scholarship alone. They must also speak to the intellectual and literary concerns of the age reviving them. Longinus spoke to an age obsessed with understanding the nature of great writing and with defining the standards of poetic excellence. His treatise was so relevant to these concerns that its popularity during the first four decades of the eighteenth century exceeds that of any other work of criticism.

Of course, various reasons help to explain the startling popularity of Longinus: his defense of poetic licence,[36] his argument that great writing requires political freedom and a high-minded citizenry,[37] and his belief that man was created to be the admiring spectator of creation—a view easily reconciled with the new interest in science.[38] At the moment, however, such explanations for the popularity of Longinus are less important to our subject than are several specific contributions to English criticism which indirectly support the development of the religious sublime. These are: 1) his influence upon the tone and methods of criticism, 2) his emphasis upon the importance of passion and imagination, and 3) his distinction between sublimity and the sublime style.

The discovery of Longinus offered hope to those who wished to change the tone and methods of English criticism. In Dryden's time, when political and literary factions multiplied quarrels, criticism often sounded shrill and belligerent. Dryden complained in 1677 that "we are fallen into an age of illiterate, censorious, and detracting people, who, thus qualified, set up for critics"—itself a deftly barbed contribution to discord—and Swift, in a similar mood, personified criticism as the child of Pride and Ridicule.[39] When gentlemen mobbed together to damn a new play, even before they had seen it, disinterested literary evaluation was all but impossible. Thus, one serious intention of Pope's *Essay on Criticism* (1711) was to propose the neglected, if obvious, standards of "*Good-Nature and Good-Sense*" as essential to the critical sensibility; and, in relating the act of criticism directly to the character of the critic, Pope, like many after him, thought especially of Longinus:

> An ardent Judge, who Zealous in his Trust,
> With Warmth gives Sentence, yet is always Just.[40]

Pope's legal metaphor—picturing Longinus as an "ardent *Judge*" —suggests a further dimension of the new idea of criticism which Longinus helped to spread: the ardency of the judge is not to be mistaken for partisan zeal but derives instead from his broad powers of sympathy, powers which inevitably temper justice with mercy. "The true critic," wrote William Smith in the notes to his translation of Longinus, "knows how to pardon, to excuse, and to extenuate."[41] Although Horace says much the same, Longinus and his practical emphasis upon the beauties (rather than faults) of composition probably did more than any other single force to civilize eighteenth-century criticism. The sublime moment of intensity excuses a variety of minor faults, while the very warmth of Longinus's style assured readers of his poetical sensibility: he himself had felt the passion of his subject. For the eighteenth century he became an embodiment of the true critic: alert to beauties and forgiving lapses.

One of Longinus's most timely contributions was in the area of terminology. In its search for a meaningful, uniform, and technical vocabulary of literary analysis, neoclassical criticism illustrates obliquely a fundamental assumption of seventeenth-century English science and philosophy: that knowledge depends utterly upon the nature of language. Both Hobbes and Locke, for example, insisted that accurate investigation requires the proper use of language, and Locke included an entire book "Of Words" in his *Essay Concerning Human Understanding* (1690), where he argues that the primary abuse of language and, consequently, of knowledge is the use of words which do not evoke "clear and distinct" ideas. No one confused literary criticism with science, but since serious literature was considered a form of knowledge, the critic, like the philosopher or naturalist, recognized the necessity of a fundamental clarity of language. The need to use words which evoke clear and distinct ideas helps to explain Addison's apparently strange syllabus for fledgling critics: "Mr. Lock's Essay on Human Understanding would be thought a very odd Book for a Man to make himself Master of, who would get a Reputation by Critical Writings; though at the same time it is very certain, that an Author who has not learn'd the Art of distinguishing between Words and Things, and of ranging his Thoughts, and setting them in proper Lights, whatever Notions he may have, will lose himself in Confusion and Obscurity" (*Spec.* 291). Like the dark and vain jargon of the Scholastic theologians whom Hobbes attacked, the inherited language of criticism often struck neoclassical writers as a confusion of mere sounds. Especially in discussing the nature of great writing, they increasingly resigned such terms as *inspiration, enthusiasm,* and *je-ne-sais-quoi* in favor of Longinian sublimity.

Longinus actually provided no clear definition of the sublime —creating a vacuum which a multitude of eighteenth-century critics rushed to fill—but he did contribute significantly to the methods of English criticism by providing what seemed like an empirical analysis of his subject. Perhaps his most important innovation, in the opinions of eighteenth-century critics, was his attention to specific passages—in contrast to the method of Horace, who dealt in generalized statements about the origin, function, and rules of poetry. "No criticism can be very instructive," judged David Hume, "which descends not to particulars, and is not full of examples and illustrations."[42] Perhaps closely associated with the shift toward particularity in eighteenth-century criticism was a declining interest in the formal and generic aspects of poetry. If Aristotle had based his notion of imitation upon the creation of probable, unified plots, Longinus and the aesthetics of intensity emphasized smaller units of composition: the individual part becomes potentially more important than the design of the whole—especially as criticism looked beyond the Aristotelian categories of drama and epic. Further, when Longinus could locate sublimity in a speech by Demosthenes, in a lyric by Sappho, and in a single line from Genesis, it was obvious that sublimity potentially transcended genre; and, while eighteenth-century critics agreed that sublimity was most appropriate to the "greater" literary forms—epic, tragedy, and the Pindaric ode—their admiration for the sublime could extend (as Joseph Priestly's did) even to scattered passages from *An Essay on Man.* Indeed, some modern scholars would argue that Longinus not only helped to topple traditional formalism in poetry but also inspired the creation of an entirely new kind of verse: the sublime poem. If we restrict our view to criticism, however, one other result of the stress upon particular passages ought to be cited. With formal considerations of lessening interest, the success of a given passage was judged implicitly by its power to excite the passions of the reader. Thus in an era fond of deducing general laws for poetry, the affective poetics of

Longinus reinforced the native pragmatic strain in English criticism which distrusted abstract rules and universal propositions: if French drama, with its meticulous observation of the Unities, did not move the passions of an English audience, Dryden argued, then its formal consistency was in vain. The traditional rules and procedures of criticism, of course, were not transformed radically or abruptly; nor is Longinus wholly responsible for the changes which occurred. But his popularity did help to augment the eighteenth-century desire for literary innovation, and perhaps the best way to suggest his effect upon the methods of English criticism is to examine a specific example: Addison's *Spectator* papers on *Paradise Lost.*

Addison's criticism of Milton begins with a traditional division of the poem, based upon Le Bossu's *Traité du poème épique* (1675), into the Aristotelian categories of fable, characters, sentiments, and language. He discusses each category in a separate paper, but after treating fable and character he announced a change of method: "In my next," he wrote at the end of his second paper, " I shall go through other parts of *Milton's* Poem; and hope that what I shall there advance, as well as what I have written already, will not only serve as a Comment upon *Milton*, but upon *Aristotle*" (*Spec.* 273). Sentiments and language, Addison perceived, are subjects which respond better to Longinian analysis than to the methods of Aristotelian criticism; thus, even while preserving the framework of Aristotle's fourfold division, he infuses it with another critical perspective. In addition, after completing the dutiful fourfold division of the poem, he devoted his final twelve papers to a book-by-book discussion of the "beauties" of *Paradise Lost*—a method at that time unparalleled in English criticism. After using Aristotle to prove that Milton's poem is a regular and well-constructed work, he shifted to Longinus to prove that it is sublime. In fact, by proposing three different passages as "most sublime" Addison attests more to his Longinian enthusiasm for Milton than to any desire for final judgment. Considering the importance of his essays on Milton, both in establishing the reputation of *Paradise Lost* and in shaping the methods of English criticism, Addison's understanding of Longinus must be viewed as a decisive force in the development of eighteenth-century English criticism.

Longinus's stress upon passion and imagination as essential aspects of the poetic process equals or exceeds in importance his contributions to the methodology of criticism. One of the greatest values of the *Peri Hupsous*, if such things can be measured, was its presentation of a detailed, technical, and illustrated discussion of great writing in a context which ignored both supernatural inspiration and the interaction of Fancy and Judgment. In providing his English admirers with a nonmystical and nonmechanical explanation of the poetic process, Longinus also happily satisfied the belief of the age that poetry is not simply the result of a psychological process but necessarily involves a highly conscious exercise of craftsmanship. While the *Peri Hupsous*, then, stressed the necessity of innate powers of feeling and of imagining, it demonstrated how these powers might be expressed through specific effects which well-endowed poets could achieve by art. The combination proved irresistible to most eighteenth-century readers, who particularly enjoyed a poetry which expressed the human passions through the use of visual images.

The stress upon passion and imagination in the poet not only improved upon other current accounts of the poetic process but also implied significant, although often unrealized, changes in the idea of the poet's intention. Most critics early in the eighteenth century considered the poetic process as guided ultimately by a preconceived moral purpose: the growth of the poem reflects the poet's sure understanding of his final didactic function. For Longinus, the function of poetry is ethical rather than moral or didactic. It involves a calling forth of greatness from within rather than a laying-on of virtue from without. The old "teach and delight" formula quietly disappears. If most eighteenth-century critics squeezed the sublime into a moralistic framework, praising its social utility, some, especially late in the century, dissociate sublimity from the Popean conception that poetry must make men better. Perhaps James Beattie best suggested the liberating possibilities of Longinus in asserting that "the test of sublimity is not moral approbation, but that pleasurable astonishment wherewith certain things strike the beholder."[43] The power of striking, when divorced from any moral or ethical intentions, can lead to excess as unfortunate as the worst faults of didacticism, and the flagrantly amoral implications of Longinian aesthetics had to await the genius of another age. But in essentially ignoring the didactic role of poetry, Longinus did help to inspire changes in eighteenth-century poetry and criticism. As the century proceeds, we hear less about the poetic process as governed by a moral and formal teleology. Rather, as for Longinus, the first requirement of the poet is that he be able to imagine vividly and to feel strongly.

Eighteenth-century poets and critics, while not desiring or wholly understanding the moral liberation which Longinus offered, did respond favorably to the argument that imagination and passion are the essential qualities of the sublime poet. By imagination they meant either the process of perceiving visual images or, less frequently, the images themselves. The emphasis, at any rate, is on pictorial qualities, and Longinus was particularly careful to stress the complementary roles of imagination and passion in producing the sublime. Horace had argued in a famous passage that the poet who wishes to make his readers weep must first weep himself (Ars 102–3). Longinus, in a chapter which Boileau entitled "Des Images," argues that the poet's power of arousing passion derives from his imaginative abilities, so that "by an enthusiasm and by an extraordinary exertion of the soul, it seems that we see the things of which we speak and place them before the eyes of those who listen."[44] The mere reader or listener, through the poet's powers of imagination, is transformed into an eyewitness, presumably experiencing emotions much like those which the real scene would have evoked. Actually, this strategy had been long familiar under the old rhetorical device of *enargeia* which, as Quintilian describes its operation, "makes us seem not so much to narrate as to display, while we are moved as much as if we were present at the scene itself" (Institutio 6.2.32). With the discovery of Longinus, this older strategy was revived by eighteenth-century poets and, enlisted among the properties of the imagination, made one of the prerequisites of sublime verse. Thus, shortly after reading Longinus, Dryden was moved to write that "imaging is, in itself, the very height and life of Poetry."[45] Later, Addison and Joseph Warton made the interaction of sight and feeling the cornerstone of their aesthetic theories. The importance of Longinus in sparking this reevaluation of passion and imagination in poetry cannot be easily overstated.

As passion and imagination came to be regarded as necessary aspects of the sublime, a number of poets and critics began to discover a new kind of sublimity in the long-admired poetry of the Bible. The habit of citing the Bible as a locus of Longinian sublimity begins shortly after the appearance of Boileau's translation. English critics previously had expressed a random appreciation of biblical imagination. Sidney, for example, praised David for "his notable *Prosopopeias*, when he maketh you, as it were, see God comming in his Maiestie; his telling of the Beastes ioyfulnes, and hills leaping."[46] Such observations, however, usually occurred in the context of conventional discussions of biblical rhetoric. After 1674, the critical analysis of biblical imagery became a growing fashion as is illustrated in the criticism of Boileau's contemporary Father Bouhours. In 1671, Bouhours had published a dialogue concerning the *je ne sais quoi*, suggesting a vague relationship between literary and theological "grace" and dealing mainly in generalities.[47] In 1687, Bouhours began to write specifically of the sublime and offered a suggestive discussion of biblical imagery:

> As for me, said Philanthus, I have seen no *pictures* like those which David made of a turn of fortune: "I myself have seen the ungodly in great power and flourishing like a green bay tree." "I went by and lo he was gone: I sought him but his place could nowhere be found." Observe how far David goes. All [that] poets have said of the decay of Troy, of Rome, and of Carthage, is that nothing was left but the places where those famous cities were situated. But David tells us that the very place where the impious was in the highest pitch of fortune is no more.[48]

Although Bouhours does not provide a lengthy explanation of the passage he cites from David, his discussion does reflect a potential for original analyses both of the poetry of the Bible and of modern poetry in general.

The passage from Bouhours illustrates not only a new critical interest in the poetry of the Bible but also a device which became standard in discussions of biblical sublimity. As in Du Bartas's remarks on poetry, the recommendation of Christian subjects often turned upon religious sentiment alone. "Pagan subjects are invariably false, Christian subjects are true," poets argued in defense of their Christian poems. Theological truth, not relative poetic merit, thus becomes the standard of literary judgment. Bouhours's comparison of classical and biblical imagery, on the other hand, makes no mention of truth or falsehood. The judgment depends entirely on literary merit; David's imagery, he believes, is both more explicit and more astonishing than the imagery of classical writers. This juxtaposition of biblical and classical passages became a regular exercise in eighteenth-century discussions of the sublime, and almost every such comparison argued that the sublimity of the Bible far surpassed that of any classical writer. Putting aside for the moment any considerations of the Bible's inspired truth, eighteenth-century critics nearly all agreed that the Bible was—on its poetic merits alone—the richest treasury of the sublime.

Longinus's main contribution to eighteenth-century critical theory was his important distinction between sublimity and the sublime style. In emphasizing this distinction, however, Boileau's "Préface" was more influential than the *Traité* itself. Providing the clarity of definition which appealed to the rational spirit of neoclassicism, Boileau explained the meaning of Longinian sublimity by carefully limiting application of the term:

> We should understand, then, that by the "Sublime" Longinus does not mean what orators call the sublime style: rather, he means that extraordinary and that marvelous which strikes us in a discourse and which causes a work to elevate, to ravish, and to transport. The sublime style always requires grand

words; but the Sublime can be found in a single thought, in a single figure of speech, or in a single turn of phrase. A work can be in the sublime style without, however, being Sublime— that is, having nothing of the extraordinary or the surprising.[49]

As Boileau notes, sublimity is not essentially a matter of language but of conception; its presence is measured not by the level of diction but by the effect of thoughts, images, or particular words upon the emotions. Grand diction has no necessary connection with true sublimity. In fact, high-sounding words, Boileau implies, probably will dampen rather than excite the feelings.

Boileau's sharp distinction between sublimity and the grand style came at a crucial moment, for in France and in England the high style was under attack for its violation of chaste, simple, clear expression.[50] The Royal Society advocated a "Mathematical plainness"[51] in scientific discourse, and, with fancy rhetoric often associated with the excesses of religious dissent, Joseph Glanville summarized the first rule of preaching in four words: "it should be PLAIN."[52] A few years later, Pope applied the same standard to poetry. False eloquence, he wrote, is like a prism, scattering indiscriminately its "gawdy Colours." True expression, on the other hand, is like the purity of light, which "Clears, and improves whate'er it shines upon."[53] Significantly, in deploring the ornate, pretentious rhetoric of their day, Frenchmen such as Balzac, Méré, Pascal, and Fénelon[54] frequently exalted as a model of style the parables of Jesus. Boileau's "Préface" gave additional impetus to this movement and to the development of the religious sublime by its discussion of the sublimity of Genesis 1:3—"And God said, Let there be light: and there was light."

Boileau helped to establish the fiat lux passage as the touchstone of eighteenth-century sublimity. His source was Longinus himself, who had quoted Genesis 1:3 to illustrate how references to divine power can ennoble works of art. To Englishmen, the sublimity of the biblical passage was so apparent that Dugald Stewart noted at the beginning of the nineteenth century, " 'Let there be light, and there was light,' has been quoted as an instance of sublime writing by almost every critic since the time of

Longinus."[55] As loyal Christians, of course, eighteenth-century critics would have been drawn to the passage in Longinus without Boileau's help; but the passage became even more than predictably familiar because of a controversy which Boileau's Preface inspired concerning the relationship of plainness to sublimity and the literary intentions of Moses.[56] Few Englishmen, however, doubted the sublimity of *fiat lux*. Poets throughout the century echoed its rhythm and language to create an aura of biblical elevation. In a serious mood, Pope in *Windsor-Forest* rose to the climactic lines:

> At length great ANNA said—Let Discord cease!
> She said, the World obey'd, and All was Peace!

In a mood of gentle irony, he portrayed Belinda ruling the microcosmic game of Ombre with Anna-like divinity: "*Let Spades be Trumps!* she said, and Trumps they were."[57] Besides suggesting that the Bible must contain a wealth of other sublime thought and expression, the *fiat lux* passage assumed independent life as the recognized epitome of the sublime.

In hailing the *fiat lux* passage as the pinnacle of sublimity, eighteenth-century critics were following Boileau rather than Longinus. For Longinus, reference to divine power was only one of numerous ways to achieve sublimity. For Boileau, the passage from Genesis was "the most proper"[58] example to illustrate the true sublime. He further emphasized the difference between true sublimity and the sublime style by juxtaposing an inflated paraphrase of Genesis 1:3 against a literal translation. The simple power of the literal version shone by comparison. The high-sounding paraphrase, Boileau wrote, was an example of the sublime style; the literal translation shows the power of true sublimity. Then he added a revealing comment: "We should understand by the Sublime in Longinus the Extraordinary, the Surprising, and, as I have translated it, the Marvellous in a discourse."[59] By expanding Longinus's title to the *Traité du Sublime, ou du Merveilleux dans le Discours*, Boileau implicitly associated the concept of sublimity with the ancient critical tradition of "the marvellous." The association of the sublime with the marvellous, however, did not merely color the idea of sublimity with a certain amount of critical respectability. Together with Boileau's choice of Genesis 1:3 as the best example of true sublimity, it also related the sublime to a current French literary quarrel concerning what was called "*le merveilleux chrétien.*" This quarrel, in which Boileau himself was directly involved, substantially affected the eventual development of the religious sublime.

LE MERVEILLEUX CHRÉTIEN

The controversy over *le merveilleux chrétien* accompanied the remarkable French interest in Christian and biblical epics during the last half of the seventeenth century. Tasso and Du Bartas provided the spark for early activity in the religious epic, but between 1610 and 1650 interest seemed to dim. Then in 1653 the *Moyse sauvé* by Saint-Amant and the *Saint-Louis* by Le Moyne initiated a period of frenzied activity.[60] The French scholar René Bray provides a summary of the alarming mass of sacred poetry published after 1650:

> Then, and I consider only the most important, Godeau produced his *Saint-Paul* and Scudéry his *Alaric* in 1654; in 1656, the first twelve "chants" of *La Pucelle*; in 1657, the *Clovis* of Desmarets; in 1658, *Constantinus* by Mambrun and a second part of Le Moyne's *Saint-Louis*; in 1660, the *David* of les Farges; in 1661, the *Ignatiade* of le Brun; from 1663 to 1665, *Samson, David, Jonas,* and *Josué* by Coras; in 1664, le Laboureur's *Charlemagne*; in 1666, *Marie-Madeleine,* in 1670, *Esther,* in 1673, a second part of *Clovis* (all three by Desmarets); and finally in 1673, the *Eustachius* of L'Abbé. Eighteen poems in twenty years, fourteen of them in the first dozen years. Certainly that constitutes a fashion. All concern Christian subjects, half drawn from modern history, seven from the Old Testament. Tasso has not lacked admirers.[61]

The first years of this determined effort to revive the religious epic coincided with the exile of Charles and his court in France. English men-of-letters, thus, were well aware of the movement to forge a strong, direct alliance between religion and epic poetry. But the French epics themselves were less important to the development of the religious sublime than was the controversy which they inspired. Most of the French epics, as René Bray has observed, were accompanied by learned essays full of theory. Inevitably, these essays discussed the question of *le merveilleux*.

"The marvellous," according to the critic René Rapin (1621–1687), "is everything which is contrary to the ordinary course of nature." [62] Since the time of Aristotle (*Poetics* 1460a), it was thought to be a proper ingredient of tragedy and of epic. Tasso, in fact, had declared that the marvellous was the essential characteristic of epic writing. Thus any epic poet who regarded critical tradition was compelled to include in his poem an assortment of preternatural beings and events. Nevertheless, the seventeenth-century poet who sought to include the marvellous in his epic faced potentially conflicting demands.

The main difficulty regarding the marvellous was the general requirement that poetry embody a principle of verisimilitude or probability. An epic, while it must contain the marvellous, must also conform to the accepted definition of art as an imitation of nature. All epic writers, to some extent, have struggled with the problem of making their marvels believable. The general solution seems to have been a recognition by writers and readers that a certain amount of preternatural activity is expected (and, hence, probable) within the epic context. Dryden suggested an additional solution, arguing that the poet can legitimately create unknown beings from the materials of memory and imagination: the centaur exists potentially in every mind through the combination of two natural images, man and horse. [63] But this solution conflicts with Horace's famous dictum forbidding irrational combinations such as women who end like fish (*Ars* 1–5), and it hardly answers the sterner challenge to the use of the marvellous indirectly advanced by English advocates of the new science.

As historian and apologist for the new science in seventeenth-century England, Thomas Sprat proudly announced the demise of a superstitious or magical view of nature. The work of the Royal Society, Sprat boasted, confirms that now the "cours of things goes quietly along, in its own true channel of *Natural Causes and Effects.*" [64] Sprat, of course, was not attacking poetry but defending science. In heralding the fall of "King Oberon and his invisible Army," [65] however, he did signal the direction of literary change. A *Midsummer Night's Dream* might suit the fantasy world of opera (Henry Purcell transformed it into an opera in 1692), but it offended Samuel Pepys, who like many of his contemporaries seemed to prefer the less exotic forms of current drama and poetry. The excesses of Dryden's heroic drama had been brilliantly deflated by Buckingham in *The Rehearsal* (1671), and, while the extravagance of an outmoded mythology suited the lighthearted vein of pastorals and mock genres, it could no longer sustain the dignity and truth of loftier composition. The question which perplexed seventeenth-century writers was both serious and knotty. If nature now continued along its own true channel of natural causes and effects, how could it accommodate the marvellous, everything contrary to the ordinary course of nature? Many eighteenth-century poets answered this question with the sublime in nature; floods, mountains, whirlwinds, blizzards, and volcanos possessed the literary advantage of being simultaneously natural and marvellous. French epic writers of the seventeenth century, following the example of Tasso, offered a different answer—*le merveilleux chrétien.*

The marvellous usually refers to supernatural beings (or machinery) in an epic, and some sort of supernatural machinery was considered necessary to its success. "For my part," wrote Dryden, "I am of opinion, that neither Homer, Virgil, Statius, Ariosto, Tasso, nor our English Spencer, could have formed their poems half so beautiful, without those gods and spirits, and those enthusiastic parts of poetry, which compose the most noble parts of all their writings." [66] It might be expected that Dryden would approve the use of supernatural marvels in the opera, [67] but he extended the same license to the epic as well. Gods and spirits were so necessary to epic writing that "no heroic poem," Dryden affirmed, "can be writ on the Epicurean principles." [68] Since the exploded mythology of the pagans, however, could be condemned as ridiculous and improbable in a modern poem, Dryden urged that modern poets turn to their own religion for believable gods and spirits. This argument Dryden might have borrowed directly from Tasso and from the French controversialists of *le merveilleux chrétien*.

By ignoring the believable marvels of Christianity, Dryden argued, Christian poets "have not hitherto been acquainted with their own strength." He advised the poet to take his machines from the Old Testament. " 'Tis a doctrine almost universally received by Christians, as well Protestants as Catholics," he wrote, "that there are guardian angels, appointed by God Almighty, as his vicegerents, for the protection and government of cities, provinces, kingdoms, and monarchies; and those as well of heathens, as of true believers."[69] Dryden took the argument one step further, contending that the pagan fables never achieved widespread acceptance among educated Greeks and Romans; the angels and spirits of Christianity, on the other hand, receive general belief among learned and unlearned alike. Thus Dryden transmitted to England a condensed but complete version of the arguments supporting *le merveilleux chrétien*, capsulizing essentially the same ideas which Desmarets de Saint-Sorlin poured into four separate treatises published between 1670 and 1674.

Dryden may have said comparatively little on the subject of *le merveilleux chrétien* precisely because it was a well-known aspect of a literary quarrel which, after his *Essay of Dramatic Poesy* (1688), he generally avoided: the contest between Ancients and Moderns. Defenders of the Moderns had cited the replacement of heathen mythology by Christianity as evidence of modern supremacy over ancient poetry. Dryden himself, while avoiding the polemical tone which many of the combatants adopted, proposed that a poet who employed Christian machinery "may build a nobler, a more beautiful and more perfect poem, than any yet extant since the Ancients."[70] Dryden does not predict absolute superiority for the moderns; but, considering his enormous respect for the poets of antiquity, he obviously thought *le merveilleux chrétien* to be an important and fruitful idea. His interest was soon shared by Samuel Wesley[71] and may have influenced younger men such as Dennis and Addison who attended Dryden in his latter days at Will's coffeehouse. Nevertheless, *le merveilleux chrétien* evoked significant opposition both in France and in England.

French opposition to *le merveilleux chrétien* was both theoretical and practical. The theoretical objection, summarized by Boileau in his *Art poétique* (1674), rested upon the fundamental neoclassical belief that the proper study of mankind is man. Poetry must deal with what is humanly knowable, and to fill a poem with angels, spirits, and devils is to presume to understand what God alone can know. Furthermore, Boileau and many others in France and in England thought of poetry as basically a medium for the imaginative expression of moral truths. It had no business, therefore, meddling with the higher religious mysteries of Christianity. This thinking underlies Boileau's famous denunciation of the Christian epic:

> De la foy d'un Chrestien les mysteres terribles
> D'ornemens égayés ne sont point susceptibles.[72]

Boileau's aphorism summarizes much English opposition to the mixing of poetry and religion. "The ideas of Christian Theology," Johnson wrote, "are too simple for eloquence, too sacred for fiction, and too majestick for ornament; to recommend them by tropes and figures is to magnify by a concave mirror the sidereal hemisphere."[73] As Johnson's image of the mirror suggests, the neoclassical doctrine of imitation encourages poets to treat only those events, objects, and ideas which can be known clearly and distinctly. Johnson would also agree with Boileau that even religious ideas which can be known clearly and distinctly are necessarily debased by imitation. Finally, Boileau claimed that certain scenes are simply unsuitable for poetic treatment. What merit is there, he asked, in describing Satan "always howling against Heaven?"[74] Of course, in part Boileau does not argue but asserts his objections to Christian poetry. Yet the name of Boileau was itself strong argument against mixing poetry and religion.

Failure was the practical objection to *le merveilleux chrétien*.

In a letter to Rapin, Bussy-Rabutin expressed what was doubtless one basis of Boileau's objections to Christian poetry. "I am convinced," he wrote, "that an epic poem cannot succeed in our language: one can prove it easily by examples. The *Moyse sauvé*, the *Saint-Louis*, *La Pucelle*, the *Clovis*, and the *Alaric* are ample testimony."[75] The examples are all Christian epics of the period from 1650 to 1675. The defenders of Christian poetry had to contend with a dismal succession of failures. And, because many of the theoretical defenders of Christian poetry also fathered unsuccessful poems, failure of the poet implicitly damned the critic. Thus, considering its history in France, especially Boileau's opposition and the misfortune of French religious poets, the theory of the Christian marvellous should have met a quick end in England. It did not, however. Two things helped to transform the French theory of *le merveilleux chrétien* into a basis of the religious sublime: the growing popularity of Longinus and the growing reputation of *Paradise Lost*.

THE RELIGIOUS SUBLIME: GLIMMERINGS

Referring to Boileau's strictures, A. F. B. Clark has contended that "the sickly life of the Christian epic, as a genre, might have been indefinitely prolonged in England, if the English critics had not crushed its life out with Boileau's bludgeon."[76] Actually, Englishmen tended to scoff at Boileau's bludgeon. While Boileau's criticism could explain any number of bad French epics, it could not account for the remarkable and overwhelming success of *Paradise Lost*. Samuel Wesley wrote in 1697:

> As for that Question of Boileau's, "What Pleasure can it be to hear the howlings of repining Lucifer?" I think 'tis easier to answer than to find out what shew of Reason he had for asking it, or why Lucifer may'nt howl as pleasantly as either Cerberus or Enceladus. And let any one read but his Speech, in Milton's Paradise, almost equall'd in Mr. Dryden's State of Innocence, and I'm mistaken if he's not of the same Mind; or if he be not, and it gives him no pleasure, I dare affirm 'tis for want of a true taste of what's really admirable.[77]

Wesley's loquacity hides a serious point. Despite the authority of Boileau and despite the failure of the French Christian epic, Milton's *Paradise Lost* established the success of the "divine poem" in England. Milton proved that poetry and Christianity were compatible. In fact, his epic supported the contention of those who claimed that a modern poet could surpass the ancients only if his subject were Christian. It is not so much the Christian epic which died in eighteenth-century England as the epic itself. And a main influence upon the demise of epic form was not Boileau's *Art poétique* but his *Traité du Sublime*.

Boileau's translation of Longinus appeared in the same year as the twelve-book version of *Paradise Lost*. Dryden three years later published his operatic version of Milton's poem and in the preface initiated the fashion of considering Milton and Longinus together. The popularity of the sublime soon grew inseparable from the acknowledged grandeur of *Paradise Lost*. Milton, after a period of initial neglect, soon exceeded the fame of the greatest classical poets. Samuel Wesley, for example, recognized certain epic irregularities in *Paradise Lost*, but he also insisted that it has "many Thoughts and Images, greater than perhaps any either in Virgil or Homer."[78] Wesley here does not speak of the sublimity of *Paradise Lost*, but it is significant that he praises Milton's "Thoughts and Images" rather than the larger conventional aspects of epic construction.

As long as the sublime and the marvellous were restricted to the context of epic writing, they would become the object only of poets willing to lavish the traditional time and effort. Thomas Gray, for example, once joked about the severe impracticality of his undertaking an epic, since he would finish at age seventy-four.[79] Yet, as Boileau noted, the sublime could consist in a single thought, or figure of speech, or turn of phrase. A poet who aimed at the sublime would not have to shackle himself to an epic but could crowd elevating thoughts and images into a few lines. Furthermore, as poets and critics increasingly turned to Milton and to the Bible for patterns of sublime thoughts and images, the association between religion and sublimity grew stronger. Traditional genres became vehicles for religious sublimity: the pastoral, the Pindaric ode, the biblical paraphrase, the epic, and even the poem of natural description were often infused with a biblical spirit. Sublime poetry, of course, did not have to be religious. But it frequently was. The conscious development of the religious sublime by eighteenth-century poets and critics is the subject of the remainder of this study. The carefully reasoned criticism of John Dennis, England's outspoken proponent of the religious sublime, provides the first and most extensive development of an idea which, from a shadowy and fragmented existence on the fringes of consciousness, suddenly emerged as the center of a full and audacious theory of poetry.

Chapter Two

John Dennis and the Religious Sublime

Writing with a clear understanding of the tortuous crosscurrents of Restoration criticism, John Dennis provided England, at the very beginning of the eighteenth century, with a thorough and articulate theory of the religious sublime. He was adept in both ancient and modern literary tradition, and he possessed in addition a pugnacious originality which allowed him to combine the old with the new in refreshing ways. His list of distinguished enemies, which at times included Addison, Steele, and Pope, inclines some modern readers to dismiss him as a crank. If he was at times grumpy and irascible, Dennis's contemporaries did not ignore him, and today some scholars think that Giles Jacob was correct in calling Dennis "the greatest Critick of this Age."[1] He was, with all his defects of temperament, certainly bold, original and important—qualities nowhere more prominent than in his advocacy of the religious sublime. His best works, *The Advancement and Reformation of Modern Poetry* (1701) and *The Grounds of Criticism in Poetry* (1704), argue in detail the proposition that the greatest poetry is inevitably both sublime and religious. Although some of his later criticism is marred by an eccentric inconsistency, his "argument for the religious-sublime in *The Advancement and Reformation of Modern Poetry* and in *The Grounds of Criticism in Poetry*," as Clarence DeWitt Thorpe asserts, "is his most consistent performance."[2] Surprisingly, this important contribution to eighteenth-century criticism passes almost without comment in the histories of literary theory. In attempting to correct the omission, I will consider in some detail Dennis's ideas concerning the religious sublime. Because no eighteenth-century writer ever argued for the theory of religious sublimity with such consistent force and clarity, his criticism provides a thorough introduction to ideas concerning the religious sublime which attracted poets and critics for the next hundred years.

POETRY AND PASSION

Dennis's theory of the religious sublime grows out of his general theory of poetry. Poetry, he believed, is "an Art, by which a Poet excites Passion."[3] It is difficult now to appreciate the boldness of Dennis's definition; his statement simply seems an affirmation of evident truth. Further, its importance to its own time is obscured because most of his contemporaries recognized that poetry could not ignore passion, and they developed the practice of extending the definitions of particular genres by stipulating which passion each genre was designed to evoke. The irregular ode, for example, should evoke astonishment; tragedy should evoke compassion and terror; the epic should evoke admiration. Normally, however, Augustan criticism concentrated on the formal and stylistic aspects of poetry, and most critics agreed with Aristotle that poetry is fundamentally an imitation of nature, shaped by the demands of various generic forms. Dennis greatly admired Aristotle, the Rules, and the doctrine of imitation. His early work *Remarks on a Book Entituled, Prince Arthur* (1696) is largely an orthodox Aristotelian attack on Richard Blackmore's epic irregularities. Yet Dennis went beyond Aristotle in a number of areas, particularly in defining poetry as an art of exciting passion. His assertion is revolutionary in the neoclassical period not only for what it affirms but for what it ignores. It offers a view of the nature of poetry unparalleled in its day.

Dennis rejected as inadequate the prevalent seventeenth-century theories of poetic creation: the Hobbesian theory of Fancy and Judgment and the Miltonic doctrine of inspiration. Hobbes viewed the creation of poetry, Dennis evidently believed, as too exclusively mental. Although the senses must store the memory with data, once the memory is well stocked the Hobbesian poetic process presumably takes place entirely within the mind. On the contrary, Dennis asserted, history shows that the first poetry had very little to do with the head. Among the primitive Greeks, poetry developed because "great Passions naturally threw [men] upon Harmony and figurative Language, as they must of necessity do any Poet, as long as he continues Master of them" (1:364). Modern as well as primitive poetry in Dennis's view involves something more than the operation of mental processes. If Hobbes's theory of poetic creation seemed incomplete, however, Milton's theory seemed too expansive. Dennis found no difficulty in believing the Bible was inspired directly by God, but he knew it was foolish to claim as much for modern poets. His strongest support of the theory of inspiration consists of a long quotation from Milton (1:330), but most often Dennis sought a natural rather than a supernatural explanation of poetic creation. He dismissed as blasphemous the notion that pagan poets could have been truly inspired, and he doubted the ministry of demons because " 'tis absurd to give a supernatural Cause of an Effect, of which we can give a very natural one" (1:212). Looking to man himself for the source of poetry, Dennis concluded that history and human nature both prove that poetry originates in strong passion.

Dennis's theory of poetry, while it emphasized the passions to an unprecedented degree, by no means excluded other human faculties from a part in the poetic process. To restrict poetry to passion alone would simply reverse Hobbes's error. Rather than restricting poetry to a single faculty, Dennis demanded a poetry which would express and engage "the whole Man" (1:263). By the whole man, Dennis meant man as a composite of three faculties: the reason, the passions, and the senses. When he simplified his discussion, Dennis divided man into two parts: the head and the heart. In reaching the whole man, however, poetry for Dennis must appeal primarily to the emotions. "A Poet," he insisted, ". . . is oblig'd always to speak to the Heart" (1:127), and by engaging the passions of the reader, poetry, Dennis hoped, would ultimately instruct and reform the reason (1:337). Thus his definition of poetry as passion really conceals a theory of how the head and heart, representing the main human faculties, combine in producing an experience which offers a potentially unique form of psychic integration.

Dennis devised a complex and original discussion of the nature of human passion which he probably intended to use as the basis of his projected essay on poetic genius. He never published—and probably never wrote—the essay, but his view of the relationship between genius and passion runs through all his works, sustaining the often bizarre superstructure of his individual judgments. "Poetical Genius," he wrote, in what is perhaps the topic sentence from his unknown essay on the subject, ". . . is the true Expression of Ordinary or Enthusiastick Passions proceeding from Ideas to which it naturally belongs" (1:222). This obscure distinction between Ordinary and Enthusiastic passion is central to Dennis's poetics and essential to an understanding of his theory of the religious sublime. It is probably based on Locke's discrimination between sensation and reflection as the ultimate sources of human knowledge.[4] Explaining his terms, Dennis developed a series of differences between the two kinds of passion. First, Ordinary (or Vulgar) passion results from direct and immediate sensation—whether excited by a physical object or event or by the *idea* of a particular object or event. Enthusiastic passion always results from ideas matured and complicated through meditation. Second, the sensations arousing Ordinary passion always derive from something commonplace, but in Enthusiastic passion the ideas in meditation must be removed from the ordinary course of life. Finally, the causes of Ordinary passion are always clearly and distinctly understood, while Enthusiastic passion proceeds from complex and unfamiliar ideas which are not distinctly understood—a requirement in part explaining Dennis's overuse of the word *hint*.[5]

Dennis illustrated the difference between Ordinary and Enthusiastic passion with a vivid example. Writing in *The Grounds of Criticism in Poetry*, he explained, "I desire the Reader to observe, that Ideas in Meditation are often very different from what Ideas of the same Objects are, in the course of common Conversation. As for example, the Sun mention'd in ordinary Conversation, gives the Idea of a round flat shining Body, of about two foot diameter. But the Sun occurring to us in Meditation, gives the Idea of a vast and glorious Body, and the top of all the visible Creation, and the brightest material Image of the Divinity" (1:339). The example Dennis probably based on a passage in which Lucretius, crediting only the reports of his senses, declared that "the wheel of the sun cannot be much larger nor its glow less than is perceived by our senses."[6] Lucretius's vision, Dennis thought, could stimulate Ordinary passion only. When the small disk perceived by the senses is transmuted by the process of meditation, however, it becomes for Dennis a source of Enthusiastic passion. Thus, when Dennis writes that poetry is an art of raising passion, he does not mean that poetry should be the source of merely visceral or nervous excitement. Rather he means that poetry should engage the mind and the passions simultaneously in a process of transforming perception. Although Dennis admits that not all men are capable of experiencing Enthusiastic passion (1:339), he believes that the epic, the Pindaric ode, and other poems which called for great thoughts and spirited verse require the experience of Enthusiastic passion in poet and reader.

Enthusiastic passion is necessary in the greater kinds of poetry, Dennis maintained, because it is the means of reforming both poetry and man. According to Dennis, poetry shared with man the corruptions of the Fall. Like Milton, he envisioned the Fall as a psychological event, a lapse from "the Harmony of the Human Faculties, and the Felicity of the first Man" (1:260) into a state of inner disharmony, "a cruel War between the Passions and Senses, and the Reason" (1:253). While many of Dennis's contemporaries saw the solution to man's internal disorder in the dominance of reason over sense and passion, Dennis always spoke of harmony instead of dominance. The Puritan interregnum seemed to him a powerful example of the disorder attending the mere suppression of passion by reason, and Puritan attempts to reform man failed, he wrote metaphorically, because they were "begun at the Tail, instead of the Head and the Heart." They "opprest and persecuted Mens Inclinations, instead of correcting and converting them" (1:154). Man's reformation,

Dennis believed, would come through the harmonious exercise of all the faculties, not through a straitjacket of reason. The vehicle of correction and conversion would be a reformed modern poetry, one able to express and to inspire Enthusiastic passion.

Poetry, for Dennis as for Milton, had the same function as all other arts: "to restore the Decays that happen'd to human Nature by the Fall" (1:336). But poetry, argued Dennis, had an advantage over the other arts because it attacked the problem of man's inner disharmony most effectively: "For whereas Philosophy pretends to correct human Passions by human Reason, that is, things that are strong and ungovernable, by something that is feeble and weak: Poetry by the force of the Passion, instructs and reforms the Reason" (1:337). Dennis disagreed on principle with Pope's decision to moralize his song. Poetry was to be far more than a medium for the delightful expression of moral truth. For Dennis, poetry was "the best and the noblest Art" because it made "the best Provision at the same Time for the Satisfaction of all the Faculties, the Reason, the Passions, [and] the Senses" (1:263). By satisfying the whole man, not just that aspect of man which valued didactic moral truth, poetry might be the instrument for restoring the "paradise within" which Milton had predicted. "Poetry," Dennis wrote, "seems to be a noble Attempt of Nature, by which it endeavours to exalt itself to its happy primitive State; and he who is entertain'd with an accomplish'd Poem, is, for a Time, at least, restored to Paradise" (1:264). The paradise is not local but psychological, referring to the condition in which man's "every Passion, in its Turn, is charm'd, while his Reason is supremely satisfied" (1:264). Such a view of the usefulness and nobility of poetry is rarely encountered among the better-known Augustan writers, and it seems scarcely surprising to learn that Wordsworth and Coleridge sought Dennis's works at the beginning of the next century.[7]

THE RELIGIOUS SUBLIME

Dennis's theory of Enthusiastic passion, the foundation of his general theory of poetry, also provides the basis for his argument that the greatest sublimity derives from religious ideas. Oddly, while many of his contemporaries would have rejected Dennis's account of Enthusiastic passion, they did not reject his conclusions concerning the religious sublime. One explanation of the apparent paradox involves the thoroughness of Dennis's method of proof. Whether he always did so consciously or not, Dennis often divided his proof into three parts, arguing from reason, from authority, and from experience. A reader, then, might well reject Dennis's arguments from reason, while being convinced or influenced by the arguments from authority and from experience. To appreciate the consistency and the thoroughness of Dennis's theory of the religious sublime requires following his own method of proof. Let us look first at his arguments from reason and from authority, and then at the arguments from experience.

Dennis based his argument from reason on the proposition that poetry should raise Enthusiastic passion in the reader. The greatest poetry, he argued, must therefore arouse the greatest Enthusiastic passion. By "greatest" Dennis meant both strongest and worthiest. Further, he insisted that religious ideas inevitably raised the strongest and worthiest Enthusiastic passion: "Religious Enthusiasm," he wrote, "must necessarily be greater than Human Enthusiasm can be, because the Passions that attend on Religious Ideas, when a Man is capable of reflecting on them as he should do, are stronger than those which attend on Prophane Ideas" (1:231). To support this belief, Dennis adapted Longinus's idea that sublimity demands men with great souls. Ordinary men, he argued, are capable of Ordinary passion only. Those with great souls, however, can experience the worthier kinds of Enthusiastic passion. Thus men capable of exalted meditative reflection must discover that religious ideas move the strongest and worthiest passion. In *The Grounds of Criticism in Poetry* he summarized this argument in a chain of logically connected propositions:

> Since therefore the Enthusiasm in the greater Poetry, is to hold proportion with the Ideas; and those Ideas are certainly the

> greatest, which are worthiest to move the greatest and the wisest
> Men: and Divine Ideas, or Ideas which shew the Attributes of
> God, or relate to his Worship, are worthiest to move the
> greatest and the wisest Men; because such Ideas belong to
> Objects which are only truly above them, and consequently
> truly Admirable, Desirable, Joyful, Terrible, &c. it follows,
> That the greatest and strongest Enthusiasm that can be
> employ'd in Poetry, is only justly and reasonably to be deriv'd
> from Religious Ideas (1:340).

The dogged plodding of this passage makes one long for Horace's
graceful negligence. Yet, if one grants his premise that poetry is
the art of raising Enthusiastic passion, Dennis's argument follows
with persuasive, if incomplete, logic. Other things being equal
(which they never are), the infinite, eternal, and supernatural
ideas of religion should indeed raise a greater and worthier
passion than mere human, finite, or natural ideas.

Dennis's association of religious Enthusiasm with the sublime
becomes explicit in his arguments from authority. His long dis-
cussion of Longinus confirms that Dennis considered sublimity
the highest aim and praise of poetry. But, before Dennis intro-
duced Longinus and the sublime into *The Grounds of Criticism
in Poetry*, he first cited Hermogenes, a Greek rhetorician whose
reputation in the eighteenth century is rather puzzling. Dennis
was fluent in Greek, so he was not handicapped by the paucity
of translations, although he may have had to hunt diligently to
find even a Greek text. Hermogenes had enjoyed a considerable
popularity during the sixteenth century, especially through an
Italian translation of his *Idea*, and during Archbishop Laud's
chancellorship at Oxford (beginning in 1629), Hermogenes was
one of four ancient rhetoricians specified as subjects for lectures.[8]
The other three were Aristotle, Cicero, and Quintilian, indicating
that Hermogenes was considered among the best rhetoricians of
antiquity. Dennis's use of Hermogenes probably owes more to
precedent than to originality, however, since Boileau had cited
Hermogenes several times in the "Préface," "Rémarques," and
"Notes" to his translation of Longinus. In addition, Hermo-
genes' discussion of *megathous* (greatness or magnificence) had

been previously associated with Longinus's treatment of the sublime,[9] and so it was natural that Dennis should cite Hermogenes to support his claim that religious ideas evoke the greatest enthusiasm. As he explained at some length, Hermogenes described four "kinds of Thoughts or Ideas, or Conceptions, which were proper to give that Elevation and Gravity . . . in Writing which we call Majesty" (1:341). These four categories are 1) thoughts or ideas of God, 2) thoughts or ideas concerning the works of God, 3) human qualities which are "Emanations of Divinity," such as Justice or Temperance, and 4) human qualities which are great or illustrious, such as riches or conquest. Dennis rejected the fourth category, but the other three, he believed, strongly supported his theory that religious ideas are the most powerful source of great poetry. Although he did not claim that Hermogenes' "majesty" is identical with Longinus's "sublimity," he implied as much by moving immediately from the discussion of Hermogenes to a consideration of Longinus, in which he directly associated religious Enthusiastic passion with the sublime.

Dennis's literary relationship with Longinus deserves some preliminary comment. Although Dryden had much admired Longinus and the sublime, Dennis was the first English critic to make sublimity the keystone of his poetics. With some justification, he prided himself on his alliance with Longinus; even as late as 1717, theater audiences were expected to recognize Dennis under the title of Sir Tremendous Longinus. Pope, who had a part in awarding Dennis that title, clearly chafed at Dennis's self-styled monopoly on the sublime. "See *Longinus* in my right Hand, and *Aristotle* in my left," Pope makes Dennis declare; "I am the only Man among the Moderns that support them."[10] By 1713 Pope's satire made a valid point: Longinus, like Aristotle, was the property of the age. But in the initial decade of the eighteenth century, when Dennis stood unchallenged as the foremost literary critic of his day, he was indeed the first vocal champion of Longinus and the sublime. Nor was he the mindless disciple that his enemies liked to picture him. Although Longinus had introduced him to the idea of sublimity,

Dennis was not entirely satisfied with the *Peri Hupsous*. Longinus, he believed, had failed in two essential ways. He had not fully appreciated the relationship of passion and sublimity, and he had neglected to discuss religion as the greatest source of the sublime.

Because passion was the basis of his own theory of poetry, Dennis was disturbed that Longinus had slighted the relationship between passion and sublimity. Although Longinus cited strong passion as one of the two innate requirements of the sublime writer (sect. 8), in the same section he also asserted that sublimity might exist in passages which evoked no passion whatsoever. This possibility contradicted Dennis's entire theory of poetry, and here he wholly disagreed with Longinus, expanding the particular objection into a criticism of Longinus's general method. In analyzing the sublime, Dennis argued, Longinus had considered its effects only—amazement, pride, terror, transport. Dennis sought to deal in causes as well, to show "what it is in Poetry that works these Effects" (1:223).

The universal cause of sublimity, Dennis maintained, was passion; and in explaining Longinus's notion that sublimity could exist without passion, he attributed the "error" in part to Longinus's failure to distinguish between Ordinary and Enthusiastic passion. "The Sublime," Dennis wrote, "is indeed often without common Passion, as ordinary Passion is often without that [i.e., the Sublime]. But then it is never without Enthusiastick Passion" (1:359). Dennis even argued that Longinus contradicted himself, since Longinus had already declared that strong passion was an innate requirement of the sublime writer or speaker. "Now I leave the Reader to judge," Dennis concluded after a lengthy review of the apparent contradiction, "whether *Longinus* has not been saying here all along that Sublimity is never without Passion" (1:359). Despite occasional appearances to the contrary, Dennis did not imply that he and Longinus agreed completely. Instead, he believed that his own stress upon passion as the cause of sublimity complemented Longinus's treatment of the effects of the sublime. "So that, take the Cause and the Effects together," Dennis concluded, "and you have the Sublime" (1:223).

Longinus's silence concerning the relationship between sublimity and religious ideas presented Dennis with an even knottier problem. "I now come to the Precepts of *Longinus*," he wrote, pursuing his argument from authority, "and pretend to shew from them, that the greatest Sublimity is to be deriv'd from Religious Ideas. But why then, says the Reader, has not *Longinus* plainly told us so?" (1:358). Dennis faced his dilemma honestly. His solutions, nevertheless, may seem forced. First, Dennis noted, because Longinus had failed to appreciate the necessary relationship between Enthusiastic passion and sublimity, he was hardly prepared to recognize that religious ideas produce the greatest Enthusiastic passion. Second, although Longinus did not explain the relationship between sublimity and religious ideas, the *Peri Hupsous* demonstrates that he must have intuited the relationship. In support of this contention, Dennis showed that many of Longinus's examples drew their power from religious practices or beliefs. Further, Dennis cited Longinus's description of the six chief marks of the sublime, arguing that each is most powerfully attained by the use of religious ideas. This vindication, however, still left Dennis a little puzzled at the Greek critic's lack of perception. "I must confess I have wonder'd very much, upon Reflection," he mused, "how it could happen that so great a Man as *Longinus*, who whenever he met a Passage in any Discourse that was lofty enough to please him, had Discernment enough to see that it had some of the [six] preceding Marks, should miss of finding so easy a thing as this, that never any Passage had all these Marks, or so much as the Majority of them, unless it were Religious" (1:361).

Dennis's bewilderment sounds much like oblique self-praise, but it also emphasizes the extent of his commitment to the theory of the religious sublime. Dennis needed Longinus's authority to support his own claim that sublimity is the unfailing mark of great poetry. But his contention that the greatest sublimity is derived from religious ideas did not depend upon the authority of Longinus. Although the theory might draw some support from ancient authorities, it was really the invention of Dennis's own reason and experience.

ANCIENT AND MODERN RELIGIOUS SUBLIMITY

Dennis probably suspected that appeals to reason and authority would not convince most readers that the greatest sublimity derives from religious ideas. As he wrote on another occasion, "Men of Sense are too proud to yield to Authority, and Fools are too weak to submit to Reason, but Experience, which never deceived any one, carries Conviction both for the one and the other" (1:377). Indeed, the tradition of English empiricism, from Bacon (whom Dennis quotes) to Locke (whose ideas and vocabulary he adopts), powerfully affected Dennis's critical methods. "Nothing," he once stated categorically, "is more vain than to argue against experience" (1:50). Thus, while making good use of reason and of authority, he anchored his theory of the religious sublime firmly in his own experience of literature. He remained at Cambridge, as a student and tutor, until nearly thirty, corresponded with such notable men-of-letters as Congreve and Wycherley, and attended Dryden during part of the ex-laureate's reign at Will's. This experience probably influenced his own theories of literature more than did his trip across the Alps in 1688, which Marjorie Nicolson dates as marking his real interest in the sublime.[11] The impact of the trip across the Alps is somewhat difficult to measure, especially since Dennis refers to it only in one self-consciously literary epistle. The letter does indicate that, unlike some of his contemporaries, he fervently admired the vast and rugged Alpine scenery. But the most important sources of Dennis's thought are probably more usefully sought in his reading than in his travels. Dennis, in fact, began his critical career not as a preromantic enthusiast for wild nature but as party to a worn-out literary quarrel concerning the Ancients and the Moderns.

Dennis's contemporaries knew him as a champion of the Moderns.[12] Dennis viewed himself, however, not as a combatant but as a mediator, "calming the Fury of the contending Parties" (1:209). In *The Advancement and Reformation of Modern Poetry*, he approached the old question of Ancient or Modern supremacy in a spirit of compromise. "The first Part of the following Treatise," he wrote in the Epistle Dedicatory, "was intended to shew, that the Ancient Poets had that actual Pre-eminence. . . . The Design of the second Part is to shew, That the Moderns . . . may come to equal the Ancients" (1:206–7). Dennis's position seems moderate because he granted a large measure of praise to the Ancients without simultaneously reducing the Moderns to a race of mimic pigmies. Although he considerably oversimplified the achievement of classical literature, he based his judgment of the Ancients and his hope for Modern poetry on a proposition central to his own poetics. The Ancients, he declared, were at present superior to the Moderns primarily because they had joined "their Religion with their Poetry." The Moderns, however, "by incorporating Poetry with the Religion reveal'd to us in Sacred Writ" (1:207) might eventually equal or surpass the Ancients. Pope had some reason to be irritated when Dennis vaunted "the Newness and Boldness" (1:197) of his argument.[13] Dennis's hope to restore poetry "to all its Greatness, and to all its Innocence" (1:328) by returning to Christian subjects and treatment had been anticipated by Du Bartas, Herbert, Cowley, and others.[14] In fact, although Dennis described his proposal as "a Piece of Criticism, which has, I know not how, escap'd all the French Criticks" (1:206), his argument only repeats the basic ideas of those in France who proselytized for *le merveilleux chrétien*. The plan was not at all as original as he wished to believe.

In several respects, however, Dennis's program for poetry was new and bold. He recommended the use of Christianity in poetry as part of a more comprehensive theory. No critic who had recommended Christian poetry ever did so primarily because he believed that poetry was an art of raising passion. For Dennis, poetry and Christianity were natural partners. As he wrote in the Epistle Dedicatory to *The Advancement and Reformation of Modern Poetry*, "The ultimate End of the ensuing Discourse, is to shew, That the Intention of Poetry, and the Christian Religion, being alike to move the Affections, they may very well be made instrumental to the Advancing each other" (1:207). For Dennis, the common bond between poetry and Christianity was their reliance upon passionate and suprarational persuasion and their similar designs to restore the inner harmony disrupted by the Fall. His own experience of literature convinced him that Christianity offered the most powerful source of human passion and, hence, the greatest opportunity for poetic sublimity. To prove that Christianity might elevate Modern poets to the exalted stature of the Ancients, Dennis marshaled numerous examples of sublime religious verse: from the classics, from the Bible, and especially from *Paradise Lost*.

In ransacking the classics for examples, Dennis could have simplified his task by borrowing passages cited by Longinus. Occasionally he did so. But Longinus often relied on Homer, and Dennis preferred to support his own theory from the works of Virgil. He considered the *Aeneid* to be "the most Religious Epick Poem that ever was writ in the World" (1:247), a judgment which deserves some explanation. Dennis's view of the *Aeneid* as the world's greatest religious epic rests upon his belief that regularity can be both a sublime and a religious quality of art. God's universe, Dennis believed, is all "Rule and Order, and Harmony" (1:202) and even its seeming irregularities contribute to a providential design. The poet, whose duty is to imitate the Rule and Order and Harmony of nature, must likewise exercise a providential control over the incidents and disposition of his poem. Thus Dennis challenged any of the "Enemies to Regularity" to study the *Oedipus* of Sophocles, where he would "easily discover, how the Religion that is every where intermix'd with the Play, shews all the Surprizes . . . as so many immediate successive Effects, of a particular dreadful Providence, which make them come, like so many Thunder-claps, from a Serene Heaven, to confound and astonish him" (1:201). Despite the clumsy phrasing, Dennis's meaning is plain: a poet whose careful regularity reflects the divine guidance of the universe can thereby move and astonish his readers with the force of a Longinian thunderbolt. Although for later writers sublimity became synonymous with wildness, disorder, and irregularity, Dennis found regularity a powerful source of the sublime when skillfully employed to move the passions. Yet Virgil's thoroughly praised regularity was only one aspect of his sublimity for Dennis. Like other pagan poets, Virgil frequently described the actions of various gods and goddesses. This poetic use of Greco-Roman religion seemed to Dennis a primary source of the sublimity of the Ancients.

The use of epic machinery had long been considered an important aspect of the marvellous, and the close association between the marvellous and the sublime[15] suggested that the use of epic machinery was logically related to the sublime. Indeed, throughout the eighteenth century, epic machinery often figured in discussions of the sublime. The introduction of supernatural beings in a poem was thought to add a dimension of grandeur which human actors could not supply. As John Ogilvie asserted in his "Critical Dissertation on Epic Machinery," the use of supernatural beings is the "parent of the sublime, and the wonderful."[16] Dennis, like Ogilvie, identified the sublime with the supernatural and thus he considered Virgil's use of epic machinery further evidence that the greatest sublimity derives from religious ideas. To prove his point, Dennis compared parallel passages from the *Aeneid* and from Lucan's *Pharsalia*. Lucan had deliberately excluded the old gods from his contemporary epic, a decision which Dennis believed robbed the *Pharsalia* of much potential grandeur. "The Excellency then, of Virgil's Subject," he decided, "must come from something that is not Human, and that must be from Religion; so Virgil's Greatness and his Enthusiasm comes from his Machines, and the Ministry of the Gods, and the other Parts of his Religion; and Lucan's Littleness, from his want of those Machines, and that Ministry" (1:228). Dennis's criticism of the *Pharsalia*, however, does not imply an approval of all religious machinery. Virgil, he believed, preserved his Olympians from the too human indiscretions of Homer's deities; violation of probability always threatened to transform the sublime into the ridiculous, and Dennis solemnly censured Homer for "the Extravagence of his Theology" (1:265) which shocks rather than elevates the reason of a modern reader.

As a great admirer of the classics, Dennis willingly admitted that a number of pagan poets had reached the heights of sublimity by employing ideas and images from pagan religion. But he was so determined to prove that the greatest sublimity depends upon religious ideas that he resolutely confronted even those cases which seemed least amenable to his theory. The recognized sublimity of Pindar, skeptics might assert, does not rely upon the use of religious ideas. This objection may explain why Dennis went out of his way to imply that Pindar had been divinely inspired.[17] Further, although Pindar's subjects seemed devoid of religious significance, Dennis argued that while Pindar was compelled to celebrate the triumphs of "worthless Coachmen and Jockeys" (1:332), the famous digressions allowed him to explore the sublime wonders of the supernatural. An even more perplexing poet for Dennis, however, was Lucretius—whose *De Rerum Natura* expounded the godless philosophy of Epicurus. Dennis admitted certain difficulties in dealing with Lucretius; but he argued, not too convincingly, that Lucretius really suspected that "the secret Causes of Things" (1:251) were beyond his comprehension and that the suspicion provides a meditative sublimity in passages which seem concerned with the merely mechanical working of the universe. More believably, Dennis repeated his opinion that invocations and apostrophes, as an aspect of pagan religious observance, were "most of them very Sublime, and attended with a strong Enthusiasm" (1:231). The lofty invocation to Alma Venus at the beginning of the *De Rerum Natura* proved to Dennis's satisfaction that even the poet of atomism was "most Poetical and Sublime, where he is Religious" (1:250).

The classics, Dennis maintained, offer abundant examples proving that the greatest sublimity derives from religious ideas. Yet, despite his admiration for Virgil, Pindar, Lucretius, and for the religious aspects of classical poetry, Dennis insisted that modern writers could not simply imitate the religious sublimity of the Ancients. With evident relish, he explicitly repudiated Pope's claim that the gods of Homer remain to this day the gods of poetry (2:369).[18] For Dennis, one source of poetry remained available to the Moderns which was more sublime than any which the pagan poets might have known.

The Bible and Christian tradition were for Dennis the ultimate sources of sublimity. *The Advancement and Reformation of Modern Poetry* and *The Grounds of Criticism in Poetry* are among the first works of English criticism to apply the tools of literary analysis to the study of biblical poetry. Dennis did not speak of rhetorical terms, as Peacham had; nor did he, like Wyther, resign completely any pretense of understanding the sources of biblical grandeur. He accepted the Scriptures as divinely inspired and inherently superior to any uninspired or falsely inspired poetry. But he also sought literary explanations for the superiority of the Bible. The sublime proved a particularly fortunate discovery for this purpose. Its emphasis upon transport and passion accounts for aspects of great poetry which cannot be wholly judged by reason. At the same time, however, it permits a nonmystical and nonmechanical appreciation of exalted poetry. The idea of sublimity illuminated the nature of biblical poetry for readers throughout the eighteenth century, and Dennis was no doubt influential in showing the way.

The Bible is the ultimate source of sublime poetry, Dennis believed, because it evokes the greatest possible Enthusiastic passion, enabling the reconciliation of all the human faculties. The inspired truth of the Bible thus becomes only one aspect of its poetical appeal. It was an important aspect, of course; paganism failed to equal the sublimity of the Christian religion partly because its falsity offended the modern reason. Yet poetry could also fail by being too reasonable. Deism, in Dennis's view, appealed exclusively to the reason and, hence, missed the sublime by preventing any strong movement of the passions (1:259). Christianity, however, appeals more strongly to the whole man than does either paganism or Deism: "it satisfies the Reason more, at the same Time that it raises a stronger Passion, and that it entertains the Senses . . . more delightfully" (1:266–67). Thus, for Dennis, valid literary reasons (not mere piety) supported his view that Christian sublimity excels the highest achievement of the Ancients. "I could produce a hundred Passages . . . out of Sacred Writ," he affirmed, "which are infinitely superior to any Thing that can be brought upon the same Subject, from the Grecian and Roman Poets" (1:271). In illustrating this conviction, he compared examples of biblical sublimity with parallel passages drawn from the classics.

Perhaps the most effective comparison of passages from the Bible and the classics juxtaposes descriptions of what Dennis considered the greatest possible subject: the power of God (1:267). The classical passage, which became a familiar illustration of sublimity in the eighteenth century,[19] he drew from Virgil's description of the storm in the first book of the *Georgics*. The translation is Dryden's:

> The Father of the Gods his Glory shrowds,
> Involv'd in Tempests, and a Night of Clouds,
> And from the middle Darkness, flashing out,
> By Fits he deals his fiery Bolts about.
> Earth feels the Motions of her angry God,
> Her Entrails tremble, and her Mountains nod,
> And flying Beasts in Forests seek Abode.

Virgil's sublimity, although impressive, seems insignificant to Dennis when compared with the sublimity of Psalm 18. The portion (verses 6–15) which Dennis cites is a fine example of what eighteenth-century writers meant by the phrase *biblical sublimity*:

> In my Distress I called upon the Lord, and cryed unto my God: He heard my Voice out of his Temple, and my Cry came before him, even into his Ears.
>
> Then the Earth shook and trembled, the Foundations of the Hills also moved and were shaken, because he was wroth.
>
> There went up a Smoak out of his Nostrils, and Fire out of his Mouth devoured; Coals were kindled by it.
>
> He bowed the Heavens also, and came down, and Darkness was under his Feet.
>
> And he rode upon a Cherub, and did fly: He came flying upon the Wings of the Winds.
>
> He made Darkness his secret Place; His Pavilion round about him were dark Waters, and thick Clouds of the Skies.
>
> At the Brightness that was before him, his Clouds remov'd Hail-stones and Coals of Fire.

The Lord also thundered in the Heavens, and the Highest
gave his Voice Hailstones and Coals of Fire.

Yea, he sent forth his Arrows, and scattered them, and he
shot out Lightnings, and discomfited them.

Then the Channels of Waters were seen, and the Founda-
tions of the World were discovered, at thy Rebuke, O Lord,
at the Blast of the Breath of thy Nostrils.

(1:268)

If Dennis had merely rhapsodized about the passage, his discus-
sion would have no more value in the history of criticism than
George Wyther's earlier rapture inspired by the same psalm.
Earlier critics had confessed or implied the folly of analyzing
God's revealed truth; Dennis subjected the Bible to literary
analysis by studying its particular poetic effects.

The greater sublimity of Psalm 18, Dennis argued, could be
measured by its greater engagement of all the human faculties.
"Reason," he noted, "finds its Account better here than it does
in *Virgil*; for the more amazing Effects that we see of Divine
Displeasure, the more it answers our Idea of infinite Wrath"
(1:268). The basis of this argument, as is clear in context, is
qualitative: Virgil's particular details are amazing; David's are
more amazing and, thus, better calculated to suggest in medita-
tion the idea of infinite wrath. But, while reason reflects on the
relationship between the finite and the infinite, the other facul-
ties are violently excited by the quantitative succession of con-
crete particulars. "And that which satisfies the Reason the more
here," Dennis continued, "raises the Passion more strongly, and
entertains the Senses the better, because there are more and more
amazing Effects of the Divine [Dis]pleasure" (1:269). Dennis
does not appeal to the inspired truth of the Bible as its mark of
superiority; he bases his claim on poetic grounds. Both the quality
and the quantity of "amazing Effects" are greater in the biblical
description than in the Virgilian.

Dennis, like Bouhours, found the biblical description more
sublime than the classical largely because it is more pictorial. His
praise of Psalm 18 might well be written with an eye to the chap-
ter of Longinus which Boileau entitled "Des Images."

> For how great, how lofty, how terrible, is that; *He bowed the
> Heavens and came down, and Darkness was under his Feet?*
> How much stronger than that of *Virgil, Ipse Pater,* &c.? And
> how Poetical, and how Dreadful is that, *Then the Channels of
> the Waters were seen, and the Foundations of the World were
> discovered; at thy Rebuke, O Lord, at the Blast of the Breath
> of thy Nostrils?* How terribly is the Eye delighted here, which
> is a Sense that the Poet ought chiefly to entertain; because it
> contributes more than any other to the exciting of strong
> Passion? (1:269).

For Longinus, the interaction of passion and imagination con-
tributed to the sublime; for Dennis, it *created* the sublime.
Demonstrating the greater passionate and imaginative appeal
of the Bible, he urged his contemporaries to challenge the An-
cients by utilizing the subjects and spirit of Christianity. He
knew of only one powerful objection to his proposal. "For several
of the Moderns have attempted Divine Poetry," he acknowl-
edged, "and yet some of them have been contemptible to the
last degree, and not one of them has excell'd the Antients"
(1:368). To meet this objection, Dennis drew again on his own
experience of literature. He directed readers to *Paradise Lost,*
"the greatest Poem that ever was written by Man" (1:351).

Without *Paradise Lost,* Dennis's theory of the religious sub-
lime might have seemed a feeble exercise in piety; only the prag-
matic evidence of what works could sway a generation taught to
respect the information of its senses. Practical failure, even more
than Boileau's theoretical objections, had doomed *le merveilleux
chrétien* in France.[20] But *Paradise Lost* proved that Christian
poetry could succeed. Dennis's main difficulty was that Milton's
epic suffered from public neglect. Tonson's elegant folio edition
of *Paradise Lost* in 1688 marked the first real step toward general
acceptance of Milton, but not until twenty years later did
Addison's *Spectator* essays successfully domesticate Milton's
epic. In the interim, as Raymond D. Havens points out, the "first
great protagonist of *Paradise Lost* was not Addison but the for-
gotten John Dennis."[21] Dennis's support of *Paradise Lost* was
not only earlier than Addison's but in some respects considerably

bolder. Addison attempted to reconcile Milton to current Augustan tastes for regularity; Dennis praised Milton's epic despite its irregularities (1:333). While Addison recommended Milton to a general audience, Dennis elevated him especially as a model for modern poets (1:372). For Dennis, Milton was the banner of a revolution. *Paradise Lost*, he believed, offered convincing evidence that his theory of the religious sublime could transform the nature of modern poetry.

Dennis admired Milton especially for his sublimity. "I, who have all my Life-time had the highest Esteem for the great Genius's of the Ancients, and especially for *Homer* and *Virgil*, and who admire them now more than ever," Dennis wrote in 1721, "have yet for these last Thirty Years admir'd *Milton* above them all for one thing, and that is for having carried away the Prize of Sublimity from both Ancients and Moderns" (2:221). The discovery of Longinus, for Dennis, provided a critical basis for his appreciation of *Paradise Lost*, an appreciation which must have substantially preceded his Alpine journey. Addison too found the idea of sublimity central to his analysis of *Paradise Lost*, which suggests that the public acceptance of Milton's epic depended to some degree upon the prior introduction of sublimity as a new term of criticism. Dennis was the first critic to stress Milton's sublimity, establishing the formula which, after Addison repeated it, became the standard critical response to *Paradise Lost*. He quoted lengthy passages, such as the portrait of Satan in Book One and the "morning hymn" in Book Five, which became familiar illustrations of sublimity later in the century, and even went to the absurd and regrettable length of complaining that passages which he had first cited for sublimity were introduced by subsequent critics without acknowledgment to him (2:221). Some pride seems justified, however, since Dennis first made Milton and Longinus the inseparable companions they became throughout the eighteenth century.

Dennis particularly admired, among other important aspects of Milton's sublimity, the choice of blank verse, and here too he anticipated ideas which later became accepted critical dogma. Rhyme, Dennis believed, could only "debase the Majesty and weaken the Spirit of the greater Poetry" (1:375). Long before nondramatic blank verse grew popular in England, Dennis wrote concerning *Paradise Lost*, "I am satisfied that something of its Excellence is owing to the Blank Verse. For Mr. Dryden has handled the very same Subject in Rime, but has faln so infinitely short of the Sublimity, the Majesty, the Vehemence, and the other great Qualities of *Milton*, that they are never to be nam'd together" (1:377). The rhymed couplet, Dennis thought, almost inevitably required a poet to deal in point, conceit, wit, and other primarily intellectual effects (1:127). If poetry was to reconcile man's warring faculties, however, it must raise strong Enthusiastic passion; and in order to raise strong Enthusiastic passion, it must employ an appropriately passionate verse form. The most extensive writer of blank verse between Milton and Thomson,[22] Dennis certainly followed this rule in his own poetry. The rejection of rhyme was an essential part of his general program to return poetry from its "miserably fall'n" state to "all its Greatness, and to all its Innocence" (1:328). With pardonable excess he predicted that "before this Century is half expir'd, Rime will be wholly banished from our greater Poetry" (1:379).

While Milton's use of blank verse contributed importantly to his sublimity, for Dennis the main cause of his superiority over both Ancients and Moderns was his use of Christian materials. In fact, Dennis expected Milton's superiority to be so evident that he offered little detailed analysis of its specific sources. Yet the apparent lack of commentary can be misleading, as in his discussion of Milton's description of Creation. All of his remarks seem merely to echo one claim: " 'tis plain, that *Milton* owes this Greatness, and this Elevation, to the Excellence of his Religion" (1:274). Milton's description of the earth emerging from the seas at the divine fiat caused Dennis to exclaim, "What an Image is here! and taken apparently from our Religion, which teaches us the most exalted Notions of God, and the immediate Obedience of the Creatures to their Creator" (1:275). At the blossoming forth of verdure, he repeats himself: "What an Image is here again, with which none but our own Religion could have possibly supply'd him!" (1:275). The earth then teems with animals: "What a Number of admirable Images are here . . . ? And yet, even in this Subject, nothing could have supplied a Poet with them, but so Divine a Religion" (1:277). Repetition was Dennis's favorite means of emphasis, but his comments here stress more than the single claim that Christianity provides Milton with greater images than any found in the classics.

Dennis's comment on the half-born lion pawing to free himself from the earth illuminates his concise but penetrating criticism of Milton. "Can any thing," he asks, "be more surprizingly strong, than this energetick Image?" (1:277). The phrase *energetick Image* suggests a double focus. First, it refers to Milton's use of visual imagery. Dennis particularly valued the use of clear visual images (*enargeia*) because it was the poet's best means of inspiring intense passion in the reader. "These Passions that attend upon our Thoughts, are seldom so strong," Dennis had written, "as they are in those kind of Thought, which we call Images. For they being the very lively [i.e., lifelike] Pictures of the Things which they represent, set them, as it were, before our very Eyes" (1:218). For Dennis, the sublimity of Milton depended upon the reader's feeling as if he actually witnessed the scene described. Second, the phrase *energetick Image* may also refer to Milton's use of vigorous motion (*energeia*). No images, Dennis believed, could stir the passions so strongly as images expressing movement. The mind, he explained, "can never imagine violent Motion, without being in a violent Agitation itself; and the Imagination being fir'd with that Agitation, sets the very Things before our Eyes; and consequently, makes us have the same Passions that we should have from the Things themselves" (1:218). Milton's description of Creation, one recalls, is not only visual but also vital, a picture of the world pulsing with motion. When Dennis applauds Milton's Christian version of Creation, then, he does so in the context of his earlier critical discussions of how vision and motion contribute to the sublimity of particular images. He was never content to rest his claims for Christian religious sublimity merely on the inspired truth of Christianity. When handled by a skillful poet, Christianity also supplied vivid and vigorous images which were artistically superior to anything the non-Christian religions could offer.

Dennis's admiration for Milton's religious sublimity included Milton's use of certain stylistic techniques which might be called biblical. While Augustan poets generally eschewed the biblical device of "crowding"[23] a number of different images together, Dennis applauded this very thing in Milton's description of the Creation: "What a Number of admirable Images are here crouding upon one another?" (1:277). The same idea recurs in his later comparison of Milton's adaptation of Psalm 148 with the Sternhold-Hopkins version. The homely devotion of Sternhold-Hopkins in Dennis's view utterly debased the passion and profusion of the biblical figurative language. (Pope referred to the Prayer Book psalms as winning Heaven "through Violence of Song.") Turning to Milton's adaptation, Dennis continued, "Let us now see how the Force of *Milton's* Genius hides and conceals the Assistance of Art, while these lofty Figures, at the very time that they raise and transport his exalted Soul, are lost in his Enthusiasm and his Sublimity, as the glittering of numberless Stars is swallow'd and lost in the blaze of Day" (2:39). His simile is not merely decorative. The Bible abounds with figures which might well seem as brilliant and numberless as the stars. Milton's use of this and other aspects of biblical style, Dennis implied, gives *Paradise Lost* much of its unsurpassed sublimity.

Milton proved to Dennis that, both for its truth and for its grandeur, Christianity was the single force which could revive modern poetry. "I have reason to believe," he asserted, "that one of the principal Reasons that has made the modern Poetry so contemptible, is, That by divesting it self of Religion, it is fallen from its Dignity, and its original Nature and Excellence; and from the greatest Production of the Mind of Man, is dwindled to an extravagant and a vain Amusement" (1:365). There was a vast difference for Dennis between amusement and happiness. If modern poets would only follow the example of Milton, he believed, and utilize both the sublime matter and manner of Christianity, man might yet establish a paradise within and modern poetry might yet "raise up its dejected Head, and . . . come to emulate the happiest of Grecian and Roman Ages" (1:372).

IMAGINATION, MACHINERY, AND TERROR

Imagination, or the process of creating and of perceiving visual images, was essential to Dennis's theory of the religious sublime. Images were for him the basic element of all poetic experience: images inspired passion, and without passion there was no true poetry. Further, he insisted that the imagery of the sublime poet must be clear and distinct. The phrase *clear and distinct ideas* (probably adapted from Locke) runs through his criticism like a leitmotif. He intended his early essay on poetic genius, for example, to treat particularly "the clearness, and justness, and . . . the energy of *Images*" (1:47). This passion for clarity is one of the most thoroughly Augustan aspects of his criticism. But, while rational clarity was the aim of much Augustan poetry, Dennis is allied with those, such as Addison, who emphasized the visual clarity of a poet's imagery. Throughout his life, he consistently championed a kind of poetry which would be passionate, vigorous, and, above all, visually precise.

Dennis's interest in sublimity was a main force behind his call for poetic clarity. Fustian, he knew, was the opposite of true sublimity and must be combated decisively. The combat was simply more enjoyable than usual when Pope's translation of Homer provided the occasion. Pope had translated Homer with attention to the demands of sublimity, indirectly challenging critics to fault him in this respect.[24] Dennis responded with his *Remarks upon Mr. Pope's Translation of Homer* (1717), an oleo of the serious and the trivial. At his most serious, he attacks what he considered to be Pope's failure of imaginative clarity. The simile of the bees in Book Two of the *Iliad* had been rendered by Pope:

> Dusky they spread, a close embodied Crowd,
> And o'er the Vale descends the living Cloud.

"And what," asked Dennis, "does he mean by *embodied?* What Idea to the Mind does that Word clearly and distinctly present?" (2:124). Pope's line describing Apollo particularly offended him: "*And gloomy Darkness roll'd around his Head.*" "HOMER has nothing like this," Dennis objected. "He only says, That APOLLO *descended, resembling the Night.* Nor does *gloomy Darkness rolling around the Head,* give a clear Idea of any thing; and for that Reason is . . . gross Fustian" (2:131). Not all of his criticism of Pope rings so true. He is best where his main aim is to attack Pope's lapses from the Homeric simplicity and clarity. Yet, although Dennis consistently associated sublimity with imaginative clarity, he did allow two important exceptions. These exceptions relate to his discussion of epic machinery and terror.

Machinery Dennis considered "the very Life and Soul of Poetry" (1:183). His ideas on epic supernaturalism developed in two stages. The first stage appears in his frequently Aristotelian *Remarks on Prince Arthur,* where he attacked among other things Richard Blackmore's use of Christian machinery. Citing Aristotle, Dennis argued with painful obviousness that imitation is the main source of poetic delight and instruction. His development of the cliché is not so obvious, however, and points toward his later emphasis on passion. "Now," he continued, "to be instructed by Imitation, I must be a Judge of that Imitation, which I can never be, if I have not a clear and distinct Idea of its Object" (1:105). The machines of Christianity, on the other hand, are something "of which no Man can have clear and distinct Idea's" (1:106). Dennis therefore concluded that, reasoning on the basis of Aristotle's theory of imitation, Christian machinery can be neither instructive nor delightful. To illustrate the point by contrast, he asserted that the anthropomorphic gods of heathenism could be a source of poetic delight because they do have manifest shapes, personalities, and passions. He condensed the contrast into three short sentences: "Poetry pleases by an imitation of Nature. Now the Christian Machines are quite out of Nature, and consequently cannot delight. The Heathen Machines are enough out of Nature to be admirable, and enough in Nature to delight" (1:105). The argument is logical, but it is incomplete. It ignores one issue which became increasingly important to Dennis: the idea of terror.

Dennis's mature attitude toward epic machinery can seem confused because, instead of rejecting his earlier position completely, he refined and modified it. This refinement required the introduction of two new arguments. First, Dennis now argued that probability was more important than clarity in the use of poetic machines. Accordingly, the heathen gods and goddesses, for all their visual clarity, cannot be delightful to a modern reader because they are not only false but (what for Aristotle was worse still) improbable. Dennis warned poets that in their use of machinery they must conform to the religion of their own age and country (1:369): the religious sublime, cut adrift from probabilities, threatened to sink to new depths of ridicule. Second, Dennis stressed a new aspect of Christian machinery. Because they are unknowable, he admitted, Christian machines would never be a source of imitative delight; but for the same reason they might be a powerful source of terror. While imitative delight proceeds from the recognition of what is already known, sublime terror proceeds from the apprehension of the unknown or of the partly known. Dennis paraded this idea with the relish of true discovery. "Enthusiastick Terror," he wrote, ". . . springs from the Ideas unknown to him who feels it" (1:231). Again, "Now of things which are terrible, those are most terrible which are the most wonderful; because that seeing them both threatning and powerful, and not being able to fathom the Greatness and Extent of their Power, we know not how far and how soon they may hurt us" (1:361–62). The discovery in fact influenced a century of English poets: what Christian machinery lost in delight, it gained in sublimity and terror.

Dennis's treatment of sublime terror transcends the specific question of his attitudes toward epic machinery. Samuel Monk writes, "In view of the prominence of terror, both in later theories of the sublime and in much of eighteenth-century literature, the most interesting aspect of Dennis's treatment of the sublime is his introduction of that emotion."[25] Several aspects of Dennis's idea of terror are pertinent to developments later in the century, particularly his characteristic assertion that "Enthusiastick Terror is chiefly to be deriv'd from Religious Ideas" (1:361). Since he believed that Christianity produces the greatest Enthusiastic terror, Dennis could develop an informal counterargument to Boileau's assertion, which he twice quotes,[26] that the *mystères terribles* of Christianity are not good subjects for poetry. Precisely because Christianity expresses mystery and terror, Dennis replied, it is the best possible source of the sublime. Indeed, although his own tastes were predominantly classical, Dennis's now familiar list of ideas capable of producing Enthusiastic terror might furnish the quasi-religious claptrap for a shelf of Gothic novels: "Gods, Daemons, Hell, Spirits and Souls of Men, Miracles, Prodigies, Enchantments, Witchcrafts, Thunder, Tempests, raging Seas, Inundations, Torrents, Earthquakes, Volcanos, Monsters, Serpents, Lions, Tygers, Fire, War, Pestilence, Famine, &c." (1:361). All of these ideas could arouse sublime terror, Dennis asserted, but none could be more sublime than those which showed the wrath of an angry God.

A second aspect of Dennis's idea of sublime terror which anticipated the work of later writers is his treatment of suggestiveness. In general, of course, Dennis believed that sublimity required the creation of clear and distinct images: vague diction inevitably produces fustian. Yet many of the most sublime Christian ideas resist precise visual delineation. If the mind is stored with finite and concrete images, how can a poet express the sublime, unknowable, indefinite, and terrible mysteries of Christianity? Edmund Burke answered that obscurity is one of the best means of expressing the incomprehensible. Dennis proposed a theory of imaginative suggestiveness.

The best way to transcend the finite, Dennis argued, is *through* the finite. The poet restricts himself to the concrete and the visual, but he employs them in such a way as to tease the mind beyond the consideration of specific particular details. The idea was not original with Dennis,[27] but he developed it with originality to support his theory that the greatest poetic passion is raised by ideas in meditation. His example of the sun inspiring a vision of the heavenly host (1:339) illustrated how the mind

of the reader could transform a finite image into an approxima-
tion of the infinite. A different illustration of the process appears
in his *Remarks on Prince Arthur*, where he cites Virgil's descrip-
tion of Venus in the first book of the *Aeneid*, observing that
while Virgil sketches her figure with particular details, he ne-
glects to mention her face. "A Poet, without Judgment," he con-
cluded, "would certainly have describ'd her Face. But *Virgil*
had discernment enough to see, that what he had said of her
Hair, and of her Neck, and her Mien, would set her Face before
the Reader in a more ravishing Form, than all the most beautifull
Colours in Poetry, and the most delicate exquisite Strokes of the
greatest of Masters could paint it" (1:105). Clear incomplete-
ness, not verbal obscurity, inspires the reader to meditate upon
the natural facts until they evoke an approximation of the super-
natural. Such, Dennis believed, was one main source of Milton's
greatness: "*Milton's* Sublimity is distinguish'd from that of all
other Poets in this Respect, that where he has excell'd all other
Poets in what he has exprest, he has left ten times more to be
understood than what he has exprest, which is the surest and
noblest Mark, and the most transporting Effect of Sublimity"
(2:222). The mind of the reader, rather than the diction of the
poet, makes the final leap from the imaginable to the unimagin-
able. The possibility of approaching the unimaginable and pas-
sionate truths of religion through the process of finite imagination
was for Dennis both the essence of sublimity and the ultimate
hope for the renewal of modern poetry.

THE IMPORTANCE OF DENNIS

No one has succeeded fully in measuring Dennis's impact upon
his age. The problem arises largely because Dennis was too
quixotic to inspire the tributes and discipleship which help in
retrospect to determine a writer's influence. In fact, only a critic
with nothing to lose, like Charles Gildon, could afford to call
Dennis "Master." For various reasons, Dennis was an abrasive
presence in the Age of Pope. On some subjects, such as blank
verse, he anticipated opinions which became popular only in

the second and third quarters of the century. On other matters, such as comic theory, he resolutely looked backward to the Restoration. His character, like his criticism, is a blend of laudable and lamentable qualities, and he inevitably embarrasses those who attempt either to exalt or to defame him. Testimonials, therefore, are an unsatisfactory way to judge Dennis's importance to his age. A better means is to examine the ideas which he so powerfully recommended. His ultimate importance should be measured by the importance and acceptance of his ideas, not by the jibes or cheers of his contemporaries.

Dennis's positive achievements allied him with the future. He gave England its first book-length criticism of a particular work (*Remarks on Prince Arthur*) and its first systematic theory of poetry since Sidney's *Apologie*. But his most valuable contribution was his strong endorsement of Longinus and the sublime. Before Dennis's criticism appeared, no English critic had adequately explored or expounded the idea of sublimity. Indeed, sublimity was so important to Dennis's personal theory of literature that he used the adjectives *poetical* and *sublime* (1:250) virtually as synonyms. The really valuable poetry, for Dennis, was always sublime. He is important, however, beyond merely helping to popularize the new idea of sublimity; through his emphasis upon the necessity of passion in poetry, he also anticipated and perhaps helped to bring about a general change in the nature of English critical thought. The poem as imitative artifact gradually ceases to control the main interest of critics, who increasingly study the mind and emotions of both poet and reader.

Dennis's treatment of the sublime in certain respects is brilliantly original. He deserves credit for applying the critical discussion of sublimity to the analysis of biblical poetry. Although Boileau's "Préface" undoubtedly spurred him to consider the general relationship between biblical poetry and the sublime, Boileau's main interest in the *fiat lux* passage (and the focus of his controversy with Jean Le Clerc and Pierre Daniel Huet) concerned the role of simplicity in the sublime.[28] Dennis completely altered the grounds on which Boileau had associated the

Bible with sublimity. Further, he initiated discussion of Milton's sublimity. Eighteenth-century critical recognition of the sublimity of *Paradise Lost* is more than a historical detail; it became a stimulus for the creation of a vast number of poems—from blank-verse fragments to ponderous epics. Finally, Dennis's discussion of sublimity devoted considerable attention to the idea of terror, and his related notions concerning Christian machinery and imaginative suggestiveness point the way to crucial future developments in English poetry and criticism. These "firsts" say nothing about the extent of Dennis's personal influence, but they do suggest that his work is full of ideas which become steadily more prominent in eighteenth-century poetry and criticism.

To a remarkable extent, individual aspects of Dennis's criticism were integrated parts of his enveloping theory of the religious sublime. Whether in Dennis's version or in some other, the notion of the religious sublime became a familiar part of eighteenth-century critical thought, and its acceptance finds a parallel in the creation of various recurring kinds of poetry. Eighteenth-century interest in the idea of religious sublimity results from combining forces, and it is impossible to decide—as Wordsworth wrote of his own growth—what portion of the river flows from what fountain. The loosely related opinions discussed in the first chapter were ready to be fused into something new and solid, especially with the appearance of Boileau's Longinus. Resentment of Milton's surly republicanism was dying, and with the light of reason illuminating new aspects of man and nature, the age was ready for a fresh approach to the literary qualities of the Bible. At the same time, the vast reaches of space and the apparent irregularities of nature—all associated with the sublime—became heady sources of devout religious awe. Dennis's real achievement was to fuse a number of such scattered ideas into a consistent and articulate theory of literature. He developed his theory of the religious sublime with such energy and resourcefulness that no writer of the first quarter of the eighteenth century could avoid some knowledge of it.

The author of the *Plain Dealer* (1725) was, for his own times, an ill prophet in predicting that "the Name of Mr. *Dennis*, will, long, continue to receive Honour, after his *Body* shall be Dust and Ashes."[29] Ironically, Dennis's name had turned to dust and ashes somewhat before his flesh. At his death in 1734, he seemed to one eulogist to have closed an era: having outlived the originality of his contributions to criticism and surviving only as a type of the ill-natured critic, he passed from memory as "the last Classick Wit of King Charles's Reign."[30] But Dennis deserves better treatment from the historian. If succeeding chapters prove that the idea of the religious sublime exerted a continuous pressure among eighteenth-century men-of-letters, the question of Dennis's contemporary reputation will seem relatively minor. Important ideas often watch their inventors lapse into obscurity, and general acceptance makes an idea the property of an age. What happens to the idea becomes the most serious question. Dennis supplied a necessary catalyst for change by introducing a fully articulated concept into the minds of his contemporaries. That act itself removed the religious sublime from any proprietary relationship with Dennis. And it simultaneously introduces us to a phenomenon which always remains mysteriously outside the laws of chemical combination or natural growth: the dynamics of literary change.

Chapter Three

The Critical Argument:
Consistent Aspects

The disparity between form and content in the criticism of Dennis, who recommended a poetry of passion in a prose relentlessly argumentative and rational, ought to alert us to the subtleties and contradictions inherent in a complex period. A number of established assumptions need to be rigorously questioned. For example, in beginning what I believe remains the best introductory book on eighteenth-century poetry, James Sutherland asserts that "one result of the growing rationalism of the last decades of the seventeenth century was the disappearance from poetry of all that may be comprehensively labelled the supernatural."[1] It is, of course, the virtue of introductory studies to risk generalizations which the authors recognize as extreme. Yet no valid statement should be false to the facts, and the disappearance of the supernatural from eighteenth-century poetry has no basis in fact. To ignore the more than 7,000 hymns written during the period—whether or not supported by the curious argument that hymns are not poems—is to write history which conforms to one's own taste for literature. To ignore the vast literature of the religious sublime—whether or not on the grounds that much of it fails to equal the best work of Keats and Eliot, or of Pope and Johnson—is to foreshorten and distort the real shape of the period in order to satisfy our own taste in perspective. I do not suggest that we abandon judgments of literary merit. If they are, as one of Borges's characters writes, merely "sentimental operations," we cannot afford to divorce literature from our feelings for it. Yet one essential basis of valuable judgments about the literature of an age must be a clear understanding of what was being written by the hundreds of minor figures who rarely find representation in anthologies. Consulting such writers not only disproves generalizations about the utter disappearance of the supernatural but also raises questions which otherwise would escape notice: why does religious literature of the eighteenth century lack the fire and spirit found in the poetry of Donne, of Herbert, of Hopkins? if the supernatural does not utterly disappear from eighteenth-century poetry, what new forms does it assume? and, since change implies the possibility of nonchange or stasis, what ideas and forms were so generally accepted that they provide a background of the unchanging against which to measure the experiments in literary innovation? For answers, we must examine the writing of a number of poets and critics whose interest in the religious sublime confirms what many Christians of all ages have understood: that rationalism can sharpen one's taste for the supernatural.

THE PASSION FOR REFORM

Probably every era since the Middle Ages has some claim to be called an age of reform. What characterizes the eighteenth century, then, is not the fact of reform but the particular directions which the reformist impulse took. The subject is too vast to consider here: perhaps it will suffice to indicate its range by citing as two examples the establishment of The Society for the Propagation of the Gospel in Foreign Parts and the invention of the steam engine. Somewhere between falls the religious sublime. In 1700 Dryden had written that " *'Tis well an Old Age is out,/And time to begin a New.*"[2] The following year Dennis obliged millennial expectations with publication of *The Advancement and Reformation of Modern Poetry*, a work which deserves to be seen in the context of the general Augustan passion for literary improvement: Jeremy Collier's call for the cleansing of the stage, Swift's scheme to perfect and stabilize the English language, Addison's efforts to chasten wit and to soften the manners of a factious public, Defoe's alternately inflammatory and dry-as-dust pamphlets on politics, economics, and morality, and Pope's long labor to forge the heroic couplet into an instrument of originality, flexibility, and power. In a century often split between Ancient and Modern temperaments, the desire for melioration and refining change could be expressed in a language of conservatism or of revolution. But even those who looked to the future with dismay worked diligently to refine and reform the present. Whenever the subject was how to reform modern poetry itself, someone always mentioned the religious sublime.

Much of the interest in the religious sublime, particularly during the early years of the century, came from a persistent but unallied group of reformers whose common tie was a conservative belief that poetry would be best served by returning to its original nature. This version of Augustan nostalgia, which viewed progress as a radical return to the past, particularly envisioned the reestablishment of a close and necessary bond between poetry and religion. There are good reasons why such a call should be heard. The increasingly rapid secularization of eighteenth-century life had in part shifted the focus of literature from the celestial to the earthly city. "Man," writes Basil Willey, "hitherto the immortal soul in quest of salvation, or the rational soul in quest of virtue, was now seen to be the economic or political ego in quest of wealth, power, and position."[3] The spiritual life of the nation had become more rational and less fervid; moreover, because religion was inextricably knit with politics, certain kinds of religious poetry could be as provocative as a declaration in support of Cromwell or the Pretender. Just as Steele claimed to regret the political partisanship which biased the *Tatler* (No. 271), Henry Mackenzie's periodical *The Mirror* in 1779 announced that it would not concern itself with religion. "This consideration will apply, in the strongest manner," he insisted, "to any thing mystic or controversial" (No. 42). Although Bunyan and a few others who specialized in religious literature became extremely popular, particularly among audiences of working people and Dissenters, booksellers seemed to avoid all but the most familiar religious works in collections meant for general sale.[4] The scattered *miscellanea sacra* which appeared found only a small audience.

One consistent literary objection to religious poetry was inherited from Boileau. Many English neoclassicists, although not all as vocally as Dr. Johnson, in general accepted Boileau's argument that the mysteries of Christianity were not proper subjects for poetry. In an essay sometimes attributed to Swift, an ironical author seriously advises a young poet to "turn your thoughts to HUMAN LITERATURE."[5] To attempt divine poetry, he implies, will result either in blasphemy or in failure. Various critics shared Johnson's repugnance at the mixture of Christian and pagan materials in a single poem, and when so many Christian poets fell into bathos, the *Critical Review* wearily reminded its readers, "We have often had occasion, in the course of our remarks, to observe, that the sacred and sublime truths of our holy religion are very unfit subjects for poetry."[6] Johnson's "Life of Waller" provided a pithy statement of the neoclassical objections to religious poetry, warning against the public expression of private devotion. "Man admitted to implore the mercy of his Creator and plead the merits of his Redeemer," wrote Johnson, "is already in a higher state than poetry can confer."[7] Recalling the strength of Johnson's religious beliefs, one can appreciate the strength of principle which supported his dislike of religious poetry. Influenced by neoclassical principles and by a trading-manufacturing society, most eighteenth-century poets make nature, manners, and morals—not religion—the main subject of their verse.

The partisans of secular poetry never overwhelmed their scattered but hardy opponents. Among writers who perhaps lamented the mundane spirit of the age or the limits of neoclassicism, the cry for the religious reformation of poetry echoes throughout the century. One of the most vocal reformers, of course, was John Dennis. And it is significant that the three most active successors of Dennis in the early decades of the century all acknowledged him with praise. Sir Richard Blackmore, Isaac Watts, and Aaron Hill vigorously presented the case for religious poetry during the first quarter of the eighteenth century. They were well-known figures in their own time, even if they are ignored today. Each offers a slightly different perspective for studying the arguments of the reformers.

Sir Richard Blackmore was knighted as a physician, but as a poet, too, he looked after the health of the nation. The City Bard viewed the age as fallen into wit, venery, and atheism; and to the rumbling of coach wheels, he compounded poetic cures. The subsuming fault of the age was secularism, Blackmore believed, and in his holy war against the wits, in preface after preface, he urged his contemporaries to seek their poetic inspiration in the truth and grandeur of Christianity. "I know 'tis said," he wrote, ". . . that the Christian Scheme of Religion is not so well accommodated to Poetical Writings, and therefore our Poets are oblig'd to embelish their Works with the Pagan Theology: A wretched Apology!" And with that contemptuous glance at Boileau, Blackmore proceeded to recommend the Book of Job as a model of "a sublime Stile, elevated Thoughts, magnificent Expressions . . . without the Aids of the Pagan System of Divinity."[8] The statement reveals much concerning the bases of Blackmore's ideas of reform. He consciously follows Cowley and opposes Boileau in affirming that Christianity affords the poet a wealth of materials for poetry. Also, he betrays a note of anti-paganism—which might seem odd, but was actually rather common, in an age which doted on the classics. Blackmore warns his fellow poets to sport no more with Amaryllis, simplifying the problem of reform to a kind of Hercules' Choice between Christian virtue and pagan vice.

His poetic vision was myopic, to be sure; but it is to Blackmore's credit that he recognized the need to offer readers something other than the standard fare of Augustan wits and moralists. Although he and Dennis quarreled at first, they soon grew friendly—as indeed they should have. Blackmore's consistent use of Christian materials and his constant striving after the sublime reflect his basic agreement with Dennis concerning the proper course for modern poetry. With pious zeal, he crowded his works with scenes of Christian religious sublimity and at his most successful won praise from Dennis, Steele, Addison, and Johnson for *The Creation* (1712), a poem which in 1753 Theophilus Cibber reported had "now deservedly become a classic."[9] History has quite properly ignored even Blackmore's "classic." Blackmore himself, however, should not be dismissed too quickly. In his inept way, he enlivened the issue of poetic reform for over two decades.

If Blackmore followed Cowley in calling for reform, Isaac Watts seemed to follow mainly his own inner light and the voices of scripture. He had studied Boileau and Dennis, so he knew the critical arguments for and against religious poetry; and he lauded both Cowley and Blackmore as Baconian heroes of religious verse who had proved that "the Obstacles of attempting Christian Poesy are broken down, and the vain Pretense of its being impracticable is experimentally confuted."[10] But while Cowley and Blackmore viewed the Bible as a mine of poetic materials, Watts saw it rather as a model of inspired writing. He did not believe that a poet must be actually inspired by God unless his verse is prophetic. "*David* the mere Man was a sublime Poet," he wrote, "and *God* made him a Prophet."[11] A poet will be sublime if his subject and feelings are sufficiently elevated; and modern poets, he believed, might successfully emulate the short, passionate lyrics of David without necessarily sharing his gift of prophecy. Instead of reworking biblical stories into vast epics, Watts modeled his own poetry on the spirit of the Psalms, often borrowing the pseudo-Pindaric structure of the Cowleyan ode. But subject and feeling, not structure, are the essence of poetry for Watts. "If the Heart were first inflam'd from Heaven, and the Muse . . . only call'd in as an Assistant to the Worship," he urged, "then the Song would end where the Inspiration ceases; the whole Composure would be of a Piece, all Meridian Light and Meridian Fervour; and the same pious Flame would be propagated and kept glowing in the Heart of him that reads."[12] It is well to remember that Pope, Swift, and Johnson do not reflect the poetic ideals of all their contemporaries. Although many eighteenth-century readers rejected Watts's view of poetry, his advocacy of passionate religious verse, like Blackmore's call for biblical grandeur, blended with the voices of other champions of reform.

Aaron Hill, in a gesture of apology, accompanied his poem *The Creation* (1720) with a preface addressed to Alexander Pope "concerning the Sublimity of the Ancient Hebrew Poetry, with a material and obvious Defect in the English." The serious defect which Hill found in modern English poetry was "that we study Form, and neglect Matter."[13] It is difficult to tell whether Hill intended this observation to needle Pope—implying perhaps that Pope's vaunted correctness had not yet been taxed upon matters of much importance. At any rate, Hill soon publicly praised Pope's old enemy John Dennis,[14] and there is real irony in his reminding Pope that the "most remarkable Excellencies [of the Ancients] have been found, in those Parts of their Works, which they elevated, and made more solemn, by a Mixture of their Religion."[15] The observation might have come directly from the pages of Dennis. Perhaps, on the basis of "Messiah," Hill honestly believed that Pope might desert Homer and Horace for the Hebrews; his appeal, fortunately, did not inspire Pope to compositions such as *The Creation*. In one sense, however, those who were unmoved by Watts and Blackmore might well have found Hill's argument persuasive. Hill praised the sublimity of the Hebrews not from motives of piety but because he believed that religious subjects treated in a biblical manner provided the best opportunities for modern sublimity. Pope's response to *The Creation* ("I am sure, the Person who is capable of writing it, can need no Man to judge it"[16]) is a masterpiece of genteel equivocation and no more than the poem deserves. But Hill's poetic failure is less important here than his critical intention. His preface reveals that Dennis's arguments for the religious sublime found both advocates and audiences among those who wished to reform modern poetry.

The little triumvirate of Blackmore, Watts, and Hill was not alone in calling for the religious reformation of modern poetry. Richard Steele's *Guardian*, in an essay devoted to the subject of sacred poetry, argued that "to reclaim our Modern Poetry, and turn it into its due and Primitive Channel, is an Endeavour altogether worthy a far greater Character than the Guardian of a private Family. Kingdoms might be better for the Conversion of the Muses from Sensuality to natural Religion, and Princes on their Thrones might be obliged and protected by its Power" (No. 51). The *Spectator* was not so grandiose in its claims for sacred verse, but it too emphasized that sacred poetry contributes to the reformation of manners and the advancement of piety. Readers who delighted in witty dissections of a beau's head and coquette's heart also encountered in their pursuit of instructive entertainment various specimens of divine poetry, from Pope's "Messiah" to the hymns of Watts and of Addison. Noting that the pagan poets often celebrated the attributes and perfections of their gods, Addison sounded very much like any of the reformers: "One wou'd wonder that more of our Christian Poets have not turned their Thoughts this way, especially if we consider, that our Idea of the Supreme Being is not only Infinitely more Great and Noble . . . but filled with every thing that can raise the Imagination, and give an Opportunity for the Sublimest Thoughts and Conceptions" (No. 453). Dennis at times feuded with Addison, but here he might have secretly exulted (as Addison would put it) to find his argument for the religious sublime substantially repeated in the most influential journal of the century.

Although the *Spectator* reached multitudes, one wonders who would buy Thomas Newcomb's unreadable epic *The Last Judgment of Men and Angels* (1723). The list of subscribers is impressive, however, and includes Addison's biographer, two Oxford Professors of Poetry, as well as the future author of the *Night-Thoughts*. Each of them, if he read the preface, would have encountered Newcomb's praise of Dennis and his claim that modern poets have failed primarily by "not incorporating Religion with their Poetry."[17] The same lament that "the *Poetical* Character has of late been separated from the *religious*" was echoed a few years later by John Husbands,[18] who likewise offered a volume designed to prove the compatibility of poetry and religion. The sublime poetry of the Hebrews, according to Husbands, remains the best possible model for modern poets. While Husbands avoids the argument concerning Ancient or Modern superiority, others who were active in seeking the reformation of modern poetry did not. Edward Young, while advising modern poets to reverence and to know themselves, also advised them to exploit the advantages of Christianity, "a marvelous light, unenjoy'd of old . . . pour'd on us by revelation, with larger prospects extending our Understanding, with brighter objects enriching our Imagination, with an inestimable prize setting our Passions on fire, thus strengthening every power that enables composition to shine."[19] It is easy to show by citing a few major writers that early eighteenth-century poets uniformly lauded a correct, rational, secular modern poetry. But accompanying the apparent satisfaction of many with *la bagatelle*, with the heroic couplet, with pastorals, mock genres, and verse essays, a steady pressure for reform challenged the Augustans to look beyond the glories of Rome and the pleasures of London.

THE BASES OF REFORM

The call for the reformation of modern poetry was rarely mere angry denunciation of what the reformers took to be the irreligious spirit of the age. Those who called for reform generally emphasized ideas concerning the nature of poetry which most writers shared. Four related ideas are particularly important: the antiquity of poetry, the poetry of the Bible, Miltonic sublimity, and the religious sublime. These ideas created a foundation of critical theory underlying the work of various religious poets and poetasters throughout the century.

Eighteenth-century critics shared similar views concerning the antiquity of poetry. Like Dennis, they approached the question from two perspectives: by appealing either to history or to human nature. Examining history, they often affirmed that poetry must have begun in worship. " 'Tis probable that the first Poets were found at the Altar," writes Steele in the *Guardian*, "that they employed their Talents in adorning and animating the Worship of their Gods" (No. 51). Sidney probably popularized the belief among Englishmen that the Bible contains the world's most ancient poetry,[20] and his examples—the songs of Moses and of Deborah in particular—became favorite eighteenth-century illustrations of ancient religious poetry. Aaron Hill, for example, cites the song of Moses to prove that poetry originated with God, passed to the Hebrews, and then to mankind in general. "As the oldest, and, I think, the sublimest Poem in the World, is of Hebrew Original, and was made immediately after passing the Red-Sea, at a Time, when the Author had neither Leisure, nor Possibility, to invent a new Art," Hill reasons, it must therefore be most probable that the art of poetry was given by God to Moses "by immediate Inspiration."[21] The same proposition appears in a popular magazine of the day.[22] Moses and Deborah frequently appear beside Homer and Virgil on the pages of eighteenth-century criticism,[23] and, however much readers rejected claims for divine inspiration among modern poets, the examples of Moses and Deborah were interpreted as decisive evidence that poetry, now fallen into the hands of mere wits, had originated in the worship of God.

The study of human nature also persuaded critics that the earliest poetry was religious. Dennis, one of the first to maintain that poetry originates in human passion, drew his illustrations from the early poetry of the Greeks. Later critics, in accepting the view that poetry originated in passion, supported their view by pointing to the poetry of the Bible. "Poetry in its infant state was the language of devotion and love," asserted one mid-century writer. "It was the voice and expression of the heart of man when ravished and transported with a view of the numberless blessings that perpetually flowed from God the fountain of all goodness."[24] Again the songs of Moses and Deborah provided evidence. All unanimously proclaimed the Bible a treasury of the world's most ancient poetry. And this agreement gave a powerful argument to the reformers. As Isaac Watts wrote in the Preface to *Horae Lyricae*, "It has been a long Complaint of the vertuous and refined World, that Poesy, whose Original is Divine, should be enslav'd to Vice and Profaneness; that an Art inspir'd from Heaven should have so far lost the Memory of its Birth-place, as to be engag'd in the Interests of Hell. How unhappily is it perverted from its most glorious Design!"[25] At a time when innovation still implied anarchy to many, instead of a poetic revolutionary, Watts appears as the moderate curator of an ancient tradition.

Not only does the Bible contain the world's oldest poetry,

eighteenth-century critics believed; it also contains the world's greatest poetry. Sidney no doubt helped to spread this view. But until the eighteenth century, critics generally exempted God's inspired word from conventional literary analysis. A passage from the *Critical Review* points the direction of eighteenth-century attitudes toward biblical poetry: "Several circumstances concurred to give the Scriptures this distinguishing pre-eminence. They were written in ages of primitive simplicity, when all frivolous embellishments of style were unknown. They are the productions of oriental writers, who were used to bold, metaphorical expressions and magnificent images. But, above all, the sacred writers employed their thoughts on the most exalted subjects; the excellence of the Supreme Being, the works of Omnipotence, and the dispensations of Providence."[26] The *Review* distinguishes three general qualities of biblical poetry: 1) a primitive simplicity, 2) an oriental boldness, and 3) a treatment of exalted subjects. Each of these issues, familiar topics of criticism even during the early eighteenth century, became closely associated with discussions of the sublime. Considered together, they help to explain why the Bible seemed the ultimate standard of sublimity—a view, as Samuel Monk notes, "expressed almost unanimously by critics and aestheticians throughout the whole century."[27] The unanimity of critics concerning the primitive simplicity, oriental boldness, and exalted subjects of the Bible, however, is not an isolated matter: it also created a coherent body of opinion which increased the pressure for a new kind of modern poetry.

In attributing the preeminence of biblical poets to their simplicity, the *Critical Review* praised a quality which readers admired in poets from Homer to Shakespeare. Early in the century, critics would be unlikely to describe simplicity as primitive; for Pope it is "the Mean between Ostentation and Rusticity," which in his Preface to *The Iliad* he finds "no where in such Perfection as in the *Scripture* and our Author [i.e., Homer]."[28] Addison had to struggle determinedly to shelter the rude ballad "Chevy Chase" under the pantheon of classical simplicity, and he increased the difficulty of his struggle by refusing to recognize that the ballad and the Horatian ode are characterized by different kinds of simplicity. In the absence of such distinctions early in the century, simplicity became a catchword of praise rather than a well-defined and uniform literary standard, and, like "Chevy Chase," the Bible could be endlessly praised for its simplicity without seriously raising the question whether its simplicity was of a different kind from that of Homer and of Horace. "Not to insist on every Particular," wrote John Husbands in 1731, "there are two Beauties in which the SACRED WRITINGS undoubtedly excel all other Books; I mean their SIMPLICITY, and SUBLIMITY."[29] But, whereas earlier critics, following the lead of Boileau, had generally associated biblical simplicity with the unadorned conciseness of "Let there be light," Husbands foreshadows the later interest in the relationship between biblical poetry and primitivist thought. "Let there be light" is certainly concise and simple, but it is not indecorous; the Bible, however, contains numerous passages in which simplicity is not a function of conciseness but of imagery drawn from uncultivated states of life: "And I will wipe Jerusalem as a man wipeth a dish" (2 Kings 21:13). These different forms of simplicity remained in Pope's lifetime basically undiscriminated. Yet later discriminations merely broadened—rather than subverted—current notions of biblical simplicity and sublimity. Everywhere critics agreed in praising simplicity as one main source of the sublimity of the Hebrews.

Some critics argued that the New Testament as well as the Old should be included in discussions of biblical simplicity and sublimity. This opinion drew support from a fragment attributed to Longinus which includes Saint Paul among mankind's sublime orators—a passage known early in the century (Spec. 633) and reprinted in at least one later edition of the *Peri Hupsous*. In *The Sacred Classics Defended and Illustrated*, Anthony Blackwall determined to update Longinus and dedicated himself to proving that the New Testament is just as sublime as its Hebrew counterpart. "These inestimable writings," he maintained, "have equal plainness and power. . . . They have strong sense in common words; and plainness with sublimity. They have no unnatural rants, no swelling words of vanity; but the amiable,

great and noble simplicity of language reigns in them; and they
always give their readers an undisguis'd and moving description
of all the sentiments of man's heart."[30] William Smith cited
Blackwall in the notes to his edition of Longinus,[31] and he added
his own illustrations of "Majestic Simplicity and unaffected
Grandeur" from the New Testament, praising Saint Paul some
eight times as one of the sublimest rhetoricians of antiquity. But,
despite his admiration for Paul, Smith clearly believed that the
most sublime of all New Testament utterances were those of
Jesus, whose hushing the tumultuous sea with "Peace, be still"
(Mark 4:39) and summoning commandment "Lazarus, come
forth" (John 11:43) became standard examples of sublime sim-
plicity. Supported by the authority, then, not only of Moses
and of Deborah but of Jesus himself, the reformers felt justified
in complaining that inflated periphrasis and ornate diction had
nothing to do with the sublime.

Boldness as well as simplicity was a sublime quality much ad-
mired in the poetry of the Bible. Because the Hebrews were an
eastern people, eighteenth-century writers sometimes associated
the sublimity of scripture with the acknowledged wildness and ir-
regularity of much oriental literature (*Spec.* 160). Others pre-
ferred to ascribe the boldness of scripture to the natural passion
characteristic of all early poetry. Still others argued that a certain
noble hardiesse was the predictable result of divine inspiration.
Yet, whatever the cause to which they traced the sublime bold-
ness of scripture, most critics described its effects with unerring
similarity. Hugh Blair is admirably representative:

> In general, for it would carry us too far to enlarge upon all the
> instances, the Style of the Poetical Books of the Old Testa-
> ment is, beyond the Style of all other Poetical Works, fervid,
> bold, and animated. It is extremely different from that regular
> correct expression, to which our ears are accustomed in Mod-
> ern Poetry. It is the burst of Inspiration. The scenes are not
> coolly described, but represented as passing before our eyes.
> Every object, and every person, is addressed and spoken to, as
> if present. The transition is often abrupt; the connection often
> obscure; the persons are often changed; figures crowded, and

heaped upon one another. Bold sublimity, not correct elegance, is its character.[32]

It was possible, of course, that such a belief would have no effect upon the poetry written by eighteenth-century Englishmen; many critics recognized a necessary difference between the poetry of inspired, primitive, oriental writers and that of modern secular Europeans.[33] But as "bold sublimity" increasingly came to be regarded as the touchstone of great poetry, the Bible began to seem an especially apt model for modern poets who aspired to sublimity. "Have they forgot, or were they never told," Isaac Watts asked concerning his contemporaries, "that many Parts of the Old Testament are *Hebrew* Verse; and the Figures are stronger, and the Metaphors bolder, and the Images more surprizing and strange than ever I read in any profane Writer?"[34] For many eighteenth-century poets, the road to Parnassus runs through Jerusalem.

The treatment of elevated subjects, the third characteristic of biblical poetry noted by the *Critical Review*, was like the others often associated with the idea of sublimity. Illustrating their belief that nothing is more sublime than what relates to God, critics frequently borrowed Dennis's method of juxtaposing passages from the Bible with others drawn from the classics. The Bible, announced Anthony Blackwall, is "more noble and sublime upon any subject than the . . . Classics; but never do the *Greek* and *Latin* authors look so out of countenance upon the comparison, as when the discourse is upon God and divine subjects."[35] The casual reader might hear Aaron Hill rhapsodizing upon the same theme in the *Plain Dealer* (No. 74) or meet it stated with authority in Smith's Longinus. "The Deity is describ'd, in a thousand Passages of Scripture, in greater majesty, pomp, and perfection than that in which *Homer* arrays *his* gods," writes Smith. "The books of *Psalms* and of *Job* abound in such divine descriptions."[36] Few of the many writers who repeated this dictum shared Blackmore's tacit anti-pagan convictions. Most were keen admirers of the classics who nevertheless believed that nothing was more sublime than the biblical descriptions of God.

In commending the "pre-eminence" of the Scriptures, the *Critical Review* touched upon an idea of major importance to the development of the religious sublime. The Bible not only appeared (in the metaphor of Jonathan Richardson) "a Treasure of the Sublimest Poetry,"[37] but, as use of the superlative suggests, it was also thought to be the *non plus ultra* of the sublime. "Of all writings, antient or modern," wrote Hugh Blair, "the Sacred Scriptures afford us the highest instances of the Sublime."[38] Generalizing from the single example cited by Longinus, eighteenth-century critics established the Bible as the undisputed masterpiece of sublimity. In fact, several critics explicitly argued that by attending carefully to the Bible, modern writers would discover "new Laws for the Sublime."[39] Joseph Warton in effect accepted the challenge, publishing two essays in the *Adventurer* (Nos. 51 and 57) which claimed to present newly discovered manuscripts of Longinus concerning the sublimity of the Bible. And in *The Sublime and Beautiful of Scripture* (1777), Samuel Jackson Pratt (who used the pen name Courtney Melmoth) likewise based an entire treatise on the recognized alliance between the Bible and sublimity. Both Warton and Melmoth are quite conventional in their treatments, a fact which emphasizes just how widespread was the critical agreement concerning biblical sublimity. And the agreement among critics did affect the poetry of the age. Searching the past for models, poets naturally thought of the Bible whenever they wished to be sublime.

The Bible, however, was not the only work which eighteenth-century writers automatically associated with the idea of sublimity. Throughout the century, Milton rivals the Hebrews for preeminence in sublimity. The formula "Miltonic sublimity" echoes in the work of English critics from Dennis to the Romantics. "*Milton's* chief Talent, and indeed his distinguishing Excellence, lies in the Sublimity of his Thoughts," wrote Addison (*Spec.* 279). "The characteristick quality of his poem," Dr. Johnson concurred, "is sublimity."[40] Parroted Hugh Blair, "The subject which he has chosen, suited the daring sublimity of his genius."[41] "Sublimity is the pre-eminent characteristic of the Paradise Lost," concluded Coleridge.[42] The lesser critics agreed.[43]

But critical agreement exceeded mere formulaic praise. It encompassed several particularly important ideas concerning the sources of Milton's sublimity.

Milton's sublimity, for most eighteenth-century readers, derived in large part from his treatment of a religious, and particularly a Christian, subject. "Even among the educated," writes Raymond D. Havens, "the religious aspect of Milton's work gained it no few readers and imitators in a century that laid preponderant stress on the moral and spiritual side of literature."[44] But this is too cautious. Especially among the educated, who published and read the criticism of *Paradise Lost*, Milton's characteristic sublimity seemed inseparable from his Christian subject. A few controversies diverted attention from Milton's subject; some critics wondered whether *Paradise Lost* was a proper epic,[45] and others either defended or attacked Milton's use of an unusual style.[46] Most, however, agreed with Robert Lowth that Milton "is justly accounted the next in sublimity to those poets, who wrote under the influence of divine inspiration,"[47] and they searched for the sources of his sublimity in his dependence upon the truth and grandeur of the Bible.

Milton's use of the Bible, a subject often neglected by modern readers, seemed dazzling proof of his genius to eighteenth-century admirers of the sublimity of *Paradise Lost*. In 1713 Henry Felton summarized the claim which would be heard for a hundred years:

> *Milton* himself, as great a Genius as he was, oweth his Superiority over *Homer* and *Virgil*, in Majesty of Thought, and Splendor of Expression, to the Scriptures: They are the Fountain from which he derived his Light; the Sacred Treasure that enriched his Fancy, and furnished him with all the Truth and Wonders of God and His Creation, of Angels and Men, which no mortal Brain was able either to discover or conceive; And in Him . . . of all human Writers, You will meet all his Sentiments and Words raised and suited to the Greatness and Dignity of the Subject.[48]

Felton's praise does more than direct attention to Milton's use of the Bible. In explaining that the Bible furnished Milton with all the "Truth and Wonders" of his subject, he indirectly touched upon an issue which troubled eighteenth-century writers. Epic sublimity, most agreed, demanded the presence of supernatural marvels; but an epic poem must be probable. Milton offered English critics a way to resolve the potential conflict between the demands of probability and sublimity. The incidents of his fable, Addison recounted, "though they are very astonishing in themselves, are not only credible, but actual Points of Faith" (*Spec.* 315). Dr. Johnson put the matter this way: "Of the *probable* and the *marvellous*, two parts of a vulgar epick poem which immerge the critick in deep consideration, the *Paradise Lost* requires little to be said. It contains the history of a miracle . . .: the probable therefore is marvellous, and the marvellous is probable." [49] As Milton's epic answered the needs of eighteenth-century readers for rational transport and marvellous truth, they responded by acclaiming it to be the modern classic of the sublime.

Two striking aspects of Milton's Christian subject contributed to his undisputed sublimity: the vast panorama of his action and his use of supernatural machines. To readers who believed that great images expanded the mind itself, Milton's cosmic stage seemed custom-built for sublimity. "Milton had a subject, which permitted his fancy to expatiate beyond the bounds of the world," wrote Henry Pemberton in 1738, "where the strength of his invention has formed greater and more astonishing images than any former poet, or than can be allowed to any succeeding one, whose subject confines him within the limits of human actions and powers." [50] Pemberton's observation is supported by, if not in fact borrowed from, Addison's comparison of *Paradise Lost* and the *Aeneid*. "The Plan of *Milton's* Poem is of an infinitely greater extent, and fills the Mind with many more astonishing Circumstances," Addison points out. "*Satan*, having surrounded the Earth seven times, departs at length from *Paradise*. We then see him steering his Course among the Constellations, and after having traversed the whole Creation, pursuing his Voyage through the *Chaos*, and entering his own Infernal Dominions" (*Spec.* 357). What fascinates Addison here is the sheer spatial sweep of Milton's epic. Like the expansive account of Creation in Book Seven, the image of Satan cruising among the constellations or struggling through Chaos literally opened a new dimension of space to the eighteenth-century imagination. For readers trapped on the isthmus of a middle state, the sublime cosmography of *Paradise Lost* encouraged men for a time to soar beyond the limits of their frame, exercising what Longinus had called the soul's natural love for everything greater than itself.

Milton's stage was sublime not only in its panoramic sweep but also in the supernatural beings who people it. If a survey of interstellar space is itself sublime, the sublimity increases when we view the cosmos as background for the gigantic, lonely figure of Satan. The perverse landscapes of Hell similarly lend their grotesque sublimity as a foil to the tortured figures who wander there without hope. For many critics of the age, then, Milton's carefully differentiated cast of demons, angels, and divinities added significantly to the sublimity of *Paradise Lost*. Hugh Blair can be taken as summarizing the position of the majority when he argues that "almost all the descriptions given us of the appearances of supernatural Beings, carry some Sublimity, though the conceptions which they afford us be confused and indistinct."[51] Thus even the personified abstractions Sin and Death, whose active role in the poem both Addison and Johnson protested, could parlay their confused indistinctness into sublimity. The portrait of Death, probably the most brilliant representation of obscurity until Coleridge's awesome late poem "Limbo," served as a model for a legion of similar vague terrors in the following age:

> The other shape,
> If shape it might be call'd that shape had none
> Distinguishable in member, joint, or limb,
> Or substance might be call'd that shadow seem'd,
> For each seem'd either; black it stood as Night,
> Fierce as ten Furies, terrible as Hell,
> And shook a dreadful Dart; what seem'd his head
> The likeness of a Kingly Crown had on.
>
> (2:666–73)

All here is seeming, conjecture, abstraction—or, to describe the portrait in Burke's adjectives, "dark, uncertain, confused, terrible, and sublime to the last degree."[52]

Of all Milton's supernatural figures—with the possible exception of God—none impressed eighteenth-century readers as quite so sublime as Satan. Whether they saw him as villain or hero, they rarely failed to acknowledge his unparalleled sublimity. Citing the passage from Book One in which Milton compares Satan to a proud tower, Addison declared that "there is no single Passage in the whole Poem worked up to a greater Sublimity" (*Spec.* 303). William Smith lauded the same portrait, and Burke agreed that we "do not any where meet a more sublime description."[53] But praise was not limited to specific passages. It encompassed not only Satan's stature, action, and rhetoric but also his character itself as the vengeful, insatiable adversary of God. Certainly most eighteenth-century readers, unlike today's common reader, interpreted *Paradise Lost* as embodying at least the moral truth—if not the factual account—of man's Fall, and Satan, therefore, was a figure to be feared and condemned. Yet moral condemnation never seemed to diminish the aesthetic pleasure afforded by Satan's sublimity; indeed, Satan was James Beattie's claim that "the test of sublimity is not moral approbation." "Though we always detest his malignity," Beattie allows, "we are often compelled to admire that very greatness by which we are confounded and terrified."[54] Probably a number of readers without Nathan Drake's proximity to the Romantic Satanism of the next century shared his similar sense that "while we gaze and tremble at the aweful demon, we feel a thrilling sensation of pleasurable wonder, of admiration and of horror stealing through every nerve."[55] Drake's account of his mixed feeling parallels Dennis's much earlier description of his emotions upon crossing the Alps (2:381), and throughout the century, the same men who shuddered at the overwhelming scenes of nature also enjoyed their *frissons* in secluded closets by imagining the dreadful figure of Milton's towering but ruined archangel.

The agreement concerning Milton's sublimity provided an enormous boost for those who recommended the reformation of modern poetry. Without much prodding, poets soon began to imitate Milton's example. He had proved conclusively that the spirit of the Old Testament could vivify the work of modern poets and that Boileau's objections to Christian poetry were not universally applicable. In addition, the study of Milton's style, and particularly the interest in his use of blank verse, soon affected various writers of religious poetry, who often proclaim their intention of imitating Milton's sublimity. Despite the difficulty, then, of proving the direct influence of Dennis upon specific contemporary writers, the virtual unanimity of opinion concerning the sublimity of *Paradise Lost*, the sublimity of the Bible, and the divine origin of poetry in effect vindicated the grounds upon which Dennis had based his theory of the religious sublime. Thus, although no critic after Dennis constructed an entire theory of poetry around the idea of the religious sublime, most shared a belief in the critical principles which supported Dennis's labyrinthine system. Religious ideas were inextricably connected with sublimity. Why, then, do we find so few theorists of the religious sublime?

The lack of systematic theories of the religious sublime—when most critics accepted the grounds upon which such a theory could be built—seems due to certain characteristics of eighteenth-century criticism in general. First, the more gentlemanly critics lived in dread of appearing pedantic, perhaps consciously recalling Shaftesbury's advice that "the most ingenious way of becoming foolish is by a system."[56] Others, who may have seen a lesson in Dennis's fate, probably recognized that system-makers faced an uncertain marketplace for their books. At any rate, remarks on sublimity in the first half of the century usually appear in belletristic essays, in scattered corners of general treatises, or in prefaces, dedications, and similar miscellaneous niches. Second, when in the latter half of the century writers do begin systematic studies of the sublime, the attention of many had shifted, significantly, from criticism to aesthetics, from the study of literature to the broader analysis of how beauty affects the mind of the beholder.[57] In both instances, the religious sublime lies outside of the main interests of writers on the sublime. But finally, and most important, the religious sublime did not require an elaborate theoretical system to support it. Most writers on the sublime find it perfectly logical and obvious that the greatest sublimity should be derived from religious ideas. They saw no need to encase the obvious in a shell of theory.

Eighteenth-century commitment to the idea of the religious sublime, while never again presented in Dennis's systematic fashion, generally takes several forms. Sometimes the idea is expressed as an axiom, suggesting that the writer considers its truth to be self-evident or its proof a matter of general agreement. Giles Jacob, who corresponded with various well-known authors, reflects the axiomatic approach when he declares bluntly, "Poesy is . . . most sublime . . . where the Subjects and Ideas are Religious."[58] Dennis was among his correspondents, and Jacob may have considered him adequate authority for such an uncompromising assertion. An anonymous contributor to the *Gentleman's Magazine*, however, seems to rely entirely upon the self-evidence of pure logic when, after quoting a specimen of modern religious poetry, he argues that a sacred subject provides particular advantages for contemporary poets. "For if the Spirit of the *Sublime* must rise in proportion to the Dignity of any Subject," he reasons, then "no Subjects can possibly be so proper for the *Sublime* as religious ones."[59] As if to bear out this view, that same year the *Gentleman's Magazine* sponsored a contest for religious poets which elicited a sizable quantity of sublime verse. What seems most pertinent is that the contest and the idea behind it—that religious poetry ought to be sublime—could appear so matter-of-factly in one of the most popular (and unreligious) periodicals of the day. It offers persuasive evidence that the religious sublime did not require the superstructure of a supporting system.

During the second half of the century, both critics and aestheticians reveal a familiarity with the idea of the religious sublime. James Usher and Nathan Drake can represent the critical viewpoint; Alexander Gerard and Dugald Stewart, by contrast, can illustrate the different manner in which aestheticians considered the religious sublime. Usher's *Clio*, a curious book, contains in its second edition what the author calls an "enthusiastic gentleman's rhapsody on the sublime."[60] *Rhapsody* is certainly the right word. Usher writes in the rhythmic poetic prose which accompanied the development of sentimentalism and which, as Vicesimus Knox pointed out, is "by no means correspondent to classical ideas of beauty."[61] Usher is in fact no classicist but a nascent Romantic spirit; he sees man's essential difference from beasts not in the exercise of reason or of language but in the soul's "obscure hopes, and obscure fears" of a dimly sensed transcendent power. As a critic he is caught between two worlds. "The first and noblest source of delight in works of genuis, without competition," he declared, "arises from the sublime."[62] Ravishment—not mere delight and certainly not instruction— has become the single test of great art. But he was simply echoing a commonplace when he informed his contemporaries that "the sublime cannot subsist without the awful and mighty views of religion."[63] In defense of this view, he marshaled predictable illustrations: the grandeur of the Bible, the comparison of pagan and Christian ideas of God, the paradox of Lucretius who glorified the gods whom he intended to annihilate, and the sublimity of *Paradise Lost*. Gone from Usher's account, nevertheless, is any appearance of logical argument. Dennis's careful theory has been transformed into a rhapsodic hodgepodge associating sublimity with man's feeling of religious intuitions. Yet, if this change looks to the future, the weight of old examples drawn from several generations of critical thought grounds it in the past. The condition of inbetweenness is apparently comfortable for Usher, but it hardly allows him to demonstrate either the penetration or clarity which distinguishes good criticism.

Nathan Drake's "Observations on the Calvary of Cumberland" —two essays praising Richard Cumberland's religious epic, *Calvary; or the Death of Christ* (1792)—illustrates how the idea of the religious sublime exerted a continuing hold upon English criticism. Since Cumberland had modeled his poem upon *Paradise Lost*, Drake faced the easy task of adapting to his defense of Cumberland the usual remarks concerning Milton's religious sublimity. The opening paragraph of the "Observations" sets the mood by stressing the close relationship between sublimity and religious subjects, although (having read Burke) he dutifully divides his praise between sublimity and beauty: "No species of poetry, perhaps, is more difficult of execution than the religious; the natural sublimity of the subject cannot be heightened but by very superior powers, and demands an imagination plastic in the extreme, vast and gigantic on the one hand, tender, luxuriant and beautiful on the other, which can select, and vividly delineate, objects the most contrasted, the graceful inhabitant of heaven, or the appalling possessor of hell, which can, in short, combine the force and sublimity of Michael Angelo with the sweetness and amenity of Guido Rheni."[64] Except for the discrimination between sublimity and beauty, between the stern and the tender, Drake's remarks add nothing to the theoretical basis of the religious sublime established over one hundred years before. Indeed, his observation has no basis in theory: it reflects a detached fragment of criticism, and, as James G. Nelson reveals in his study of Milton and the Victorians, the same practical equation between Milton's sublimity and his Christian subject inspired the creation of poems such as Cumberland's well into the nineteenth century.[65]

Alexander Gerard and Dugald Stewart, unlike Usher and Drake, were mainly interested in aesthetics. Their studies, however, do suggest what could happen to the theory of the religious sublime when it was approached from a new perspective. Gerard is clearly bored by the idea. He restricts his treatment of the religious aspects of sublimity to the comment that "in classing sentiments that are sublime, the first place is assigned by critics, to those which have a relation to the gods."[66] A note refers the interested reader to Hermogenes, whose ideas had so excited Dennis some fifty years before. Gerard's indifference was not shared by Dugald Stewart, however. In 1810 Stewart offered a full and original discussion of how religious associations of ideas contribute to the sublime. "Of all the associations attached to the idea of Sublimity," he declared, "the most impressive are those arising from the tendency which the religious sentiments of men, in every age and country, have had to carry their thoughts *upwards* towards the objects of their worship." [67] Stewart believed that since men habitually associate gods and Heaven with elevation, the literal meaning of sublimity (i.e., height) naturally became associated with ideas which relate to religion. Seeing in literature an accurate reflection of what men in various ages and countries have thought, Stewart filled his psychological study of the sublime with standard literary quotations demonstrating the relationship between religion and sublimity. The treasury of examples collected by critics for over a century becomes the source for Stewart's new study of how the association of religious ideas contributes to man's experience of sublimity.

One subject which particularly interested Stewart, especially after Burke had treated it at length, was the idea of terror. But instead of following Burke in calling terror the ruling principle of the sublime, Stewart considered terror in the context of his own theory of associationalism. "If the former observations be just," he noted, referring to his explanation of how the mind associates ideas, "instead of considering, with Mr Burke, Terror as the ruling principle of the *religious sublime*, it would be nearer the truth to say, that the Terrible derives whatever character of Sublimity belongs to it from religious associations." [68] The psychological principle supporting Stewart's analysis would not have occurred to Dennis. But in practice the religious sublime simply involved the recognition of certain literary effects, and various principles might be put forth to account for them. Throughout the eighteenth century, critics simply stressed the isolated observation that sublimity was intimately related to the use of religious ideas. Stewart applied the current tools of psychology to explain a relationship which generations of readers had understood. In fact, it is not his particular theory which is unusual but his recourse to theory itself. For most writers the belief that the greatest sublimity derives from religious ideas seemed as untheoretical as the statement that snow is cold.

Stewart's distinguishing virtue lies in the comprehensiveness of his equation between sublimity and religious ideas. It is a revealing mistake when he refers to Burke's theory that terror is "the ruling principle of *religious sublime*": the adjective *religious* is wholly Stewart's addition. In associating all sublimity with religion, Stewart provided a theory at the end of the eighteenth century which attempts to explain the identical phenomenon which at the beginning of the century Dennis had studied in the context of a different hypothesis. But perhaps Stewart's most suggestive idea was that a study of the relationship between sublimity and religion might explain "the poetical effect of almost all the qualities which Mr Burke, and other modern critics, have enumerated as constituents of the Sublime."[69] The idea is particularly apt quite apart from Stewart's theory of association-alism because the importance of the religious sublime cannot be deduced from a study of criticism alone. Only an analysis of certain poems and poetic effects will suggest its full impact upon eighteenth-century men-of-letters. There is no need to argue that specific poems reflect the direct influence of specific critics. The existence, after Dennis, of a large body of critical thought relevant to the religious sublime makes the search for direct influences even more than usually futile. The idea was in the air. And it is clear that certain roughly definable types of eighteenth-century poetry do reflect the poets' continuing interest in the religious sublime. The next chapter will describe and analyze the forms of sublime religious verse which remain stable throughout the century, providing one essential element for an understanding of change: the isolation of that which remains constant.

Chapter Four

Poetic Practice: Varieties of the Religious Sublime

Religious poetry which did not meet the formal requirements of existing genres was often shuffled into the catchall classification of the "divine poem." Subject and treatment, not form, are the distinguishing characteristics of eighteenth-century religious poetry. These characteristics may seem so general, however, as merely to separate poems that obviously are religious from those that obviously are not. Yet, attention to certain basic subjects and treatments also provides a means for distinguishing among different kinds of eighteenth-century religious verse. This is especially true of divine poems written with an eye to the sublime. Throughout the century, a few basic kinds of sublime religious poems reappear with frequency. These are the biblical paraphrase, the eschatological poem, poems on the attributes of God and other "Seatonian" subjects, and poetry of imaginative devotion. A study of these different poems indicates in what ways eighteenth-century writers created a new variety of sacred literature which seems particularly attuned to the critical arguments concerning the religious sublime.

THE BIBLICAL PARAPHRASE

One effect of England's Protestant tradition was to encourage the versification of scripture for the delight and solace of a lay audience. Defenders of paraphrase among its early practitioners argued that verse is retained in the memory better than prose; the versification of scripture thus helps to spread the word of God among the illiterate. But such apologetics were soon unnecessary. Sir Thomas Wyatt and Sidney could claim continental models for their own elegant versions of the Psalms; and seventeenth-century poets such as Milton and Waller turned to the versification of scripture as a normal poetic activity, without seeming to feel any mission to spread the gospel among the cottages and looms of England. In fact, much seventeenth-century biblical paraphrase is deliberately wrought to a point of high artifice, an artifice which limits its audience to the cultivated few. For the masses, the crude but manly verse of the Sternhold-Hopkins psalmody remained the plain man's pathway to Heaven. By the beginning of the eighteenth century, the versification of scripture was an established literary fashion—which is not surprising in an age which rivaled the Elizabethan in its gust for translation. Nor was piety always the chief motive for biblical translation. Although it is true that poets were versifying scripture long before the heyday of the sublime, the eighteenth-century taste for biblical paraphrase probably owes much to the discovery that the Bible is "a Treasure of the Sublimest Poetry."

There are two main varieties of scriptural paraphrase, only one of which is closely related to the idea of religious sublimity. The first is the hymn, often characterized by a regular quatrain structure and a chastity of style which permit only infrequent opportunties for the sublime. It rarely complicates direct expression with any sort of literary sophistication; indeed, many writers of hymns seem committed to the belief (expressed by Richard Mather in his Preface to The Bay Psalm Book [1640]) that "God's altar needs not our polishing." Isaac Watts could speak for many writers of hymns when he observed in the preface to his *Hymns and Spiritual Songs* (1707), "The Metaphors are generally sunk to the Level of vulgar Capacities. I have aimed at ease of Numbers and smoothness of Sound, and endeavour'd to make the Sense plain and obvious."[1] Watts's hymn "God the Thunderer—The Last Judgment and Hell," a paraphrase of the sublime Psalm 18, illustrates his principles of hymnody:

> *His sounding Chariot shakes the Sky,*
> *He makes the Clouds his Throne,*

> There all his Stores of Lightning lie
> Till Vengeance dart them down.
>
> His Nostrils breathe out fiery Streams,
>   And from his awful Tongue
> A Sovereign Voice divides the Flames,
>   And Thunder roars along.[2]

Paradoxically, while eighteenth-century critics admired the sublime simplicity of the Bible, "God the Thunderer" would strike them as a little too simple. Although the diction neither sinks nor soars, a matter-of-fact tone prevents the poem from developing an excitement equal to its subject. But Watts would defend this breach of conventional decorum on religious grounds. His hymn intentionally disappoints the literary expectations of a polite reader; it remains simple, he would argue, "lest a more exalted Turn of Thought or Language should darken or disturb the Devotion of the weakest Souls."[3]

When eighteenth-century religious poets heeded what Watts called "the politer part of Mankind,"[4] they created a second kind of biblical paraphrase which deliberately aims at the sublime. Comparison of Watts's Hymns and Spiritual Songs with his Horae Lyricae (1706) illustrates the difference quite clearly. Originally he had intended many of the poems in Horae Lyricae for inclusion in Hymns and Spiritual Songs, but he excluded them "because of the bolder Figures of Speech that crouded themselves into the Verse, and a more unconfin'd Variety of Number which I could not easily restrain."[5] Horae Lyricae, in other words, is full of spoiled hymns. Under the influence of strong feeling, poems which began as hymns came out impassioned and complex lyrics. And one remarkable characteristic of the poems in Horae Lyricae is their obvious sublimity. The restrained power of "God the Thunderer," for example, appears with more passion and literary finesse as Watts presents a similar vision for the politer part of mankind:

> His Chariot was a pitchy Cloud,
> His Wheels beset with burning Gems
> The Winds in Harness with the Flames

> Flew o'er th' Ethereal Road;
> Down thro' his Magazines he past
> Of Hail and Ice and fleecy Snow,
>   Swift roll'd the Triumph, and as fast
> Did Hail and Ice in melted Rivers flow.
> *The Day was mingled with the Night,*
> *His Feet on solid Darkness trod,*
> *His radiant Eyes proclaim'd the God,*
>   *And scatter'd dreadful Light.*[6]

I have italicized parts of the passage to show how Watts's pseudo-Pindaric stanza is composed of units somewhat similar to the quatrains of his hymns—punctuated with apparently hypermetrical, but quite contrived, hexameter and pentameter lines. Single verses still contain essentially complete or separable thoughts; and the *abba* rhyme scheme is no less artful, if less common, than the *abab* rhymes of his hymns. Yet, while much is similar, much has changed. The images are considerably bolder and more pictorial: God's chariot, dignified in "God the Thunderer" with the single ceremonial adjective *sounding*, here becomes the focus of an extended sensuous description. The change is evident in the new profusion of adjectives: pitchy, burning, ethereal, fleecy, melted, solid, radiant, dreadful. Further, the boldness of Watts's imagery does not merely consist in its greater visual appeal. A figure such as "solid Darkness," like Milton's "palpable obscure" (on which it perhaps was modeled), suggests mingled sensory experience—both sight and touch combining to render a synesthetic effect, making the image itself more complex and elusive. Meanwhile, the straightforward simplicity of individual lines brings the poem very close to what Watts's contemporaries would have regarded as the sublimity of scripture.

It is pertinent, in discussing the sublime biblical paraphrase, to recall that the activity designated as *paraphrase* allowed eighteenth-century poets considerable latitude. The relevant definition in Johnson's *Dictionary* (1755) is "to translate loosely." Thus the sublime biblical paraphrase can be either an original poem which relies strongly upon scripture for imagery, style, situation, or subject (as does "The Law given at *Sinai*") or a reasonably close reworking of specific biblical passages. The latter of these alternatives obviously requires less originality and invention, but it continued to interest many eighteenth-century poets —and for good reasons. Most poets were pious Christians to whom the Bible was certainly as familiar as the classics which they often paraphrased or imitated, and in an age of refinement the existing poetical translations of scripture seemed barbarous, antiquated, or extravagant. In his "Life of Addison," Dr. Johnson reports that Addison, like so many others of his time, planned to compose a new poetical version of the Psalms. In addition, however, certain biblical passages offered unusual opportunities for poets who specialized in the carefully turned phrase or elegant compliment to venture for a moment outside the ordered garden of neoclassicism. "To adopt the beautiful sublime of the sacred writings, particularly of the prophecies, which breathe all the wildness of an irregular genius," commented the *Critical Review* in 1761, "requires an imagination rather warm than correct; the bold and extravagant flights of genius more than the unaffecting cold accuracy of art."[7] A poet who wished to prove he could be bold and extravagant as well as elegant and correct might begin paraphrasing scripture as a sure way to achieve short swallow-flights of sublimity.

The elder Thomas Warton provides a clear illustration of how the Bible could be used by modern writers as an arena for demonstrating their poetic virtuosity. His *Poems on Several Occasions* (1748), a collection of trifles, includes amid the *nugae* "A Paraphrase on the xiiith Chap. of Isaiah." The style suddenly grows bolder. Rhyme vanishes:

> The dread Jehovah comes—before him march
> Anger and Vengeance: The polluted Land
> Shall desolated mourn, and far away
> His red Right Hand shall shrieking Sinners sweep.
> Then shall the Stars of Heav'n, the glittering Gems
> Of awful Night's dark Robe, the pale-ey'd Moon,
> The weary Pilgrim's Friend, and the great Sun,
> Who from the crystal Portals of the East
> Walks forth with tenfold Brightness cloth'd, and pours

Intolerable Day, all darken'd droop.
Earth from her Orbit shall astonisht leap,
Heav'n rock and tremble to the Throne of God.[8]

It is instructive to compare Warton's paraphrase with the original: "Behold, the day of the Lord cometh, cruel both with wrath and fierce anger, to lay the land desolate: and he shall destroy the sinners thereof out of it. For the stars of heaven and the constellations thereof shall not give their light: the sun shall be darkened in his going forth, and the moon shall not cause her light to shine" (13:9-10). Warton apparently found the denuded nouns of the King James version inherently unpoetic: land, sinners, sun, and moon thus receive the gilding of adjectives and appositive phrases carefully selected for their powers of exalting the commonplace. The passage, in fact, could be a paradigm of what might be called adjectival sublimity, for certainly the least successful method employed by eighteenth-century poets of the sublime is to heap up adjectives which express a high degree of intensity: dread, polluted, shrieking, glittering, awful, pale-ey'd, weary, great, crystal, tenfold, intolerable, darken'd, astonisht. A man who once held the Oxford Professorship of Poetry no doubt chose his words with care, confident that sheer intensity of language would transmit the sublimity of the original to cultured English readers. No doubt, too, he recognized that his passage from Isaiah almost duplicates the "God came from Teman" verses in Habakkuk which Dennis and others had praised for their sublimity. However pious his motives, the elder Warton must have admitted to himself that Isaiah offered him something more precious than mere religious instruction: the opportunity for a short, exhilarating divagation into the sublime.

Warton's kind of biblical sublimity, with its unfortunate bombast and equivocal piety, could be reproduced many times from the minor poetry of the eighteenth century. Isaiah, Habakkuk, the Psalms, and the songs of Judith, Moses, and Deborah became the models of numerous (and often very worldly) poets seeking to be sublime. Certain passages appear with comic regularity. In John Husbands's *Miscellany of Poems*, one of Dennis's favorite instances of the sublime swells with Pindaric grandeur:

> Admiring Worlds beheld with silent Fear
> The interposing Deity appear,
> As thro' the Heav'ns full royally He rode,
> High-charioting on many an harness'd Cloud,
> And on the wings of mighty Winds came flying all abroad.[9]

Milton as well as Pindar lent his authority to poems of more than usual elevation. In 1725 a correspondent to *Hibernicus's Letters* (No. 18), for instance, submits a Miltonic paraphrase of the same psalm in order "to shew how proper for Verse Divine Subjects are":

> Clouds thou mak'st thy Chariots,
> Which carried on the Wings of driving Storms,
> Proclaim the awful Presence of th' Almighty.
> Him Winds obey; and airy Meteors flash
> His Messages, to the Divine Command
> Obsequious.[10]

God in his chariot of clouds, Pestilence stalking before the enraged Deity, and innumerable other biblical descriptions of divine wrath became standard subjects for paraphrase. While any poet innocently drawn to these passages would be obliged to maintain the elevation of the original, the process often seemed to work in reverse. Poets wishing to lace their volumes with sublimity carefully included a few paraphrases from Isaiah, David, or the other biblical prophets and poets recognized for their fire and transport.

One measure of the common use of biblical passages by poets aiming to be sublime is the frequency with which critics cite these works as instances of false sublimity. The eighteenth-century champion of bathos was Sir Richard Blackmore, who had conspicuously recommended the Bible for "nobler Examples of the true sublime Stile, than any [that] can be found in the Pagan Writers."[11] Blackmore, however, consistently offended against the standard which he proposed. Commenting upon Edmund Smith's projected translation of the *Peri Hupsous*, Dr. Johnson wrote that Smith had intended to accompany it with illustrations and "had selected his instances of the false *Sublime* from the works of Blackmore."[12] From the beginning until the end of the century, critics continued to cite Blackmore's debasement of the sublime through demeaning imagery,[13] and his name looms large in the notes to Pope's *Peri Bathous*, where he frequently illustrates "the Bottom, the End, the Central Point, the *non plus ultra* of true Modern Poesie!"[14] By comparing God to a painter, chemist, wrestler, fuller, butler, and baker, Blackmore incurred a century of ridicule as "the Father of the *Bathos*, and indeed the *Homer* of it."[15] But his solace, and the solace of so many who attempted to paraphrase the Bible, was to have company in failure. As the *Critical Review* wrote in 1763 concerning James Merrick's *Poems on Sacred Subjects*, "Such paraphrases of the Scripture seldom succeed. It must be no ordinary genius that enters into the spirit and sublimity of the sacred writings."[16] Despite such warnings, however, poets too often saw biblical paraphrase as a convenient, if hazardous, shortcut to the sublime.

Poets who drew somewhat less attention to their scriptural models sometimes fared better. A looser adherence permitted both greater range for originality and an allusive, rather than direct, use of biblical materials. Perhaps no poet was more successful in this looser form of biblical paraphrase than Alexander Pope, whose name is rarely associated with the sublime. It is possible that his "Messiah" (1712) represents Pope's oblique answer to Henry Cromwell, who rather pointedly reminded him that while he had surpassed Dennis in the realm of criticism, he had yet to prove his superiority in the grander poetic forms in which Dennis specialized.[17] Whatever its genesis, "Messiah" is a fine example of a sublime religious poem which derives much of its power from an unconfining adherence to the matter and language of the Bible. Although Dennis blasted nearly every major poem which Pope wrote, from *An Essay on Criticism* to *The Dunciad*, he never mentioned "Messiah"—even though after 1717 there could be no doubt concerning its authorship.

Most readers must have recognized what the *Critical Review* called "the blaze of sublime description, with which the Messiah of Pope is gloriously invested."[18] Pope himself strikes the keynote in his opening couplet:

> *Ye Nymphs of Solyma! begin the Song:*
> *To heav'nly Themes sublimer Strains belong.*

The earthly themes of the preceding four pastorals had been sung in a smooth middle style. But religious subjects, as Dennis had argued, require an elevated treatment. By invoking the nymphs of Jerusalem (Solyma)—rather than the conventional maidens of pastoral—Pope at once announces his shift from fable to truth, from delight to sublimity. His allusions to Virgil and to Isaiah also prepare his readers for a higher flight. Dennis had praised the fourth eclogue as "very Sublime" (1:233), particularly because of its clearly religious nature. Yet eighteenth-century critics seem to underplay Pope's debt to Virgil. Vicesimus Knox, for example, who certainly appreciated Pope's use of Virgil, asserted that his poem "derived its chief merit from Isaiah." [19] Nor was Knox alone in tracing Pope's principal debt to the Old Testament.

Joseph Warton's criticism of "Messiah" recalls other discussions of the religious sublime. He praised the poem as a brilliant exception to Pope's usual practice. "Our author," he wrote, ". . . was with justice convinced, that the Scriptures of God contained not only the purest precepts of morality, but the most elevated and sublime strokes of genuine poesy; strokes, as much superior to any thing Heathenism can produce, as is Jehovah to Jupiter." [20] Pope has dignified "Messiah" above all of his works, Warton implies, by utilizing the inherent sublimity and truth of Christianity. Although Wordsworth [21] could dismiss Pope's diction as extravagant and absurd, most eighteenth-century readers would have agreed with Steele that Pope had preserved "the sublime heavenly spirit" [22] of Isaiah throughout the poem. Indeed, the concluding lines are a triumph of religious sublimity:

> *The Seas shall waste; the Skies in Smoke decay;*
> *Rocks fall to Dust, and Mountains melt away;*
> *But fix'd His Word, His saving Pow'r remains:*
> *Thy Realm for ever lasts! thy own Messiah reigns!*

While the brilliance is all Pope's, the impulse to write this sort of poem, or to write it in this way, must be traced in part to the work of critics such as Dennis who argued the necessary relationship between religion and sublimity.

A great many biblical poems could be exhumed to show how frequently eighteenth-century poets exploited the relationship between religion and sublimity. Only upon occasions, however, did poets—whether closely or loosely following scripture—manage very happy results. One such occasion deserves attention here, both for its fame and for its interesting use of religious sublimity. Addison's poem *The Campaign* (1705), which glorifies Marlborough's victory at Blenheim, contains one of the most renowned similes in eighteenth-century literature. As the battle rages around him, the Duke is compared to a serene angel of Providence:

> So when an Angel by Divine Command
> With rising Tempests shakes a guilty Land,
> Such as late o'er pale Britannia past,
> Calm and Serene he drives the furious Blast;
> And, pleas'd th'Almighty's Orders to perform,
> Rides in the Whirl-wind, and directs the Storm.[23]

Addison no doubt calculated the effect which his simile would have. "No passage in *The Campaign* has been more often mentioned," wrote Dr. Johnson, "than the simile of the Angel."[24] Steele discussed it in the *Tatler* (No. 43) as an illustration of true sublimity, and Hugh Blair declared it "a truly Sublime"[25] image. The use of the supernatural for a single stroke of emphasis frees Addison from the epic machinery of good and bad spirits which encumbers Dennis's *Britannia Triumphans* (1704), written to celebrate the same occasion and to illustrate his theory of the religious sublime. Equally effective is Addison's attempt to create a scriptural language. The last line gains significantly in power when we hear the echo of the prophet Nahum: "the Lord hath his way in the whirlwind and in the storm" (1:3). One wishes that all those who ransacked the Bible for sublimity had caught its spirit so well.

Addison's use of Nahum is clearly not an example of paraphrase but of allusion. Yet the effect of Addison's allusion does not depend so much upon our recognition of a particular context as upon our sense that the line sounds somehow biblical. The fame of Addison's line in the eighteenth century offers one measure of his success.[26] It is much easier to sound biblical in a single line or short passage, however, than in an extended paraphrase. Nevertheless, this difficulty did not dissuade poets from the attempt. Throughout the century they paraphrased long biblical passages famous for sublimity. And, predictably, nearly all proved unequal to the spirit of the original. In translating what the *Critical Review* called some of "the most affecting and sublime passages from the Psalms and Prophets," John Farrer could do no better than most poets of the age. "All these tinsel ornaments," concluded the *Review*, "this glow of poetical colouring, added by our translator, it is evident, only mars the beautiful sentiment, and destroys the dignity and simplicity of the original."[27] Boileau's clear assertion that a vast difference exists between the sublime style and true sublimity failed to convince an unfortunate number of eighteenth-century poets. And nowhere was their error more evident and disastrous than in their attempts to paraphrase the Bible.

ESCHATOLOGICAL POETRY: SUBLIMITY AND THE LAST THINGS

Although eighteenth-century poetry often seems wholly committed to the city of man, many poets were also deeply concerned with the essential religious issues of holy living and holy dying. Dr. Johnson, as usual, sounds authoritative in telling Boswell, "Sir, there is a great cry about infidelity: but there are, in reality, very few infidels."[28] Literature belonged mainly to the faithful, especially early in the century. "The truly popular authors between 1690 and 1700, to judge from the frequency with which they were reprinted," Amy L. Reed has written, "were Jeremy Collier, Bishop Taylor, Archbishop Tillotson, John Bunyan, Richard Baxter, and George Herbert. The favorite subjects were 'the four last things,' i.e., death, judgment, heaven, and hell."[29] What was true at the beginning of the century continued, to a somewhat diminished degree, to reflect the reading habits of many in the later decades. For example, in *Serino: or, The Character of a Fine Gentleman*, James Foxton notes that his callow Grandison is a devotee of the arts, four of his favorite poems being *Paradise Lost*, Blackmore's *Creation*, Watts's *Horae Lyricae*, and Edward Young's *Poem on the Last Day*.[30] It is not surprising to discover Blackmore and Watts among the favorite poets of a gentleman with a taste for religious verse; but the inclusion of Young might strike modern readers as odd, if not morbid. Young's theme, however, is a familiar one in the eighteenth century, and poets were quick to recognize the relation between sublimity and the last things.

John Pomfret reveals in interesting ways the double vision of many eighteenth-century poets. His most popular work, "The Choice," is a mild Horatian celebration of the middle road to earthly contentment. But Pomfret also knew that human life cannot offer lasting joy. "Every wise Man . . . will consider this Life only as it may conduce to the Happiness of the other," wrote Addison, "and chearfully sacrifice the Pleasures of a few Years to those of an Eternity" (*Spec.* 575). Pomfret surely agreed. In "Dies Novissima: or The Last Epiphany"—published after his death in 1702 in his *Poems on Several Occasions* (often reprinted) —he considered the period when choice is no longer possible:

> See beck'ning from yon cloud, he stands,
> And promises assistance with his hands.
> I feel the heavy rolling God
> Incumbent, revel in his frail abode.
> How my breast heaves, and pulses beat!
> I sink, I sink beneath the furious heat.

The gentle parson, who preferred his sycamores in "a stately row," now imagines a condition in which all human order dissolves:

> Forward confusion shall provoke the fray,
> And nature from her antient order stray;
>   Black tempests, gath'ring from the seas around,
>   In horrid Ranges shall advance;
> And, as they march, in thickest sables drown'd,

> The rival thunder from the clouds shall sound,
> And light'nings join the fearful dance.
>
> (1746 ed.)

This nightmarish vision of the Last Day in part underlies the Augustan rage for order. The impetus for Pomfret's poem is not merely a longing to let his imagination bolt with his reason. The poem derives its character from his understanding that the idea of the Last Day requires a poetic flight of sublimity. Nor was Pomfret alone in recognizing both the poetic and devotional power of his subject. Poems on the Last Day and related subjects became one of the century's favorite exercises in religious sublimity.

Even relatively early in the century, as Pomfret's poem indicates, writers liked to imagine cataclysmic upheavals of nature. Thus, well before the publication of Thomson's *Winter* (1726) signaled the first popular success of the new poetry of natural description, readers enjoyed the vivid descriptions of sublime and prodigious aspects of nature in Thomas Burnet's well-known *Sacred Theory of the Earth* (1684): "Here are Lakes of fire and brimstone: Rivers of melted glowing matter: Ten thousand Volcano's [sic] vomiting flames all at once. Thick darkness, and Pillars of smoke twisted about with wreaths of flame, like fiery Snakes. Mountains of Earth thrown up into the Air, and the Heavens dropping down in lumps of fire."[31] Burnet's vision of the Conflagration is not far removed from the predictable succession of prodigies which fill the poems of natural description. Writing to David Mallet concerning Mallet's manuscript poem "The Excursion," Thomson assured him that "sublimity must be the character of your piece." He also included some specific advice: "Here if you could insert a sketch of the deluge, what more affecting and noble?"[32] Any flood, properly handled, would contribute to the sublimity of Mallet's poem. But Thomson recommends "the" Deluge as especially sublime, not just because it is the largest inundation on record but because it directly involves the mysterious terrors of Christianity. The Deluge is not an eschatological subject—although flooding frequently appears in the Last Day poems—but similarly monumental forces are unleashed in the poetry of the last things to guarantee an appropriate aura of sublimity.

Edward Young and Samuel Catherall both responded to current eschatological interest by composing sublime poems on the subject of the Last Day. Young's *A Poem on the Last Day* (1713) received added notice by appearing in the *Guardian* essay on sacred poetry (No. 86). As his Dedication to Queen Anne indicates, Young had calculated the advantages of his subject. "There is no Subject more Exalted, and Affecting, than this which I have chosen; it's [sic] very first Mention Snatches away the Soul to the Borders of Eternity, Surrounds it with Wonders, Opens to it on every hand the most Surprizing Scenes of Awe, and Astonishment, and Terminates it's view with nothing less than the Fulness of Glory, and the Throne of God."[33] For modern readers, Young's choice of rhymed couplets undercuts the grandeur of his vision. Catherall, on the other hand, humbly calling himself a "mean Follower of Great Milton," chose blank verse as the fitting medium for his *Essay on the Conflagration* (1720), no doubt because it seemed more flexibly attuned to the passion of his theme. "For my own Part," he wrote, "I never pretended to set forth an exact, and regular Poem upon a Subject so Copious, and truly Sublime."[34] As Catherall indicates, the taste for sublimity was not restricted to poems of natural description. If asked to name subjects appropriate for sublime poetry, most eighteenth-century poets and critics would invariably include a series of explicitly religious topics, especially those concerned with the last things.

Perhaps the most popular eschatological subject among sublime poets was the Day of Judgment. If the order and infinitude of nature revealed by the telescope could evoke sublime thoughts and feelings, so too could the vision of the heavens rolled together like a flaming scroll. Unlike the sedate admiration which Addison (*Spec.* 339) and others thought to be the appropriate response to a philosophical contemplation of the universe, the idea of the world's final dissolution usually produced the sublimity of terror. As Thomas Leland declared, without a hint of uncertainty in his style, "There is no grander or more awful subject, on which a writer or speaker can be employed, than that of the Deity executing his justice, publicly and sensibly, upon his offending creatures."[35] It is hardly surprising that poets in search of grand and awful subjects would consider writing about the Last Day. In fact, the subject was inherently so powerful that writers concerned with the Day of Judgment were taxed more to control than to excite the emotions. Isaac Watts achieved one of the most judicious blends of excitement and control when he restrained his poem "The Day of Judgment" through the metrical discipline of English Sapphic verse:

> Hark the shrill Outcries of the guilty Wretches!
> Lively bright Horror and amazing Anguish
> Stare thro' their Eye-lids, while the living Worm lies
>   Gnawing within them.[36]

The deft conjunction of a medieval vision and a classical form saves the poem from mere sensationalism and is perhaps what William Cowper recalled when he praised Watts as often "sublime in his conceptions and masterly in his execution."[37] Yet an unclassical indistinctness ("Lively bright Horror") and vague emotionalism ("amazing Anguish") support Dr. Johnson's view that "the thought of the LAST DAY makes every man more than poetical by spreading over his mind a general obscurity of sacred horror, that oppresses distinction and disdains expression."[38] Like much eschatological verse, Watts's poem seems closer to Edmund Burke's ideas of sublimity than to the ideas of Boileau.

Burke's belief that terror is the main source of sublimity suggests the rationale behind a number of Last Day poems. Dennis had recommended a suggestive incompleteness in the use of images to produce terror and terrible sublimity, but Burke went substantially further. Vague words, as well as incomplete images, are for Burke one of the poetic sources of terror, a view he justifies by arguing that poetry is often designed "to display rather the effect of things on the mind of the speaker, or of others, than to present a clear idea of the things themselves."[39] A poet writing on the Last Day might find this notion attractive; the old injunctions about imitating nature cannot mean much to the poet whose subject is the unique and unknowable occasion of nature's expiration. Analogy likewise fails. Thus the poet may ultimately trust that vague evocative language, rather than clear visual description, will convey his sense of the unimaginable—as Aaron Hill seems to have done in *The Judgement-Day, A Poem* (1721):

> Worlds *against* Worlds, *with clashing* Horror driv'n,
> Dash *their* broad Ruins *to the* Throne of Heav'n!
> Thro' *flaming* Regions *of the* burning Air,
> Down rain *distilling* Suns, *in liquid* Rills,
> Mix'd *with* red Mountains of unmelted Fire!
> Hissing, *perplex'd, with* Show'rs of Icy Hills,
> And Cat'ract Seas, *that* roar, *from* Worlds still higher;
> Mingled, *like driving* Hail, *they* pour *along*,
> And, thund'ring, *on our* ruin'd *System* fall!

It has been argued that Hill uses religious verse chiefly "as an outlet for his craving to be expansive and sublime."[40] Nothing could be truer. Yet it is possible to recognize in Hill's *The Judgement-Day* a struggle which partly redeems his lack of skill. He was, however inept, one of the few early poets of the religious sublime to understand the potential conflict between the language of neoclassical poetry and the choice of eschatological subjects. As he writes in his Preface, "When we let our Fancy loose, on this frightful Discovery, we conceive an Indistinct and astonishing Idea of something, horribly prodigious, and which is too mighty for our Grasp. But it bursts from our very Approach, and overflows Humane Thought, when we would draw it into Description!"[41] In pursuing a sublimity of the unimaginable, Hill matches his description of ultimate disorder with a massive dislocation of normal Augustan poetic practice—far beyond the requirements of Pindaric grandeur. The violent motion, jarring numbers, and jumbled, indistinct images create an impression (but not a picture) of total chaos, a subject which proved darkly irresistible in an age of mathematics.

The same readers who admired Ossian in the 1760s might

have praised Hill's *The Judgement-Day*, but strict neoclassical
temperaments found little to enjoy in the Last Day verse. The
most trenchant ridicule of such productions is undoubtedly
Swift's posthumously published "The Day of Judgement." Like
many of the works it satirizes, it begins with the poet rapt above
the earth where he witnesses a vision of the world's last hours.
Swift's main target, however, is not the poetic manner or quality
of the Judgment Day poems: it would be hard indeed to satirize
a poetic manner which, by neoclassical standards, was already
deformed to the point of self-ridicule. Instead, Swift attacks the
habits of mind which could approve and create such poems. As
the trembling sinners huddle before the throne of God, each
hoping to see the others damned, the poem ends with God's an-
nouncement that the Judgment will not take place:

> *I to such Blockheads set my Wit!*
> *I damn such Fools!—Go, go, you're bit.*[42]

Swift's serious point is not that the Judgment may not occur.
Rather, he employs the shock of such a thought to expose the
vaunting pride of those who think they understand God's ulti-
mate ends. A Lilliputian in Brobdingnag could not be more
contemptible than one little paltry mortal at the Last Judgment,
Swift implies, and the habit of imagining the Last Day from
man's point of view is but one more instance of the absurd vice
of pride. "We should often . . . annihilate our selves before [God]
in the Contemplation of our own Worthlessness and of his
transcendent Excellency and Perfection," wrote Addison. "This
would effectively kill in us all the little Seeds of Pride, Vanity
and Self-conceit" (*Spec.* 531). The fools who extend their self-
love even to the Day of Judgment hardly entertain a just idea of
their own worthlessness. And the poet who fills his Last Day
poems with scenes of human terror, Swift would argue, simply
encourages the perpetuation of a foolish, dangerous error of
perspective.

Swift's dislike of the Last Day poems proceeds from a worthy
religious impulse, but their defenders could cite equally pious
motives. To the Puritan conscience, obsessed with individual sal-

vation, a poem such as Watts's "The Day of Judgment" might touch the heart with saving power. At the same time, Thomas Newcomb could envision the Last Day as an epic subject appropriate for the advancement of both literature and piety. Newcomb's *The Last Judgment of Men and Angels* (1723), a twelve-book epic after the manner of Milton, purports to follow Dennis and the Ancients in using religious ideas to excite "those Violent and Enthusiastick Passions of Fear, Terror, and Astonishment, which 'tis the Aim of Heroick Poetry chiefly to produce."[43] In fact, the relationship between sublimity and the last things was so widely recognized that Joseph Trapp's pedestrian *Thoughts upon the Four Last Things* (1734-1735) could be criticized for failing to exploit "so many occasions of rising to an elevated sublimity."[44] Perhaps the vogue for eschatological verse, despite the Spartan tastes of the major poets, can best be suggested by a contest in the *Gentleman's Magazine* for the twelve months beginning July 1734. "Be it known to all men by these presents," began the announcement, "that the sum of *Fifty Pounds* will be given to the person, who shall make the best *Poem*, Latin or English, on *Life, Death, Judgment, Heaven* and *Hell*, viz. all the said subjects jointly, and not any single one independent of the rest."[45] One year after the publication of Pope's *Essay on Man*, the nation's poets were encouraged to look beyond the study of mankind.

The *Gentleman's Magazine*, like most of its successors, rooted itself in the diurnal and the mundane. Its first editor, Edward Cave, talked as if he viewed the contest for sacred poets almost as a form of public atonement. But certainly, too, he expected to profit from the interest in eschatological verse. Writing to Isaac Watts, he described the stipulated topics in a significant phrase as "five sublime subjects,"[46] and probably he hoped that poets would imitate Watts's own fiery models of the religious sublime. When the submitted poems were finally published in an "extraordinary" edition (July 1735), however, the results were not explosive. Much of the verse was rhymed, rational, and didactic—no doubt a tribute to the influence of Pope. Yet, if large doses of reason and morality were appropriate to such philosophical

themes as life and death, most of the contestants also recognized
the need to be sublime.

When their focus shifted to visions of Judgment, Heaven, and
Hell, the poets' manner altered dramatically. Fired by such
elevated themes (or at least by the knowledge that they must
appear to be fired), the winning poets stretched themselves on
the rack of the religious sublime. The first-place poem draws the
Judgment with admirable restraint:

> Messiah comes—before th' avenging God
> Red fires consuming roll, a dreadful flood,
> While clam'rous ruin of dissolving skies,
> And flaming earth th' astonish'd throng surprize.[47]

Reading the second-place poem, however, a patron of Cave's
gentlemanly pages would have suddenly encountered dread
prodigies in the sky, floods of sulphur, ten thousand thunders,
and the blaring trump of doom, while Christ descended before
his eyes and shouting angels shook the world's frame. After such
excess, the fourth-place poem seems almost classically chaste
and simple:

> Each being nature's stated course forsakes,
> Seas deluge 'round, and earth's foundation shakes;
> Stars drop from heav'n; the glorious source of light,
> Darkling, fore-dooms an ever-lasting night.[48]

These poems, and others like them, do not claim our interest as
works of art, but they should remind us that interest in sublimity
during the century is not restricted to the enjoyment of moun-
tains, storms, and inundations.

In addition, Last Day poems such as those published in the
Gentleman's Magazine can help to illuminate important works
of art which do survive. The mighty, chilling last lines of Pope's
Dunciad, for example, lose much if we miss their allusive terror:

> The sick'ning stars fade off th'ethereal plain . . .
> Art after Art goes out, and all is Night. . . .
> Thy hand, great Anarch! lets the curtain fall:
> And Universal Darkness buries All.[49]

"Pope is not thinking of an actual night," Geoffrey Tillotson has written, "but of the night in the mind of man when a curtain of intellectual darkness is being let fall."[50] Yet Pope is thinking of an actual night—of the darkness following the Last Judgment, when the stars drop from heaven and even the sun expires. His "Messiah" had envisioned "God's eternal Day" as ultimately succeeding the bleak midnight of "Winter." But in the *Dunciad*, there is no provision for a renewal of the creative light. The dunces roused by "Fame's posterior Trumpet" (4.71)—a scatological parody of the Trump of Doom—cannot comprehend the terror of an eternal *fiat nox*. Like Swift, Pope creates the maniacal vision of a world without Redemption as his ultimate comment upon modern emptiness and vanity. Although the lines would be awesome enough without assistance from analogy, by borrowing the mood and imagery of the Last Day poems, Pope paints the triumph of the "uncreating word" (4.654) in a manner which appropriately intensifies its terror and sublimity.

THE ATTRIBUTES OF GOD AND 'SEATONIAN' VERSE

When they were not paraphrasing the Bible or contemplating the terrors of the Last Day, a number of eighteenth-century religious poets busied themselves in describing the sublimest of all possible subjects, the being and attributes of God. One initial difficulty, of course, was the unanimous belief that men can never understand what Sidney had called the "incomprehensible excellencies" of God. Addison repeated for readers of the *Spectator* the familiar story of Simonides' perplexity upon being asked to describe the Deity. Simonides first requested a day to consider the matter; when that time expired, he asked for two more days; then three, and so on. With each additional extension, wrote Addison, he discovered that "he waded but the more out of his Depth; and that he lost himself in the Thought, instead of finding an End of it" (No. 531). Hobbes expressed somewhat the same idea in the language of contemporary philosophy. "Whatsoever we imagine, is *Finite*," he argued. "Therefore there is no Idea, or conception of any thing we call *Infinite*.

No man can have in his mind an Image of infinite magnitude; nor conceive infinite swiftness, infinite time, or infinite force, or infinite power. . . . And therefore the Name of God is used, not to make us conceive him; (for he is *Incomprehensible*; and his greatnesse, and power are unconceivable;) but that we may honour him."[51] Although Hobbes and Simonides reach an identical conclusion regarding the unimaginable nature of God, Addison had a reply which could free his contemporaries from the apparent necessity of resigning all unrevealed knowledge of God.

Because the question raised by Simonides and Hobbes is as much epistemological as religious, Addison appropriately drew his response from Locke's *Essay Concerning Human Understanding*, the bible of eighteenth-century psychology:

> If we examine the *Idea* we have of the incomprehensible supreme Being, we shall find, that . . . the complex *Ideas* we have both of God, and separate Spirits, are made up of the simple *Ideas* we receive from Reflection; v.g. having from what we experiment in our selves, got the *Ideas* of Existence and Duration; of Knowledge and Power; of Pleasure and Happiness; and of several other Qualities and Powers, which it is better to have, than to be without: When we would frame an *Idea* the most suitable we can to the supreme Being, we enlarge every one of these with our *Idea* of Infinity; and so putting them together, make our complex *Idea of God* (*Spec.* 531).

For Locke, man can conceive of infinity by reflecting on the mind's ability to repeat single ideas endlessly. In Addison's version of Locke, man achieves an idea of God by multiplying laudable human qualities by infinity. Although he admitted that God might well possess virtues and attributes unknown to man, even a necessarily partial and limited idea of God was both possible and desirable. In general, most eighteenth-century religious poets seem to have shared Addison's confidence. The Deity was transformed into a composite of various human qualities raised to the nth degree. He became in Blake's terms a kind of

Human Abstract, but a Being nonetheless both imaginable and sublime.

Poems on the attributes of God achieve their greatest vogue during the middle decades of the century, beginning about the time when the reputation of Longinus reached its zenith.[52] Critics agreed that the pagan poets were most sublime in describing their gods and goddesses. Why then should Christian poets be reluctant to glorify God? With the cult of sublimity well established in England, poets naturally turned to what many believed the sublimest possible subject. In addition, as writers began to analyze various qualities which contributed to the sublime, they concluded that almost every such quality reached its apogee in God. For example, power had always been associated with sublimity. In 1747 John Baillie observed that "it is in the *Almighty* that this Sublime [of power] is compleated, who with a *Nod* can shatter to Pieces the *Foundations* of a *Universe*, as with a *Word* he called it into *Being*."[53] Majesty and splendor were thought to be aspects of the sublime. Anthony Blackwall referred his readers to Job for the ultimate examples of those qualities.[54] Even moral and intellectual abstractions such as benevolence, heroism, justice, and virtue found a place in discussions of sublimity. Inevitably, these too achieved their most exalted form in the Deity. The effects of such thought soon appeared in sublime poems on the nature of God. Henry Fielding, otherwise a man of taste and judgment, had a strange affection for a work by Samuel Boyse entitled *Deity: a Poem* (1739). His enjoyment of Boyse's poem, however, would not have seemed strange to many of his contemporaries. In 1737, for example, they would have encountered in the *Gentleman's Magazine* a similar work entitled "A Poem on the Divine Attributes."[55] One can hardly imagine less promising topics for poetry than those which the anonymous poet dutifully explored: 1) Existence and Immateriality, 2) Wisdom and Power, 3) Unity, 4) Eternity and Independency, 5) Immutability, 6) Providence, 7) Omnipresence, 8) Liberty, 9) Goodness, and 10) Justice. Yet such was the stuff of other sublime religious poems which took as their subject the various attributes of God.

Perhaps inspired by poems such as Boyse's *Deity*, or perhaps by the charity of Sir Richard Blackmore, who offered funds for the writing of divine poetry at Oxford,[56] an obscure alumnus of Cambridge named Thomas Seaton in 1738 added a fateful paragraph to his will, regarding the disposition of his Kislinbury estate. The rents of the estate he devoted to the establishment of a poetry contest at Cambridge. Seaton not only specified that the nature of the poems be religious; he also specified the appropriate subjects—which "shall for the first year be one or other of the perfections or attributes of the supreme being, and so the succeeding years, till the subject is exhausted."[57] When the judges ran out of divine attributes or perfections, Seaton instructed them to propose as subjects "either death, judgment, heaven, hell, purity of heart, &c. or whatever else may be judged . . . to be most conducive to the honour of the supreme being, and recommendation of virtue." The rents of Seaton's Kislinbury estate provided a generous cash prize for the winning poet; and so that the honor of the supreme being should not languish within the walls of Cambridge, each year's winning poem was published, thus assuring critics an annual opportunity to regret the performances of modern religious poets.

Seaton's contest had one immediate effect. It supplemented the livelihood and hastened the recognition of Christopher Smart, then a young Cambridge wit and resident of Grub Street. After an extended lawsuit questioned the wisdom of Seaton's legacy, the prize was offered for the first time in 1750, when, as for the next few years, it fell to Smart. The poems, rightly, are not among the most admired works of Smart. But they are skillfully done, and an understanding of his early apprenticeship to these conventional forms of sublime religious verse helps to illuminate the real originality of his later work. His first winning poem, "On the Eternity of the Supreme Being," does little more than exploit the sublimity long associated both with God and with eternity.[58] Not taking any chance of being outsublimed, however, Smart adds a somewhat gratuitous terror in describing the Last Day:

> A day shall come, when all this Earth shall perish,
> Nor leave behind e'en Chaos; it shall come

> When all the armies of the elements
> Shall war against themselves, and mutual rage,
> To make Perdition triumph; it shall come,
> When the capacious atmosphere above
> Shall in sulphureous thunders groan, and die,
> And vanish into void; the earth beneath
> Shall sever to the centre, and devour
> Th' enormous blaze of the destructive flames.[59]

The feverish, incremental rhetoric, the vaguely Miltonic diction, the conscious extravagance—all suggest that Smart is laboring to please his judges with a conventional piece of religious sublimity. Those who misunderstood his intentions might have been enlightened by the parody of Smart's poem written by his Grub-Street rival William Kenrick; it contained an "Interpretation" designed to explicate the poem "for the Sake of the Herd of Readers, who are void of a Taste for the Sublime."[60]

But even dancing in chains, Smart moved with style. Avoiding the epic machinery of gods and angels, he infused his poems with a different kind of dramatic tension. "On the Power of the Supreme Being," the winning entry in 1753, provides a good example of Smart's mastery of the religious sublime. A few years after the poem appeared, Edmund Burke discussed at length the close relationship between sublimity and the idea of power; and in discussing divine power, he had reason to cite Psalm 114: "Tremble, thou earth, at the presence of the Lord."[61] Burke's choice of example was hardly original, and Smart too could draw on the same familiar illustrations of sublimity. His poem begins,

> "Tremble, thou Earth!" th' anointed poet said,
> "At God's bright presence, tremble, all ye mountains!
> "And all ye hillocks on the surface bound!"
> Then once again, ye glorious thunders, roll!
> The Muse with transport hears ye.

Transport, as Boileau noted, was thought to be one of the effects of the sublime, and it is clearly the effect that Smart wishes his poem to have on the reader. Despite its sensational beginning, however, his poem does not continue like the fustian works which

Pope attacked in the noise-making contest in the *Dunciad*. Instead, it develops through an unobtrusive but forceful transition from Old to New Testament conceptions of divine power.

The continuity as well as the contrast between Hebrew and Christian ideas concerning religion is central to much of Smart's poetry. "On the Power of the Supreme Being" draws attention to its Hebrew beginning not only by quoting from Psalm 114 but also by paraphrasing the age's favorite example of Hebrew sublimity:

> *Hark! on the winged whirlwind's rapid rage,*
> *Which is and is not in a moment—hark!*
> *On th' hurricane's tempestuous sweep He rides*
> *Invincible, and oaks and pines and cedars*
> *And forests are no more.*

Gradually, however, Smart's focus shifts from instances of the terrible might of the Old Testament Jehovah to the quieter mysteries of Christianity's sustaining God. The New Testament mood of thoughtful admiration then yields easily to a consideration of God's active creating power. The turbulent sublimity of the Old Testament subsides before the gentler wonders of the Incarnation. Christ succeeds Jehovah:

> *"Let there be peace!" (he said,) and all was calm*
> *Amongst the warring world—calm as the sea*
> *When, "Oh be still, ye boisterous Winds!" he cried,*
> *And not a breath was blown, nor murmur heard.*

If it requires real virtuosity to weave such disparate moods into a single poem, Smart remains dextrous to the end, concluding with the promise of man's Redemption—the ultimate example of Christ's "miracles and might." From the wrathful power of Jehovah as sung by David to the sustaining, creative, and saving grace of God embodied in the Son's "immortal prowess," Smart's poem is a remarkable model of controlled sublimity—sublimity contained within a developing poetical argument.

It is tempting to dwell upon Smart's Seatonian poems if only because they are so much superior to the winning entries for the rest of the century. Yet the other poems in their own day were read, criticized, and sometimes even praised. Vicesimus Knox, lamenting the decline in religious poetry in the second half of the century, remarked that he did not know "a collection of poems, on divine subjects, more laudable than those of the Seatonian poets."[62] Abandoning the divine attributes and perfections after 1758, the Seatonians exercised their talents on a number of miscellaneous divine subjects, from theological abstractions such as death and repentance to specific scenes or events from Christian history. The Creation, the Deluge, the Destruction of Nineveh, the Nativity, the Conversion of Saint Paul, the Day of Judgment, the Redemption, and Heaven are some of the topics which they treated. And, with only a few exceptions, most of the winning poems demonstrate their authors' conscious attempts to be sublime.

The nature and reception of the Seatonian poems might be best summarized in the words of Vicesimus Knox: "They have raised meteors, but not created suns."[63] He used the word *meteors* as a conventional synonym for the false sublime. Other contemporary reviewers were equally persuaded that in their pursuit of sublimity the Seatonian poets were misled by false fires. In 1765 the *Critical Review* scored "The Conversion of St. Paul" by John Lettice for its "affected sublimity."[64] The next year the *Monthly Review* lamented "The Crucifixion" by Thomas Zouch as "another production of the Kislinbury estate, and by no means superior to the general produce of that unfortunate farm."[65] Thus John Roberts was simply upholding Seatonian tradition when he invented the line " 'Cease rain!' pronounc'd th' Almighty; the rain ceas'd." The *Monthly Review* chastised with ironic moderation. "We fear," they wrote, "that this imitation of a beautiful and *simple* expression in Scripture, will not impress the mind of the reader with that sensation of sublimity, which it, doubtless, was intended to produce."[66] But the best gloss upon the Seatonian poems is Pope's description in the *Peri Bathous* of the variety of modern poets he classified as porpoises. "The *Porpoises*," Pope explained, "are unweildly [sic] and big;

they put all their Numbers into a great *Turmoil* and *Tempest*, but whenever they appear in *plain Light*, (which is seldom) they are only *shapeless* and *ugly Monsters*." [67] Pope included Dennis among the porpoise-poets; and had he known of Roberts and the Seatonians, he might have added them as well. The *Monthly Review* did what it could to classify Roberts: "The author appears to be labouring to make his verse, like his subject, vast and profound. He wishes to be great, and he becomes unwieldy." [68]

There is much to ponder in the fate of the Seatonian poets. Their consistent failure in writing sublime religious poetry may well have signaled to better poets the need for significant change. No doubt Smart himself soon recognized the limitations of religious verse which achieves the sublime at the cost of impersonality and abstraction. Omniscience, omnipotence, eternity, benevolence, and similar topics offer poets with any possibility of failure a kind of endless rope in which to get tangled. Even the less abstract Seatonian subjects almost equally resisted poets who sought grandeur and elevation in a conventional, impersonal, descriptive sublimity. If individual Seatonian pieces may have been "laudably intended to turn the attention to sacred poetry," [69] one reads them today with the recognition that inept forms of piety do a positive disservice to religion. Like the biblical paraphrase, the eschatological verse, and the poems on the nature and attributes of God, the Seatonian poems tended to duplicate themselves without assistance from genius or study. The result was a predictable, mechanical sublimity which mocked Dennis's bold hope for the advancement and reform of modern poetry.

IMAGINATIVE DEVOTION: ADDISON, THOMSON, YOUNG

John Baillie wrote in 1747, "We often confess the *Sublime* as we do the *Deity*; It fills and dilates our *Soul* without being able to penetrate into its *Nature*, and define its *Essence*." [70] Baillie's analogy between man's experience of God and his experience of the sublime—although he does not develop it further—provides a convenient point of departure for considering one other important kind of eighteenth-century sublime religious verse. Devotion and sublimity, for a number of writers, were not only analogous but also interpenetrating experiences. One recalls Thomas Gray's much quoted response to mountain scenery: "Not a precipice, not a torrent, not a cliff, but is pregnant with religion and poetry."[71] Yet, while many poets and critics instinctively sensed a relationship between sublimity and devotion, the nature of the relationship was explained most clearly and influentially by Joseph Addison.

Addison had a continuing interest in devotional poetry. In addition to his hymns which appeared in the *Spectator*, his Latin poem on the Resurrection had been published several times and exhausted three editions in the first year of its translation into English. Nicholas Amhurst, the translator, referred to the poem as a "useful and sublime"[72] entertainment—adjectives which surely would have pleased Addison, who planned to devote his retirement from politics partly to the writing of divine poetry. Addison's poetry, however, is less important to a study of the religious sublime than are his critical essays. His discussion of the complementary roles of reason and imagination in the process of devotion is linked intrinsically to his discussion of the sublime. These discussions provide an illuminating context for studying the work of James Thomson and Edward Young, two of the most popular and now neglected poets of the eighteenth century.

Addison, like others of his age, praised the potential of human reason so long as the mind stayed within moderate bounds, not soaring into airy abstraction nor sinking into useless minutiae. He believed that any reasonable man who contemplated the natural order could affirm confidently that nature everywhere reveals the hand of its intelligent Creator. Such in fact is the rational process which leads the irreligious Robinson Crusoe to deduce the existence of God while he sits meditating by the sea. But, if Addison praised reason as capable of affirming the existence of God (and as necessary to prevent worship from degenerating into mere enthusiasm), he also insisted that devotion requires the assistance of two additional, indispensable forces: imagination and Revelation.

Robinson Crusoe again offers a convenient illustration of the necessity of imagination and Revelation in order for man to arrive at a proper relationship with God. Crusoe is properly and (so far as possible) unwaveringly devout only after his experience of a terrible dream vision and his providential discovery of a Bible supplement his rational proof of the Deity. Oddly enough, it is the imaginative experience, the dream vision, which is the variable (and, hence, crucial) aspect of Crusoe's conversion. The Bible and reason are both a birthright of man; he need only claim them in order to derive their benefit. The imagination is no less a birthright, but its potential for religious service is less reliable and less consistent. Yet it is overwhelmingly important. As Addison noted of the imagination, God can "so exquisitely ravish or torture the Soul through this single Faculty, as might suffice to make up the whole Heaven or Hell of any finite Being" (*Spec.* 421). Without the assistance of imagination, faith may be rational and properly grounded in Revelation; but will it be passionately alive? The imagination assures that it will.

Addison's description of a mind elevated in a state of proper devotion further helps to suggest the necessary link between imagination and religious experience. "Devotion," he wrote, "opens the Mind to great Conceptions, and fills it with more sublime Ideas than any that are to be met with in the most exalted Science; and at the same time warms and agitates the Soul more than sensual Pleasure" (*Spec.* 201). Although the essay on devotion appeared well before the famous *Spectator* series on the Pleasures of the Imagination (*Spec.* 411–21), much of the Imagination series already existed in manuscript.[73] Thus, in defining the pleasures of devotion as distinct from those of reason and sense, Addison might have been paraphrasing his own description of the pleasures of the imagination, which are "not so gross as those of Sense, nor so refined as those of the Understanding" (*Spec.* 411). Imagination and devotion, for Addison, have much in common. Inevitably they are found to impinge upon each other.

Addison distinguishes imagination from reason in two ways: it is more immediate and also more closely related to sense and feeling. Both characteristics make the imagination particularly appropriate to the state of devotion. Reason may function with intuitive immediacy in an ideal Houyhnhnm land,[74] but in the world of man, it necessarily hobbles by discursive and logical steps. The imagination, on the other hand, operates with un-fallen immediacy: "It is but opening the Eye, and the Scene enters. The Colours paint themselves on the Fancy, with very little Attention of Thought or Application of Mind in the Be-holder" (*Spec.* 411). Despite their different manners of opera-tion, however, reason and imagination can work in harmonious cooperation, and this harmony is especially necessary in the state of devotion. Addison illustrates this point indirectly in a story borrowed (via Cicero) from a lost treatise of Aristotle: "*Aristotle* says, that should a Man live under Ground, and there converse with Works of Art and Mechanism, and should afterwards be brought up into the open Day, and see the several Glories of the Heav'n and Earth, he would immediately pronounce them the Works of such a Being as we define God to be" (*Spec.* 465). It is important to note that the reason has prepared for the moment of imaginative perception by its painstaking study. Without this preparation, the experience itself would be potentially meaning-less. At the moment of vision, however, the reason is passive. Simply by opening his eyes, the viewer approaches a state of imaginative devotion.

The imagination differs from the reason not only in the im-mediacy of its operation, Addison argues, but also in its reliance upon sensory experience and in its direct relation to the passions. Reason, of course, must work ultimately with materials derived from the senses. But it works effectively only by weighing the evidence of all the senses; and (to use Locke's terms) it relies as much upon the complex data of reflection as upon the simple data of sensation. The imagination, by contrast, is for Addison mainly allied with the sense of vision—either recording images supplied by sight or recollecting ideas stored in the memory. Although the reason can and must consider abstract ideas which are the product of reflection, the imagination is restricted to whatever is vivid and visible. In this way, too, the imagination is particularly suited to the state of devotion which Addison describes as often inspired by direct visual experience. "Faith and Devotion," he writes, "naturally grow in the Mind of every reasonable Man, who sees the Impressions of Divine Power and Wisdom in every Object on which he casts his Eye" (*Spec.* 465). The imaginative perception of nature leads directly to the experience of devotion.

Through its close relationship with vision, the imagination links itself with men's feelings. As writers had insisted for centuries, we feel strongly what we see clearly. This link between vision and feeling in turn suggests a further explanation of the close relationship between imagination and devotion. "The Devout Man," Addison affirmed, "does not only believe, but feels there is a Deity. He has actual Sensations of him; his Experience concurs with his Reason; he sees him more and more in all his Intercourses with him, and even in this Life almost loses his Faith in Conviction" (*Spec.* 465). Reason and Revelation offer man various assurances concerning the existence and nature of God. But the devout man strengthens his faith through feeling, feeling inspired by imaginative perception. Without understanding this relationship between imagination and devotion, a modern reader might be puzzled when Addison concludes his series on the imagination by observing "what an infinite Advantage this Faculty gives an Almighty Being over the Soul of Man, and how great a measure of Happiness or Misery we are capable of receiving from the Imagination only" (*Spec.* 421). Eighteenth-century poets, however, understood the implications of Addison's remark: they deliberately engage the imagination in the service of religious feeling.

Addison's ideas concerning imaginative devotion have much to do with the sublime, as indeed we might expect, since "greatness" is for Addison one of the three sources of imaginative pleasure. Although the term *sublime* is not generally applied to external nature until the 1740s,[75] Addison uses *greatness* to describe the same scenes and objects which later writers would call *sublime*, and he seems to prefer *greatness* to *sublimity* mainly because the former term is more precise, referring specifically to

physical immensity, while *sublimity* implies a number of meta-
phorical applications of greatness: greatness of soul, of thought,
of action, of language, and many others. *Greatness*, then, is a
special subclass of *sublimity*, and both, through their powers of
affecting the imagination, provide access to devotional experi-
ence. Two well-known passages from the *Spectator* offer a good
occasion for exploring the nature of the link between devotion
and sublimity: the first is Addison's famous ode "The Spacious
Firmament on High," the second a description of his thoughts
upon seeing a storm-tossed sea.

"The Spacious Firmament on High" is not, as is too often
maintained, simply a physico-theological hymn to reason. Ap-
pearing at the end of a *Spectator* essay on the nature of devotion,
it in part serves to illustrate Addison's ideas concerning the close
relationship between imagination and devotion. His model for
the poem is the Prayer Book version of Psalm 19 (verses 1–4) in
which the heavens declare the glory of God. This theme, of
course, delighted contemporary physico-theologians, who be-
lieved that every aspect of nature reflected the purpose and de-
sign of the Creator. If man simply exercised his reason upon the
visible universe, he would discover the inevitable order and
rationality of creation. As Addison himself wrote in the essay
which precedes his poem, "The Supream Being has made the best
Arguments for his own Existence, in the Formation of the
Heavens and the Earth, and these are Arguments which a Man
of Sense cannot forbear attending to, who is out of the Noise and
Hurry of Human Affairs" (*Spec.* 465). The repetition of the
word *Argument* is important, for it implies the operation of
reason and logic. Yet devotion means for Addison more than
rational theology. It means as well the engagement of the imagi-
nation. And the imagination is engaged most powerfully when
greatness or sublimity compels its attention.

Far from extolling human reason, Addison's poem reduces man
to an awed spectator of God's might. The firmament itself, not
man, proclaims the existence of God. The sun, not man, "pub-
lishes" the wondrous tale of divine creation, and the stars "con-
firm" the tidings. The universe, rather than man, has become the

conscious agent. Addison's tendency to imagine inanimate nature as acting upon man parallels his deliberate shift in controlling metaphors. In the ode, he no longer considers nature as providing "Arguments" for the existence of God but as engaged in a form of imaginative activity. The heavenly bodies are singing a song, repeating a tale. They are appealing to the senses and to the imagination, not primarily to the reason. Addison notes, of course, that the song is overheard by "Reason's Ear." But unless that figure is the century's most awkward personification, it must mean that the reason is essentially passive, receiving and assenting to the pleasures of the imagination, not actively performing the analytic and deductive tasks which are its usual function. Perhaps the clearest expression of the idea which Addison's poem embodies appears in Burke's treatise on the sublime. "Whenever the wisdom of our Creator intended that we should be affected with any thing," Burke explains with Addisonian confidence in his understanding of God's intentions, "he did not confide the execution of his design to the languid and precarious operation of our reason; but he endued it with powers and properties that prevent [i.e., act in advance of] the understanding, and even the will, which seizing upon the senses and imagination, captivate the soul before the understanding is ready either to join with them or to oppose them."[76] In reacting to the sublimity of nature, Addison discovers imaginative support for his rational belief concerning the existence and nature of God: his experience concurs with his reason. This process, modified slightly, underlies a second example from the *Spectator* which illustrates Addison's ideas of imaginative devotion.

Spectator 489 also describes an experience of sublimity in nature, although the natural scene is not the sedate majesty of the heavens but the turbulent grandeur of a stormy sea. The essay has clear affinities with the essay on devotion which contains "The Spacious Firmament on High"; it begins by referring to the account of greatness in the Pleasures of the Imagination series and concludes with a biblical hymn. Disguising himself as a correspondent, Addison offers a theological interpretation of storms at sea:

A troubled Ocean, to a Man who sails upon it, is, I think, the biggest Object that he can see in Motion, and consequently gives his Imagination one of the highest Kinds of Pleasure that can arise from Greatness. I must confess, it is impossible for me to survey this World of fluid Matter, without thinking on the Hand that first poured it out, and made a proper Channel for its Reception. Such an Object naturally raises in my Thoughts the Idea of an Almighty Being, and convinces me of his Existence, as much as a Metaphisical [sic] Demonstration.

Scholars usually quote this passage to illustrate how sublimity in nature so often in the eighteenth century turns men's thoughts toward God. What has not been stressed about the passage is that it reflects the same distinction between rational and imaginative perception which characterizes Addison's idea of devotion.

The Pleasures of the Imagination series develops around a distinction so basic and simple that it is often overlooked. "A beautiful Prospect," Addison writes in his first essay on the imagination, "delights the Soul, as much as a Demonstration; and a Description in *Homer* has charmed more Readers than a Chapter in *Aristotle*" (*Spec.* 411). Viewing a landscape and reading Homer are forms of imaginative activity, as opposed to the rational process involved in following a demonstration or Aristotelian argument. Thus, when Addison in *Spectator* 489 claims that the sight of a turbulent sea convinces him of God's existence "as much as a Metaphisical Demonstration," he is comparing two ways of knowing the Deity: through rational analysis and imaginative perception. *Spectator* 489, then, asserts the importance and validity of imaginative experience in strengthening faith. Simply by opening his eyes to the sublimity of nature, a reasonable being can achieve a new power of religious conviction, one made accessible by the imagination, rendered persuasive by the feelings, and ultimately confirmed by the understanding. As Addison wrote in the sentence summarizing his reaction toward the troubled sea, "The Imagination prompts the Understanding, and by the Greatness of the sensible Object, produces in it the Idea of a Being who is neither circumscribed by Time nor Space." The rational lessons of innumerable sermons, treatises, and arguments are verified by the imagination: in fact, the imaginative experience of sublimity provides a vital impulse for the renewal of religious conviction.

The ideas which Addison developed concerning imagination, devotion, and sublimity provide a meaningful context within which to read James Thomson's massive poem *The Seasons*. A work so diverse, of course, commands more than a single context, and it is impossible here to provide more than a partial view of its bounty. Yet even a limited view, restricted to Thomson and the religious sublime, is well worth attempting, for it will to some degree counterbalance the modern emphasis upon Thomson's interest in science and his relation to deistic thought.

"In estimating Thomson's relation to science and philosophy," Alan Dugald McKillop has cautioned, "we should remind ourselves that he began with a complex of religious and literary motives . . . broad Presbyterianism and the Old Testament, strains of thought from Neoplatonism and Shaftesbury, the rational ethics of Locke and Addison, enthusiasm for Milton and Virgil, and, we may add, the Longinian theory of the sublime applied to religious poetry by Watts, Blackmore, and Hill."[77] This last aspect of his poetry has been most neglected by modern scholars. *The Seasons* owes a great deal to poets and critics concerned with the religious sublime. It will not do to argue that Thomson's interest in nature proves his disinterest in other sources of sublimity. Although he apparently disagreed with Addison that a reader often "finds a Scene drawn in stronger Colours, and painted more to the Life in his Imagination, by the help of Words, than by an actual Survey of the Scene which they describe" (*Spec.* 416), their disagreement is not over the validity of nature poetry. When in *Spring* Thomson asks "But who can paint/ Like Nature?" he implies what no major Augustan writer would dispute: that God's art (nature) inevitably transcends the poet's ability to imitate it.[78] But the poet's art of imitation, despite its secondary status, nevertheless carries with it a worthy purpose, because the poet can help us not only to see nature but also to understand its significance. Poetry of natural description thus implies for Thomson much more than painting with words.

It means, in Pope's phrase, looking "through Nature up to Nature's God." In this sense *The Seasons* is a devotional poem which, like a number of hymns, uses the description of nature as its vehicle. And, although Thomson rightly proclaims his own originality among modern writers in making nature itself the subject of his poem, both the Preface to *Winter* and his own practice throughout *The Seasons* illustrate his indebtedness to familiar literary sources for many of his ideas concerning the sublime.

The preface which Thomson added to the second edition of *Winter* belongs to the tradition of arguments such as Aristotle's *Poetics* and Sidney's *Apologie* defending poetry against those who attack its right to exist. More importantly, the basis of his defense is essentially religious. Sidney had cited the biblical poets and prophets as evidence that poetry need be neither trifling nor false. Thomson's defense of poetry as a "divine art" rests on the same foundation: to despise poetry altogether, he insists, would be declaring against "what has charmed the listening world from Moses down to Milton."[79] His choice of exemplary poets is not dictated solely by alliteration; like David, both Moses and Milton were regarded as types of the sublime religious poet. In fact, Thomson's friendly concern for Dennis, when the old critic had fallen on evil days, probably stems in part from the kinship of their ideas concerning poetry. "Let poetry once more be restored to her ancient truth and purity," he implored in words reminiscent of Dennis; "let her be inspired from heaven, and in return her incense ascend thither."[80] Lest a reader mistake the kind of poetic reforms he recommended, Thomson quoted in his preface a passage from Aaron Hill's *The Judgment-Day*. It was from works such as Hill's that he drew many of his ideas about sublime poetry. Although Thomson's enthusiasm for rugged outdoor scenery contributed much to his understanding of the sublime, his interest also extends to several essential literary sources—particularly to Milton and to the Bible.

Patrick Murdoch observed in 1762 that Thomson "owed much to a religious education; and . . . his early acquaintance with the sacred writings contributed greatly to that *sublime*, by which his works will be for ever distinguished."[81] Thomson's appren-

ticeship to the sublime can be illuminated by watching his early
struggle to embody a biblical spirit in a form which proved
resistant:

> *The heavens and all the wide-spread orbs on high*
> *Thou like a curtain stretched of curious dye;*
> *On the devouring flood thy chambers are*
> *Established; a lofty cloud's thy car,*
> *Which quick through the ethereal road doth fly*
> *On swift-winged winds that shake the troubled sky.*[82]

The first and final lines catch something of Thomson's mature
speed, grandeur, and directness; but the vaguely Miltonic diction
clashes with the awkward rhymed couplets. It is true, as Johnson
noted, that the blank verse of Thomson is not the blank verse of
Milton. Yet the famous storm in *Winter* shows how, in a manner
something like Milton's, Thomson learned to control a biblical
vision within the wider sweep of the verse paragraph:

> *Huge uproar lords it wide. The clouds, commixed*
> *With stars swift-gliding, sweep along the sky.*
> *All Nature reels: till Nature's King, who oft*
> *Amid tempestuous darkness dwells alone,*
> *And on the wings of the careering wind*
> *Walks dreadfully serene, commands a calm;*
> *Then straight air, sea, and earth are hushed at once.*[83]

Much of the power comes from Thomson's ability to keep his
eye upon the object, making the reader, in Dr. Johnson's words,
"wonder that he never saw before what Thomson shews him,
and that he never yet has felt what Thomson impresses."[84] The
image of nature's King riding the whirlwind, however, he owes
to the well-established conventions of the religious sublime.

The storm in *Winter*, like other violent and sublime scenes
throughout *The Seasons*, reflects Thomson's special interest in
terror. As Samuel Monk has noted, "Thomson filled each suc-
cessive edition of *The Seasons* with increasingly long passages
which aimed at evoking terror before the vast and destructive
forces of nature."[85] Clearly, this increasing use of terror is partly

the product of Thomson's sense of the shifting taste of eighteenth-century readers. But there are other reasons for Thomson's interest in sublime terror, reasons closely related to the strongly devotional aspects of *The Seasons*.

Terror in the eighteenth century was an emotion which often turned the mind toward God. Dennis, in fact, had argued that terror was itself evidence for the existence of God. "Let any Man shew me where Terror is mov'd to a Heighth," he challenged, "and I will shew him that that Place requires the Belief of a God, and particular Providence" (1:183). The phrase *particular Providence* implies that for Dennis terror proves the existence of an immanent Deity, one actively present in the universe and directing its affairs—not, therefore, identical with the retired God of the Deists. Thomson's own faith contained deistical elements, but his emphasis upon terror in *The Seasons* hardly accords with the theology of the Deists, at whose hands (as one modern critic has written) the "ancient Deity was rapidly stripped of such stern attributes as vengeance, if not justice, and regarded merely as the Spirit of Benevolence."[86] For Thomson, the Deists' view was too simplistic to account for the "varied God" he saw embodied in the different seasons. Nature and God, he believed, are mysteriously terrible as well as benevolent. The plague and sandstorm of *Summer*, for example, involve the destruction of much that is beautiful and good:

> Nor stop the terrors of these regions here.
> Commissioned demons oft, angels of wrath,
> Let loose the raging elements. Breathed hot
> From all the boundless furnace of the sky,
> And the wide glittering waste of burning sand,
> A suffocating wind the pilgrim smites
> With instant death.[87]

It helps to know that Thomson's demons are "commissioned," but that knowledge cannot explain *why* they are commissioned. Thomson forces his readers to experience Job's bewilderment and sense of loss when innocent shepherds, pilgrims, and lovers are crushed by the terrible might of nature. Yet he intends that, like Job, the reader should pass through terror to affirmation, affirmation which is especially durable because it has been made in the face of seemingly irrational catastrophe. In refusing to comfort us with explanations, Thomson succeeds in demonstrating God's mysterious power so convincingly that terror inspires its own kind of imaginative religious awe.

It seems likely that one reason for Thomson's frequent use of storms, floods, and other terrible prodigies of nature was to raise what William Smith, citing the tempest in Psalm 107, called "that fervency of devotion, which such grand occurrences are fitted to raise in the minds of the thoughtful." [88] This use of sublimity in *The Seasons* reflects, if indirectly, Addison's ideas concerning imaginative devotion. For Addison, the imaginative experience of nature was an essential means of strengthening faith. For Thomson, poetry itself becomes a means of strengthening faith because it is a means of communicating, as in *The Seasons*, an imaginative perception of nature. "The best, both ancient and modern, poets have been passionately fond of retirement and solitude," he observed in the preface to *Winter*. "The wild romantic country was their delight. And they seem never to have been more happy than when, lost in unfrequented fields, far from the little busy world, they were at leisure to meditate and sing the works of nature." [89] This is not mere Horatian longing for the Sabine farm. The "wild romantic country" is the domain of the sublime; and the religious meditation which it inspires is the product of a unique form of poetic vision.

For Thomson, as for Addison, to meditate upon the works of nature was inevitably to approach a state of devotion. As Thomson describes the process in *Spring*,

> Pure Serenity apace
> *Induces thought, and contemplation still.*
> *By swift degrees the love of nature works,*
> *And warms the bosom; till at last, sublimed*
> *To rapture and enthusiastic heat,*
> *We feel the present Deity, and taste*
> *The joy of God to see a happy world!* [90]

It is mistaken to assume that nature for Thomson is merely the setting for meditations which might exist independent of the surroundings. The setting, imaginatively perceived, gives rise to the meditations. Nor are these meditations identical with the rational theology of the Deists and physico-theologians. Instead, the imaginative perception of nature results in a new interfusion of thought and feeling. "The Devout Man," Addison had argued, "does not only believe, but feels there is a Deity." Thomson asserts, "We feel the present Deity." For both men, the imagination prompts the understanding; and the resulting condition is neither purely rational nor purely passionate. It is something of both, superior to either alone. Less formal and explicitly Christian than the process of meditation which influenced certain earlier religious poets,[91] more rational and directly religious than the shadowy intimations which inspired Wordsworth, it hangs between—a uniquely Augustan form of devotion. As Thomson explains to George Lyttelton in the lines which conclude the passage quoted above,

> These are the sacred feelings of thy heart,
> Thy heart informed by reason's purer ray.[92]

The feelings are sacred because they provide access to divine knowledge, but they are not (as they were often to seem later in the century) independent of the guidance of reason. Reason and feeling combine to inspire a concerted faith, faith sparked and sustained by the imaginative perception of nature.

Various aspects of nature, not merely its patently sublime aspects, are capable of sparking the process of imaginative devotion. Yet contemporary readers were most impressed by Thomson's use of the sublime, which, as Patrick Murdoch noted, was the characteristic by which his works will be "for ever distinguished." In Theophilus Cibber's *Lives of the Poets*, Robert Shiels called attention to "the tow'ring sublimity of Mr Thomson's style,"[93] and one eighteenth-century study of Thomson, unique only in the length of its treatment, contains an entire chapter entitled "On the Sublimity of the Seasons."[94] Both in its style, including its biblical and Miltonic manner, and in its subject, particularly in its emphasis upon the great and terrible aspects of nature, *The Seasons* proclaimed its self-evident sublimity. What modern readers have been slow to acknowledge, however, is that the sublimity of *The Seasons* is tied so closely to its religious vision. *The Seasons* is not merely a poem about nature. It is also about a particular way of looking at nature. And to the man who looks at nature with a certain kind of imaginative vision, sublimity becomes a means of elevating the soul to a state of passionate devotion.

There is no reason why a poem about nature should conclude with a hymn, but the devotional context of *The Seasons* makes Thomson's concluding "Hymn" particularly appropriate. His survey of the unfolding year consistently coaxes the reader toward a faith renewed by experience of the sacred feelings of the heart, and the "Hymn" stands as a culminating statement of that faith. Like the admired "morning hymn" of Adam and Eve in *Paradise Lost*, it is modeled on Psalm 148; and in his "Illustrations on Sublimity" James Beattie argued that except for "an unguarded word or two"[95] it was in no way inferior to Milton's. Yet the symphony of praise which nature offers the Creator forecasts the climactic sublimity of Thomson's final line: "Come then, expressive Silence, muse his praise." Ever since the rediscovery of Longinus, poets and critics had been fond of inventing their own parallels to the silence of Ajax and Dido. As Beattie contended, "It may seem strange, and yet it is true, that the sublime is sometimes attained by a total want of expression: and this may happen, when by silence . . . we are made to understand, that there is in the mind something too great for utterance."[96] Whatever science and reason contribute to man's understanding of nature in *The Seasons*, ultimately man's powers of explanation are exhausted, and the exhaustion of rationality itself implies a consequent failure of language. If, as Restoration and eighteenth-century writers never tired of claiming, speech is the mark of man's rationality, then the contemplation of God, whose nature transcends the powers of human reason, necessarily involves eighteenth-century poets in recognizing the limitations of words. Even the ceremonial language of devotion at last, for Thomson, becomes an inadequate response to a mystery too powerful for speech. Awed silence, acknowledging the incompetence of human explanation, remains the only possible expression of praise which does not circumscribe the Deity in the language of man. Instead of heaping up adjectives to reach the sublime, Thomson proceeds in reverse fashion to strip away language until the result is what Ralph Cohen has finely called his "poetry of silence." [97]

The devotional possibilities of sublimity were explored most ingeniously by Edward Young, whose long poem *The Complaint: or Night-Thoughts on Life, Death, & Immortality* (1742–1746) rivaled *The Seasons* for popularity in the middle decades of the century. Young began his career as a religious poet with his *Poem on the Last Day* (1713) and his *Paraphrase on Part of the Book of Job* (1719), both decidedly in the manner of the religious sublime. Then after a mildly successful venture in tragedy and satire, he returned to divine poetry with the *Night-Thoughts*. Its fame was such that fifty years after its publication Coleridge could be found savoring its delights—reading a single page, then walking outdoors to muse upon it. "Young," he reportedly said, ". . . was not a poet to be read through at once." [98] Today Young is hardly read at all. He deserves attention, however, not because his poem is likely to be read again with pleasure but because we ought to understand what eighteenth-century readers found in it to admire.

Young was valued by his contemporaries for two qualities above all, qualities summarized in Joseph Warton's description of him as a "sublime and original genius." [99] Sublimity and originality were the foundation of his success. His originality is reflected in his choice of form; as Wordsworth noted, [100] the *Night-Thoughts* cuts across traditional lines, virtually creating its own genre. William Duff appropriately offered Young a place in his *Essay on Original Genius*, where he described the *Night-Thoughts* as a work "in which the most sublime spirit of Poetry predominates." [101] Yet Duff, like others who praised Young's sublimity, noted that the poem had a peculiarly uneven quality. Nathan

Drake best characterized this odd texture when he described Young as a poet with "powers inferior to Milton, turgid, obscure, and epigrammatic, yet with occasional sallies of imagination, and bursts of sublimity that course along the gloom with the rapidity and brilliance of lightning."[102] Chiaroscuro, not sublimity, is the chief characteristic of his poem. Drake's phrase has a further aptness in suggesting that Young's sublimity comes in "bursts," for if Young tried to sustain the sublime—somewhat in the manner of Milton—he failed conclusively. Yet the author of the *Poem on the Last Day* surely knew how to sustain the sublime if that was his purpose. Thus the uneven use of sublimity in the *Night-Thoughts* may itself be the result of a conscious plan. It is worth asking why Young apparently found an interruptive and discontinuous sublimity particularly appropriate to the religious purpose of his poem.

The *Night-Thoughts* has a dramatic focus which allies it with various Restoration and eighteenth-century works of Christian apologetics.[103] Young in effect argues the truth of Christianity against the objections of both atheists and Deists. The argument achieves a dramatic tension because he places the objections to Christianity in the mouth of a protean young sinner named Lorenzo. Atheist and Deist by turns, Lorenzo is a complex adversary who must be opposed with a shifting series of arguments and demonstrations. Because Lorenzo alters his roles or combines them from time to time, often abruptly, there is no use in seeking a methodical structure in the case presented against him. The occasion of his poem was real not fictitious, Young contended, and probably he intended a certain formless spontaneity in his presentation to suggest a mind coping with passion too real for method. A logical structure is surely not what Coleridge, or earlier readers, sought in the *Night-Thoughts*.

Yet it is possible to schematize, in a simplified but understandable way, Young's strategy in the *Night-Thoughts*. When Lorenzo assumes the mantle of atheism, Young marshals against him the standard arguments from design. By appealing to Lorenzo's proud reason, he proves that nature everywhere reveals the ordering purposes of its Creator. At this point, however, his strate-

gy is incomplete. He has argued Lorenzo from atheism to Deism.
He still must bring him from Deism to Christianity. But Lo-
renzo, as one committed to reason, will not be argued into faith.
Young's dilemma resembles that of several generations of English
divines: how can intelligent rationalists be induced to take the
mysterious leap of faith? Young's solution leads him to a radical
revaluation of the idea of feeling and to a unique application of
the sublime.

"As the eighteenth century wore on," Basil Willey argues, "it
was discovered that the 'Nature' of man was not his 'reason' at
all, but his instincts, emotions, and 'sensibilities.' "[104] Young
does not go as far as Willey's generalization suggests. To reject
reason's claim upon man would cripple the very arguments which
he had used to convince Lorenzo that a Deity does exist. Thus,
without rejecting the claims of reason, Young simply insists that,
in addition, sense, passion, and feeling can provide a legitimate
access to truth. "Our Senses, and our Reason, are Divine,"[105] he
asserts in the Night-Thoughts, boldly countering the traditional
objections that feeling is unreliable at best. As he asks at one
point,

> Think you my Song, too turbulent? too warm?
> Are Passions, then, the Pagans of the Soul?
> Reason alone baptiz'd? alone ordain'd
> To touch Things sacred? Oh for a warmer still![106]

Where reason proves insufficient to convince Lorenzo of the
truth of Christian mystery, Young without hesitation invokes
the aid of feeling. With epigrammatic majesty he instructs his
opponent,

> To feel, is to be fired,
> And to believe, LORENZO! is to feel.[107]

Convinced that feeling is a legitimate mode of inspiring belief,
Young no doubt concluded that in the sublime he had a ready-
made instrument for moving the passions of Lorenzo and for
bringing him from doubt to affirmation.

Young, like Thomson, seemed particularly interested in using the sublime to evoke the emotion of terror. There are good reasons, beyond his penchant for graveyard sensationalism, why Young should have given terror such prominence in his poem. Dennis, who first called attention to the close relationship between sublimity and terror, offers an explanation of the most important reason. He argues that "as Terror is one of the violentest of all Passions, if it is very great, and the hardest to be resisted, nothing gives more Force, nor more Vehemence to a Discourse" (1:361). As the passion "hardest to be resisted," terror is an appropriate weapon in Young's attack upon Lorenzo's resisting reason. It is hardly surprising that Young's "bursts of sublimity" should be most prominent, then, in the culminating "Night Ninth," in which Lorenzo's long deferred conversion at last takes place.

The sublimity of "Night Ninth" depends upon portrayal of many of the same scenes which Young had described in his *Poem on the Last Day*. Unfettered by the rhymed couplets of the earlier poem, he relies upon the sensuous spell of alliteration and the rhetorical passion of eighteenth-century tragedy to warm and elevate his style. The effect, while sometimes silly, at times can be rather impressive:

> *Amazing Period! when each Mountain-Height*
> *Out-burns Vesuvius; Rocks eternal pour*
> *Their melted Mass, as Rivers once they pour'd;*
> *Stars rush; and final Ruin fiercely drives*
> *Her Ploughshare o'er Creation!*[108]

The image of the ploughshare, which Beattie commended for its sublimity, lends a primitive and striking finality to Young's vision of the Last Day. "The driving of a plow over a field is not a grand object," Beattie admits. "Yet the figure conveys a sublime idea to those who know, that some antient nations, when they meant to destroy a city, not only razed the buildings, but plowed up the foundation; to intimate, that it was never to be rebuilt any more."[109] Young manages to avoid the excessively confused and jumbled imagery of Aaron Hill's description of Judgment;

the verse is strong, clear, and vivid. In fact, part of the control implicit in the passage may derive from Young's conscious purpose in presenting it. He is not laboring simply to create a mad crescendo of sublimity. Rather, he is making a calculated effort to engage the imagination of his rationalist opponent; and by engaging Lorenzo's imagination, Young ultimately intends to awaken him to the truth which is affirmed by feeling.

Young himself clearly explains the strategy behind his use of sublimity in "Night Ninth." Describing the world's ultimate dissolution, he declares to Lorenzo, "*This* strikes, if aught can strike thee." [110] Sheer astonishment is the effect which he pursues. And in detailing his own reactions to the scenes before them, Young offers Lorenzo a paradigm for salvation:

> Shall Man alone, whose Fate, whose final Fate,
> Hangs on that Hour, exclude it from his Thought:
> I think of nothing else; I see! I feel it!
> All Nature, like an Earthquake, trembling round!
> All Deities, like Summer's Swarms, on Wing!
> All basking in the full Meridian Blaze! [111]

The connected exclamations "I see! I feel it!" reflect a long history of critical thought which Young has diverted to the service of religion. The imagination ("I see!") inspires the passions ("I feel it!"), imparting a lifelike reality to the scene described. The idea of the Last Day no longer exists in the mind of Lorenzo as a quaint piece of religious conjecture unprovable by reason. What the reason might attempt to deny is, by the force of astonishment, proved upon the pulses. In a passage which might be said to summarize Young's attitude toward the religious uses of sublimity, he announces,

> Know This, LORENZO! (seem it ne'er so strange)
> Nothing can satisfy, but what confounds;
> Nothing, but what astonishes, is true. [112]

This test of truth would not have occurred to Pope, but it is the article of faith upon which Young grounds the strategy of the *Night-Thoughts*. If to be fired is to believe, to be astonished is to be saved. The traditional leap of faith is made by an act of the imagination. Passion, evoked by the sublime, works a converting magic on the soul of Lorenzo.

If modern readers wish to dismiss Young's poem, they should dismiss it with understanding. Yet his intentions are widely misconstrued. Probably the most common objection to the *Night-Thoughts* is that prose, not verse, is the proper vehicle for religious ratiocination. Young, however, should not be convicted too quickly of ignoring important differences between prose and verse; in his *Conjectures on Original Composition*, in fact, he described the differences in a manner which many of his critics would accept. "There is something in Poetry," he argued, "beyond Prose-reason; there are Mysteries in it not to be explained, but admired; which render mere Prose-men Infidels to their Divinity."[113] Prose, Young implies, is the province of reason and explanation. Poetry is the realm of admiration and mystery. This distinction suggests why it was essential for Young that his defense of Christianity should be a poem, because only poetry could express the mysteriousness which is for him a vital part of Christian truth. Thus devotion for Young absolutely requires the igniting spark of imagination and feeling; and poetry, rather than prose, is the only proper medium for the exercise of these essential powers. "Man's Science," he asserted in the *Night-Thoughts*, "is the Culture of his Heart,"[114] and in his own poetry he labored to forge a saving alliance between poetic feeling and the mysteries of Christianity. His controlled "bursts of sublimity" are a dramatic means of jarring Lorenzo from his rational disbelief and doubt into passionate affirmation. And, as among increasing numbers of poets in the second half of the century, they affirm Young's basic and un-Augustan assumption that "Man must soar."[115]

Young's assertion that "Man must soar" provides a convenient ending to this chapter because it reminds us that much Augustan satire derives its chief energy from ridiculing man's attempts to transcend the limitations of his sense and reason. John R. Clark has coined the term "Icarian pattern" to describe the major trope underlying Swift's *Tale of a Tub*: the soaring and plummeting movement which traces the speaker's unsuccessful quest of mysteries too refined for sense and reason.[116] For Pope, as for Swift, the attempt to strain too high, whether through excess of reason or fancy, inevitably produces a plunge into bathos, madness, or the lower depths of inhumanity:

> Go, wond'rous creature! mount where Science guides,
> Go, measure earth, weigh air, and state the tides;
> Instruct the planets in what orbs to run,
> Correct old Time, and regulate the Sun;
> Go, soar with Plato to th' empyreal sphere,
> To the first good, first perfect, and first fair;
> Or tread the mazy round his follow'rs trod,
> And quitting sense call imitating God;
> As Eastern priests in giddy circles run,
> And turn their heads to imitate the Sun.
> Go, teach Eternal Wisdom how to rule—
> Then drop into thyself, and be a fool![117]

Like Swift's Laputans—who have one eye turned inward and the other aimed toward the zenith—Pope's proud adversaries in *An Essay on Man* fail in the one art toward which all other eighteenth-century arts aspire: the art of living. As Rochester phrased the extreme Augustan position with characteristic pungency,

> Our Sphere of Action, is lifes happiness,
> And he who thinks Beyond, thinks like an Ass.[118]

Pope wisely excluded from *An Essay on Man*, on the advice of the philosopher George Berkeley, an address "to our Saviour": the Christian dispensation, Warton records Berkeley as saying, did not come within the compass of his plan. Pope himself explained as much to Spence. "Some wonder why I did not take in the fall of man in my *Essay*, and others how the immortality of the soul came to be omitted. The reason is plain. They both lay out of my subject, which was only to consider man as he is, in his present state, not in his past or future."[119] In excluding from his subject both man's immortality and his fall, Pope deliberately centered his poem in the present state of humanity, where ethical moderation releases man from the potentially endless rising and falling cycles of the Icarian pattern. Young, despite his great admiration for Pope, clearly understood his own divergence from Pope's example. "Man too he sung," he wrote of Pope in the *Night-Thoughts*: "Immortal Man I sing."[120] And in choosing *immortal* man as his subject, Young marks a change of direction away from the earth-centered ethics and aesthetics of the major Augustan writers. This change, although at first tentative, incomplete, and almost imperceptible, manifests itself in various experiments with the religious sublime.

Numerous earlier writers of the religious sublime, of course, had concerned themselves with "Immortal Man." Pomfret's "Dies Novissima" is quite typical of other poems which, explicitly or implicitly, treat man as a creature of eternity as well as of time. But Pomfret's most popular poem by far was "The Choice"— Johnson thought that perhaps no composition in English had been oftener perused—and thus the staggering popularity of the *Night-Thoughts* suggests that the ethics of moderation and of limitation were no longer sufficient to sustain the religious and literary aspirations of a great many readers. The sublime always implied the possibility of rising above the ordinary limitations of humanity to a vision of wholeness or to a passionate experience of the mysterious. But generally this potential, in Pomfret and in most other writers early in the century, is carefully circumscribed within an accepted order of subordination: man always returns from his precarious moment of illumination to accept the necessities of his limited condition. "Submit" is the imperative of *An Essay on Man*. In Young, however, and in some other poets of the religious sublime during the second half of the century, the ethics of resignation are partially subverted by a belief that man is not only a "spectator" of creation—and the detachment of Mr. Spectator reflects an entire way of viewing the world—but, more importantly, he is a *participant* in a mysterious, divine, and on-going process. Instead of resigning his will to God's as the primary act of worship, man attempts to elevate his spirit in order to increase his sense of participation with the divine. In this effort, the religious sublime found a new usefulness and ultimately a new appearance.

That Young's contemporaries could excuse defects in the *Night-Thoughts* which are painfully obvious to modern readers suggests that he offered his own age something vitally important, something more immediately valuable than felicities of style or intelligible structure. He told them to trust their feelings; he told them that passion is evidence of truth; he told them that the consolation for loss is not found in resignation alone but in participation with the divine; he told them that man's destiny is not to pick a middle way between extremes but to soar above them. While the importance of these ideas helps explain his contemporary fame, it cannot today excuse his poetic failures. Criticism, however, must do more than lament failure. It should also try to understand the reasons for failure. The defects of the *Night-Thoughts* are, as Ezra Pound wrote of his failures in the *Cantos*, "the defects inherent in a record of struggle,"[121] and for Young the struggle primarily involved the attempt to find a language appropriate to his ideas. His solution might be called the exclamatory sublime: a series of declarative statements, punctuated primarily by question marks and exclamation points, which derive their intensity from a rising tone of voice. The effect, for most readers, is a disagreeable sensation of being shouted at. When the matter of the communication is compelling—Thoreau's "simplify!" or Carlyle's "work!"—the exclamatory sublime finds its uses. But the haranguing styles of Thoreau and of Carlyle remain effective largely because both writers had a finely developed sense of language. They use words complexly, often employing etymological puns as a means of showing how language can tap deeper levels of experience and consciousness than men encounter in ordinary life. Young had no sense of language.

The failure of language in the *Night-Thoughts* involves more than Young's failure alone. His effort to create a new style implies a recognition that Pope's couplets, so expressive of an ethics and an aesthetics of limitation, would not suit a different view of man. The experimentation with new kinds of poetry in the second half of the century reflects more than a shift in taste: it reflects a changing view of man himself. Thus, when Joseph Warton demotes Pope to the second rank of English writers, his reason is that satire and didactic poetry—forms rooted in the conception of man as a limited creature in need of constant instruction and correction—are not the highest kinds of verse. Although he admits that Pope excels his immediate contemporaries, Warton concludes his two-volume study with the assertion that "there are parts and passages in other modern authors, in Young and in *Thomson*, for instance, equal to any of Pope; and he has written nothing in a strain so truly sublime, as the *Bard* of Gray." [122] The poetry of Christopher Smart or the Ossian poems of James Macpherson, like Gray's *The Bard*, demonstrate how eighteenth-century poets experimented with new forms of the sublime in order to find a language appropriate to changed views of man's place. Gray through nostalgia for a vanished past, Smart through a combination of personal vision and Hebrew poetics, Macpherson through the re-creation of a bardic voice—all seek to use sublimity in new ways. Their experiments provide a further exploration of eighteenth-century literary change and ultimately create a context for understanding certain Romantic transformations of the religious sublime.

Chapter Five

Changes in Poetry
and Criticism

In the second half of the eighteenth century, declining interest in most forms of explicitly religious poetry hastened the demise of the religious sublime. Its eventual failure, however, was implicit in its association with a set of conventional subjects, forms, and techniques. Sublimity, like novelty, dulls through repetition; and one's tenth Pindaric ode concerning the Last Day may not strike the mind with wonder. The idea of the religious sublime did not die in the last half of the century, but it was doomed largely to survive at the hands of unimaginative poets and critics who simply repeated the labors of the past. Yet there was one way in which the religious sublime achieved a renewed vigor. It became associated with certain of the fresh principles which in the second half of the eighteenth century were changing the nature of English poetry and criticism.

SENTIMENT AND SUBLIMITY

The revaluation of feeling in the second half of the eighteenth century changed the nature both of religion and of literature. The Methodist and Evangelical movements imparted a new fervor to religious experience in general. Feeling and religion became nearly equivalents. This close alliance is illustrated by an announcement in the *Mirror* (1779) explaining that the periodical would not treat matters of religion: "This consideration," the journal stated, "will apply, in the strongest manner, to any thing mystic or controversial; but it may, perhaps, admit of an exception, when religion is only introduced as a feeling, not a system, as appealing to the sentiments of the heart, not to the disquisitions of the head" (No. 42). In literature, too, the sentiments of the heart became for many the only reliable standard of judgment. "I cannot help thinking," wrote Vicesimus Knox, "that the effect which a literary work is found to produce is the best criterion of its merit; and that sentiment or feeling, after all that has been urged by theoretical critics, is the ultimate and infallible touchstone to appreciate with precision the works of taste and genius."[1] Both art and nature in the later eighteenth century are suffused with the soft glow of feeling. Nor did sublimity escape transformation.

The traditionally close relationship between the sublime and the pathetic encouraged sentimentalists to blur their essential differences. As a result, sentiment and sublimity to some degree blended into one. Nowhere was this confusion more apparent than in the religious poetry of the later eighteenth century. In fact, one emblem of confusion is the new "poetical prose" popularized by James Hervey's *Meditations and Contemplations* (1746). The similarities between Hervey and Edward Young are hard to miss; and there is a relentless logic behind Thomas Newcomb's decision to publish, in 1757, a version of Hervey's *Contemplations* done "after the Manner of Dr. Young." Newcomb, an admirer of Dennis, announced in his Dedication what hardly needed saying—that Hervey's work contains "some of the most sublime and elevated strains of piety and devotion; such as, if attentively perused, must affect the most unfeeling, and warm the coldest bosom."[2] To the sentimentalists, sublimity no longer implied the stern grandeur of Milton or the chaste simplicity of Boileau but whatever in art or nature contributes to strong excitement of the feelings.

The religious poetry of the sentimentalists defies a sympathetic reading; yet, in order to demonstrate how men of feeling transformed the sublime, two typical instances deserve some comment. The first reflects a little-known aspect of later eighteenth-century culture: that is, the curious taste among English readers for certain kinds of German religious literature. To judge from current English periodicals, the most popular of those writing in

German were Johann Bodmer (1698–1783), the Swiss poet, critic, and translator of *Paradise Lost*, who greatly influenced eighteenth-century German verse; Salomon Gessner (1730–1788), also Swiss, whose *Der Tod Abels* (1758) was translated into English in 1761; and Friedrich Klopstock (1724–1803), whose *Messias* (1748–1773) appeared in an English translation beginning in 1763. By 1772 the *Monthly Review* could report that the work of Bodmer, Gessner, and Klopstock had "met with success in this country."[3] Its success has something to do with English interest in sentimental sublimity.

Klopstock, as the best known of the trio, can speak for all three—especially as his *Messias* was accompanied with an essay on divine poetry and with a preface by its English translator. Joseph Collyer, the translator, lost no time in advising English readers of the "amazing sublimity"[4] of Klopstock's poem. He even apologized for any flaws in the translation by attributing them to the grandeur of his task. "Indeed, in the prosecution of this work," he wrote, "I have frequently been fill'd with sensations too big, too sublime for utterance; but happy will it be, if, where I have been unable to reach my own ideas, this work raises such great and inexpressible sensations in the minds of my readers."[5] Collyer's cloudy account is an apt prelude to Klopstock's essay "On Divine Poetry," which undertakes a few remarks on "the most sublime kind of poetry" for the benefit of those unschooled but ideal readers "who are guided only by the pure unbias'd sentiments of nature, and a good heart."[6] As might be expected, Klopstock's remarks hover about a single theme: the sublime poet must touch "the tender feelings of the heart" and give "strong emotions to the soul."[7] "Doing this by the force of religion," he asserted, "is a new species of the sublime."[8]

In truth, English readers could have found nothing new in the use of religion to evoke the sublime. After the work of Young and Hervey, even the oppressively close relationship between sublimity and pathos should have been familiar. Nathan Drake offers a perceptive description of Klopstock (and suggests what English readers liked about *The Messiah*) in observing that while Klopstock lacks "the stern and gigantic sublimity of Milton, [he] still elevates the mind by the vigour and novelty of his fiction, and is certainly more tender and pathetic than the English Bard."[9] Klopstock's version of the Crucifixion confirms Drake's account of him: "The earth was silent at the descending twilight, and as the gloom increas'd, deeper was the silence. Terrifying shades and palpable darkness came on. The birds ceas'd their notes, and sought the thickest groves: the very insects hurry'd to their retreats, and the wild beasts of the desarts fled to their lonely dens. A death-like silence reign'd through the air. The human race, standing aghast, look'd up to Heaven. The darkness became still more dark. What a night in the midst of day!"[10] Burke might have commended the use of darkness and silence to achieve sublimity, but the effect of the scene seems closer to Klopstock's own description of his intentions—to pour "sublime sensations into the hearts of the redeem'd."[11] The quest for sensation determines Klopstock's treatment, as it must also have determined the reactions of his readers.

A passage from Richard Cumberland's epic *Calvary* (1792) provides a second opportunity for examining the sentimental transformation of the religious sublime. More in the manner of Dennis than of Young, Cumberland interweaves the action of various spirits and devils with the progress of his poem. "The most poetical parts of the work are those in which the author introduces the infernal spirits," affirmed the *Monthly Review*. "Here he frequently catches no small portion of the fire and sublimity of Milton."[12] Indeed, one main reason for the popularity of Cumberland's poem may have been the appearance of Satan, who bears some likeness to Milton's mighty devil. But his portrait of Satan, in a passage which the *Monthly Review* commended for its "terrible sublimity,"[13] shows how Cumberland had improved upon Milton:

> And ever and anon he beat his breast,
> That quick and short with lab'ring pulses heav'd.
> One piteous look he upward turn'd, one sigh
> From his sad heart he fain had sent to heav'n,
> But ere the hopeless messenger could leave
> His quiv'ring lips. . . .[14]

The transformation of Satan mirrors the sentimental transformation of the religious sublime.

It is not infusion of strong feeling into religious experience which is offensive about the sentimentalists, nor is it their belief that the feelings are a surer guide to truth and human happiness than is reason. Mrs. Thrale reports that Johnson invariably "burst into a flood of tears" whenever he read the line "*Tantus labor non sit cassus*" from the "Dies Irae,"[15] and his power of friendship surely indicates an almost Shandean responsiveness to human feeling. Yet Johnson's deep feeling never trivializes its objects, as is so often the case among the sentimentalists. If, as Goldsmith wittily observed, Johnson's little fishes would all talk like whales, the transformation reveals a truth about his refusal to diminish, through the inadequacies of language, anything for which he felt affection. This refusal, of course, appears most evident in his reiterated criticism of religious poetry: to describe the divine—in any language except the ceremonial phrases of orthodox worship—is to diminish it. Perhaps only a reading of the religious literature of the sentimentalists can do justice to the perceptiveness of Johnson's belief. When Johnson began to write, the religious sublime had hardened into a mechanical exercise which even the most contemptible poets could master. And whatever novelty was to be gained through the tears of Satan represented a net loss for poetry and perhaps for religion as well. Fortunately, sentiment such as that of *The Messiah* or of *Calvary* was not the only new force altering the nature of eighteenth-century verse. Other ideas offered possibilities of rejuvenating the sublime and of guiding poets around the dead end implicit in Johnson's criticism of religious poetry. The originality of Macpherson, Smart, Blake, Coleridge, and Wordsworth appears partly in their ability to create new forms of the religious sublime by breathing a fresh spirit into worn-out materials.

PRIMITIVE SUBLIMITY: LOWTH, BLAIR, AND OSSIAN

Robert Lowth, one of the most original, important, and today least-known of eighteenth-century critics, delivered his official lectures as Oxford Professor of Poetry from 1741 until 1750. The lectures were published first in 1753 in their original Latin form. Not until 1787 did they appear in English. Yet the English translation, entitled *Lectures on the Sacred Poetry of the Hebrews*, did little to augment Lowth's already solid reputation as a critic. The *Critical Review* began its notice of the translation by saying, "Our praises cannot add to the credit of Dr. Lowth's Lectures, nor render them better known," and the *Monthly Review* agreed: "The well-earned celebrity of Bishop Lowth's Lectures, renders any commendation of them, on the present occasion, superfluous, if not impertinent."[16] The thoroughness and originality of Lowth's *Lectures* make them a landmark of Hebrew scholarship; and, not surprisingly, he devoted several individual lectures to discussing aspects of Hebrew sublimity. These lectures, while repeating many ideas familiar to early proponents of the religious sublime, advance significantly beyond the work of other critics. They were one stimulus for important changes in the nature of eighteenth-century verse.

Lowth's discussion of Hebrew sublimity was most conventional in analyzing subjects which contribute to the sublime. Like many critics before him, he argued that religious subjects are inherently the most sublime. Because the subjects of Hebrew poetry are invariably religious, it followed that the Hebrew poets must excel all others in sublimity. "As far as respects the dignity and importance of the subject," he wrote, "they not only surpass all other writers, but even exceed the confines of human genius and intellect. The greatness, the power, the justice, the immensity of God; the infinite wisdom of his works and of his dispensations, are the subjects in which the Hebrew Poetry is always conversant, and always excels."[17] But, as Lowth wisely allows, the sublimity of the Hebrews is not wholly dependent on subject, for a number of modern poets unintentionally demonstrated that excellence in the poet is as important as sublimity in the subject. Thus, in explaining the particular power of the Hebrews to reach the sublime, Lowth introduced two additional arguments concerning Hebrew poetry which, although not entirely original, he made seem boldly inventive through the precision and detail of his analysis, moving his *Lectures* far beyond the jargon of standard eighteenth-century criticism. The sublimity of the Hebrews depends particularly, he argued, upon strong passion in the poets and upon the "naturalness" of their expression.

Lowth is reminiscent of Dennis in his insistence that passion is the source both of poetry and of the sublime. "Some passions may be expressed without any thing of the sublime," he wrote; "the sublime also may exist, where no passion is directly expressed: there is however no sublimity where no passion is excited."[18] Lowth's analysis of Hebrew sublimity, then, proceeds from his premise that the essence of the sublime is its power to arouse passion in the reader. Despite his caution in conceding that sublimity is governed by the reader's response, not necessarily by the poet's own experience and expression of strong feeling, he clearly most admires the poetry of the Hebrews for its intense and personal overflowing of religious emotion:

> Here indeed a spacious field presents itself to our view: for by far the greater part of the sacred poetry is little else than a continued imitation of the different passions. What in reality forms the substance and subject of most of these [Hebrew] poems but the passion of admiration, excited by the consideration of the Divine power and majesty; the passion of joy, from the sense of Divine favour, and the prosperous issue of events: the passion of resentment and indignation against the contemners of God: of grief, from the consciousness of sin; and terror, from the apprehension of Divine judgment? Of all these, and if there be any emotions of the mind beyond these, exquisite examples may be found in the Book of Job, in the Psalms, in the Canticles, and in every part of the prophetic writings.[19]

Only Isaac Watts among earlier writers seems to have felt so deeply Lowth's conviction that the sublimity of the Hebrews is essentially lyrical—"a continued imitation of the different passions"—and depends fundamentally upon the presence of strong feeling in the poet. Epic machinery, eschatological subjects, "crowded" imagery, periphrasis, and Miltonic diction obsessed most eighteenth-century sublime religious poets. Lowth offered a different analysis of what constitutes biblical sublimity, one which looks forward to the passionate adoration of Smart's *Song to David*.

Lowth's analysis of passion as a source of sublimity complements his discussion of the "naturalness" of Hebrew verse. To the conventional view that religious subjects arouse strong passion in the reader, Lowth added a distinction which earlier critics had rarely wished to make explicit. The emotion excited by religious subjects, in both poet and reader, is "natural" feeling. "In other instances," he wrote, "Poetry appears to want [i.e., require] the assistance of *art*, but in this to shine forth with all its *natural* splendour."[20] The "naturalness" of Hebrew verse, Lowth believed, contributes most to its unrivaled sublimity. In explaining this belief, he subtly redirected the discussion of religious sublimity, allying the sublimity of the Hebrews with the new interest in primitivism, the study of "natural" cultures.

Writers for years had, of course, recognized that Hebrew verse lacked the polish of later poetry; like Homer and Shakespeare, the Hebrews were admired exceptions to the neoclassical rule of correctness. But, although in part they thought the sublimity of the Bible a consequence of the artlessness of early poetry in general, most critics before Lowth ignored the close relationship between biblical poetry and the culture of the Hebrews. Lowth changed that. "We must endeavour as much as possible," he wrote, "to read Hebrew as the Hebrews would have read it."[21] In his *Lectures on the Sacred Poetry of the Hebrews*, formulaic praise of the "magnificent plainness" and "terrible simplicity" of biblical poetry yields to a detailed explanation of how the customs and conditions of a primitive society contribute to the sublimity of its verse.

For Lowth the Bible is sublime because it contains the natural language of the heart—a language which must be poetic because it is figurative and which must be figurative because it is passionate. With his passions fired by thoughts of God, the biblical poet expressed his feelings without restraint or artifice, drawing his imagery from the "natural" surroundings and affairs of a primitive people:

And I will wipe Jerusalem,
As a man wipeth a dish:
He wipeth it, and turneth it upside down.
(2 Kings 21:13)

Although he acknowledged the "meanness" of the image, Lowth also declared, "I do not scruple to pronounce it sublime."[22] He insisted that readers not attribute the sublimity of the Hebrews to art, "which above all things is due to nature alone,"[23] and by stressing the relationship between sublimity and natural passion, he in effect expanded the idea of the sublime to include figures not only great and ennobling (like Addison's angel in *The Campaign*) but also "natural" to the passionate imagination of a primitive poet.

Although the modern reader will find fault with aspects of Lowth's analysis of Hebrew poetry, his contemporaries were deeply impressed. Its scope, seriousness, and intelligence outstrip all earlier treatments of biblical poetry, and its account of Hebrew versification (to be discussed later in relation to Smart) remains the basis of modern scholarly opinion.[24] But perhaps Lowth's most important contribution, in which he was aided by William Smith, Bishop Warburton, and other admirers of biblical poetry, was to destroy the notion that sublimity requires conformity to a single standard of diction, of imagery, and of subject. To experience the sublimity of "I will wipe Jerusalem," he insists, requires an act of historical imagination: "We must read Hebrew as the Hebrews would have read it." If any such principle had guided his idea of sublimity, the elder Thomas Warton, for example, could never have produced his modernized paraphrase of Isaiah in which the moon becomes "the weary Pilgrim's Friend." But beyond changing the principle of biblical translation, Lowth's *Lectures* implied a view of sublimity which he himself might have rejected because of its revolutionary possibilities. If one accepts, however, the principle that sublimity must be understood within a context of cultural independence, free from the standards developed by a particular age or country, then a basis exists for arguing that individual poets themselves are free to create their own standards of sublimity. The reader of *Jubilate Agno*, in effect, is challenged to abandon the standards of eighteenth-century culture and to "read the *Jubilate* as Smart would have read it." If Smart did find such implications in Lowth's *Lectures*, which he greatly admired, his reception by contemporary readers suggests that few shared his insights. Most discovered excitement enough in Lowth's detailed treatment of the relationship between biblical sublimity and primitivist thought. Thus, when Hugh Blair wrote his *Critical Dissertation on the Poems of Ossian* (1763), which he based upon the confidence that Ossian was a primitive poet, he was unavoidably drawn to consider the question of Ossianic sublimity in the context of Lowth's discussion of the Hebrews.

Blair had read Lowth with attention. His *Lectures on Rhetoric and Belles Lettres* contains a discussion of Hebrew poetry which begins with a tribute to Lowth's "learned Treatise."[25] There is, in fact, nothing in Blair's account not to be found in Lowth. He agreed that Hebrew imagery is "in a high degree, expressive and natural,"[26] and, comparing modern poetry with the Bible, he argued that its "superfluities and excrescencies of Style, were the result of imitation in after times; when Composition passed into inferior hands, and flowed from art and study, more than from native genius."[27] Like Lowth, he affirmed that the Bible affords "the highest instances of the Sublime."[28] But he went somewhat beyond the letter of Lowth's *Lectures*, although not beyond the spirit, in declaring that the greatest sublimity will *invariably* be found in the literature of primitive cultures:

> I am inclined to think, that the early ages of the world, and the rude unimproved state of society, are peculiarly favourable to the strong emotions of Sublimity. The genius of men is then much turned to admiration and astonishment. Meeting with many objects, to them new and strange, their imagination is kept glowing, and their passions are often raised to the utmost. They think, and express themselves boldly, and without restraint. In the progress of society, the genius and manners of men undergo a change more favourable to accuracy, than to strength or Sublimity.[29]

The relationship between primitivism and sublimity which Lowth had developed at length seduced Blair into an error which few modern readers are willing to forgive: his defense of the fraudulent Ossian poems.

Blair bases his analysis of Ossian upon his appreciation of Hebrew sublimity. Believing that sublimity is most often the product of a primitive society, he concluded that the deliberate sublimity of the poems marked them as genuinely primitive. James Macpherson, the "translator" of Ossian, helped to mislead the unwary by observing in his notes various biblical parallels to phrases in the text. Nor was Blair unique in finding that the poems breathe, as another critic put it, "a sublimity truly scriptural." [30] Persuasive evidence in the poem supported Blair's assumption that Ossian matched, almost point for point, the sublimity of the Hebrew poets.

"The works of Ossian," Blair wrote in his *Lectures on Rhetoric and Belles Lettres*, ". . . abound with examples of the Sublime." [31] In the *Critical Dissertation* he studied at length the sources of Ossian's sublimity, inevitably discovering parallels between Ossian and the Hebrews. Conciseness and simplicity were touchstones of biblical sublimity; Blair argued in the *Critical Dissertation* that "Ossian is always concise" [32] and that the "simplicity of Ossian's manner adds great beauty to his descriptions, and indeed to his whole Poetry." [33] Certain kinds of imagery were held to contribute to the sublimity of the Bible; Blair noted, "A resemblance may be sometimes observed between Ossian's comparisons, and those employed by the sacred writers." [34] Almost everything that Blair wrote concerning Ossian's use of hyperbole, personification, apostrophe, allegory, and epithets resembles passages from Lowth regarding the sublimity of the Hebrews. Only in discussing the question of Ossian's use of the supernatural did Blair part company with Lowth. But there, too, he continued to think of Ossian as a counterpart of the Hebrews; and where Lowth failed him, Blair turned for aid to another contemporary critic of the sublime.

Edmund Burke's ideas concerning the sublime strongly influenced Blair's treatment of the Ossianic supernatural. Particularly important for Blair were Burke's notions of obscurity and terror. Arguing that sublimity requires an "approach towards infinity," Burke asserted that a "clear idea is therefore another name for a little idea."[35] "It is one thing to make an idea clear," he insisted, "and another to make it *affecting* to the imagination."[36] Obscurity, for Burke, was one means of blurring the clear outlines of things, creating in the imagination of the viewer an impression of boundlessness and infinity. He developed this notion further by stressing the close relationship between obscurity and terror—calling the latter in fact "the ruling principle"[37] of the sublime. The famous vision of Eliphaz from the Book of Job he chose to illustrate the relationship. But while for Burke the vision of Eliphaz simply illustrated a psychological principle, for Blair it complemented Lowth's ideas concerning the sublimity of the Hebrews. He quickly recognized the usefulness of Burke's illustration, and of his ideas concerning obscurity and terror, in accounting for Ossian's treatment of the supernatural.

Blair discussed the idea of obscurity in his *Lectures on Rhetoric and Belles Lettres*, relating Burke's psychological principle to familiar notions concerning the religious sublime:

> Obscurity . . . is not unfavourable to the Sublime. Though it render the object indistinct, the impression, however, may be great; for, as an ingenious Author has well observed, it is one thing to make an idea clear, and another to make it affecting to the imagination; and the imagination may be strongly affected . . . by objects of which we have no clear conception. Thus we see, that almost all the descriptions given us of the appearances of supernatural Beings, carry some Sublimity, though the conceptions which they afford us be confused and indistinct. Their Sublimity arises from the ideas, which they always convey, of superior power and might, joined with an awful obscurity.[38]

In illustration of this idea, Blair chose Burke's own example— the vision of Eliphaz. To read the passage aloud is to understand why Blair associated Ossian with the Hebrews: "In thoughts from the visions of the night, when deep sleep falleth on men,

Fear came upon me, and trembling, which made all my bones to shake. Then a spirit passed before my face; the hair of my flesh stood up: It stood still, but I could not discern the form thereof: an image was before mine eyes, there was silence, and I heard a voice, saying, Shall mortal man be more just than God?" (Job 4:13-17). In its rhythms, language, and vague supernatural terror, the passage might have come directly from the pages of Ossian. Only one thing prevents it from being truly Ossianic: the mention of God.

Ossian's failure to reveal any knowledge of a Supreme Being taxed the ingenuity of his defenders. Because many critics believed that poetry originated in the worship of God, Ossian's silence on matters divine might call into doubt his stature as a primitive. Macpherson himself noted, "It is a singular case, it must be allowed, that there are no traces of religion in the poems ascribed to Ossian; as the poetical compositions of other nations are so closely connected with their mythology."[39] He argued, in explanation, that all secular "Gallic" poetry shares this characteristic. But Blair offered a different argument. While Ossian does not acknowledge the idea of a Supreme Being, Blair pointed out, he does introduce ghosts and spirits—the literary equivalents of pagan machinery and Christian marvels. He cited a number of passages to show that the appearances of ghosts are "among the most sublime passages of Ossian's poetry."[40] Imitating critics who juxtaposed classical and Christian descriptions of God, Blair compared passages from Ossian and Homer, concluding that "Ossian's ghosts are drawn with much stronger and livelier colours than those of Homer."[41] In Blair's view, only the Bible could match the supernatural terrors of Ossian; and as if to confirm that belief, he cited, once again, the sublime vision of Eliphaz.

Blair praised, in addition to Ossian's ghosts, the weird superior powers and spirits which influence the destiny of his heroes. Their obscurity, he felt, simply made them more sublime. He particularly recommended Ossian's description in "Carric-Thura" of the spirit Loda. "I know no passage more sublime in the writings of any uninspired author,"[42] he commented. Although Blair thought the passage too well known for quotation, citing it will show why he compared it implicitly with the inspired poetry of the Bible: "The flame was dim and distant; the moon hid her red face in the east. A blast came from the mountain, and bore, on its wings, the spirit of Loda. He came to his place in his terrors, and he shook his dusky spear.—His eyes appear like flames in his dark face; and his voice is like distant thunder." [43] Macpherson's note to the passage is revealing. "There is a great resemblance," he rightly observed, since he created the resemblance intentionally, "between the terrors of this mock divinity, and those of the true God, as they are described in the 18th Psalm." Here the religious sublime appears in a new disguise, justifying Wordsworth's quip that Ossian was a phantom "begotten by the snug embrace of an impudent Highlander upon a cloud of tradition." [44] But Blair doubtlessly was not so much deceived by Macpherson as self-deceived. Reading Ossian in the context of the long critical tradition of the religious sublime, like many critics after him he refused to believe that a poem which fit his theories so well could not be genuine.

The conclusion to Blair's discussion of the Ossianic supernatural shows how thoroughly he guided himself by criticial tradition:

> Notwithstanding the poetical advantages which I have ascribed to Ossian's machinery, I acknowledge it would have been much more beautiful and perfect, had the author discovered some knowledge of a supreme Being. . . . For the most august and lofty ideas that can embellish poetry are derived from the belief of a divine administration of the universe. . . . The absence of all such religious ideas from Ossian's poetry, is a sensible blank in it; the more to be regretted, as we can easily imagine what an illustrious figure they would have made under the management of such a genius as his; and how finely they would have been adapted to many situations which occur in his works. [45]

Mere piety does not cause Blair to argue that ignorance of a Supreme Being creates a "sensible blank" in the poetry of Ossian.

The argument is based mainly upon expectations aroused by the long tradition of the religious sublime. What is most disappointing about Blair's account, however, is not his dependence upon critical tradition but his inability to view the Ossianic supernatural as part of a general variation of the religious sublime. Probably the best view of this variant appears in an essay by George Richards, a schoolmate of Charles Lamb, who in 1789 won the Oxford English Prize Essay with his composition "On the Characteristic Differences between Ancient and Modern Poetry, and the several Causes from which they result." Richards's wordy title, however infelicitous, is an accurate introduction to his comparison of the ancient and modern supernatural. "The mythology of the ancients is simply interesting and attractive," he writes, "but frequently weak in its parts, and formed too closely upon the models of human characters: but the Gothic machinery, by its wild and original air, conveys us into scenes beyond the limits of mortality, and introduces us to personages not familiarized to the general perceptions of man." [46] The phrase Gothic machinery offers a fine description of the new supernatural marvels which, while allied to the tradition of the Christian marvellous, create a special kind of religious sublimity during the last four decades of the century.

The interest in a distinctive "Gothic machinery," one different from both the traditional Christian and classical systems of divinity, is an essential aspect of the general trend toward Gothicism in the later eighteenth century, a trend which the poems of Ossian helped to spread. To explore the subject in any detail would require a lengthy study of both the novel and the drama, where Gothicism especially flourished. For our purposes, it is sufficient here to suggest that a movement usually considered antithetical to most neoclassicists has important points of similarity with the poetics of religious sublimity, with which the major Augustan writers were well acquainted. Once men agree that sublimity is the touchstone of great poetry, and once they agree that religious ideas are inherently the most sublime, then the appreciation of Ossianic ghosts and spirits requires only the impetus of a broadened taste for the supernatural; the grounds for approval already exist. Thus, Bishop Hurd insisted that although Shakespeare is always great whatever his subject, "even he is greater when he uses Gothic manners and machinery than when he employs classical: which brings us again to the same point [made earlier], that the former have, by their nature and genius, the advantage in producing the *sublime*."[47] The only misfortune in the popular gusto for "Gothic machinery" was that it implied a debasement as well as an expansion of taste for the supernatural. When a majority of eighteenth-century readers preferred Ossian's kind of religious sublimity, it became very difficult indeed for them to enjoy or to understand the genuinely Hebraic spirit of Christopher Smart.

PRAISE AND PROPHECY: THE SUBLIMITY OF CHRISTOPHER SMART

Smart's two best works, A *Song to David* (1763) and *Jubilate Agno* (begun in 1759 but not published until 1939), reflect his understanding both of Lowth's *Lectures* and of the tradition of the religious sublime. He praised Lowth's criticism as "one of the best performances that has been published for a century,"[48] and it is certain that Lowth helped him to surpass the conventional sublimity of his Seatonian exercises. "Generally, what Smart took from Lowth's *Lectures*," Robert D. Saltz explains, "was a way of adapting his psalmistic vision to forms recognized as Hebraic. . . . It freed him from the deadening weight of the conventions of Miltonic language and syntax, which, most critics would agree, mar the Seatonian poems; and it guided him to a style that had all the characteristics of Longinian sublimity and the sanction of scriptural tradition."[49] Yet Smart's reading of Lowth, while it released him from certain burdens of the past and guided him toward a more vigorous style, must be only a beginning for a study of Smart's sublimity. Whatever Lowth taught him, he did not show Smart poems resembling A *Song to David* and *Jubilate Agno*. The sublimity of Smart's best works, while embodying some of the ideas inspired by his reading of Lowth, develops in ways consistent with his personal vision of the world and of his role as poet. By examining these two aspects of his later work, it should be possible to understand the distinctive tone which makes Smart's religious sublimity different from that of any poet of the age.

Smart's view of the world is like that of the Franciscan or mystic who sees a profound spiritual unity comprehending the diverse and fractured phenomena of existence. Since all nature is of God, it is therefore suffused with the spirit of God; from the vast to the minute, from the angelic to the brutish, from the comprehensible to the mysterious, nature is not simply matter in motion but the manifestation of the divine spirit. In this outlook, Smart differs from the contemporary physico-theologians whose catalogs of natural lore he often appropriates for his own purposes. Nature, to the physico-theologian, is viewed primarily as evidence of the doctrine of fitness: he sees in nature data confirming God's orderly design for creation. In emphasizing purpose, the physico-theologian approaches nature more like a scientist than a mystic. Smart, on the other hand, is not primarily interested in discovering evidence of God's design; he seeks, instead, signs of his existence, aspects of his Being, participation in his inexplicable ongoing processes. The physico-theologian is, in Addison's term, a "spectator" of God's finished handiwork. Smart is a communicant in the mystery of God's continuous presence in nature.

Smart's vision of the world affects his conception of the poet's role. The poet is, for Smart, essentially an interpreter. His task is not to imitate nature—the standard eighteenth-century definition of the poet's role—but to serve as an intermediary between unawakened mankind and the divine mystery which he has been privileged to understand. The role is not entirely comfortable, for the poet is often cut off from the sympathy and understanding of his contemporaries, but it cannot be either ignored or deferred. Johnson ridiculed as "fantastick foppery" the idea that poets could write only at certain times; Smart, without pressing claims for his own inspiration, always seems *compelled* to write. This compulsion eighteenth-century readers would have "explained" as the result of Smart's madness. Denied paper, the legend went, he wrote *A Song to David* by scratching it onto the wainscotting of his cell with a key. But Smart's urgent tone is probably less the result of insanity than the sign of a deep seriousness of intention. Very few other eighteenth-century poets give an impression of being compelled to write out of any experience save profound leisure. But Smart's role as interpreter demands communication. And, equally important, it helps to determine the impulse embodied in *Jubilate Agno* and *A Song to David:* the necessary act of prophecy and praise.

In both poems the act of prophecy and praise is a unified performance, a single function composed of two main elements. For the purpose of analysis, however, it seems proper to discuss each poem as stressing a separate element of the dual function. Although such a division to some degree falsifies the integrity of each work, it will permit us to examine more closely Smart's idea of the poet's role. And it is Smart's role, rather than his rhetoric, which ultimately determines the sublimity of his major poems.

A Song to David is essentially a poem of praise—or, as Smart himself described it, a song of "affection and thankfulness to the great Author of the Book of Gratitude, which is the *Psalms* of David the king."[50] Like David, the archetypal sublime poet, Smart writes a hymn of adoration, fulfilling through his own act the worship which God requires of all his creatures. Thus, in repeating the duties required of Christians, he concludes the list by exhorting:

> *Praise above all—for praise prevails;*
> *Heap up the measure, load the scales,*
>   *And good to goodness add:*
> *The gen'rous soul her Saviour aids,*
> *But peevish obloquy degrades;*
>   *The Lord is great and glad.*[51]

The impulse to praise gives the poem a unity which, while not mirroring the symmetry of a Palladian villa, hardly justifies the observation by the *Critical Review* that Smart had constructed "a fine piece of ruins."[52] There is, then, a serious point to his ironic rejoinder, in a note which he added to his *Poems,* that the *Song* "is allowed by Mr. Smart's judicious Friends and Enemies to be the best piece ever made public by him, its chief fault being the EXACT REGULARITY and METHOD with which it is conducted."[53] Smart, I suspect, recognized that eighteenth-century theories of the mathematical harmony and proportion of the creation in effect imposed upon God the puny standards of human beauty. Exact regularity and method, at least as the *Critical Review* understood them, were things to be unlearned: "For in my nature I quested for beauty," Smart wrote of himself, "but God, God hath sent me to sea for pearls."[54] The unity which Smart perceives lies deeper than the harmonious proportions of Augustan beauty. Indeed, the profusion of competing accounts of the poem's "unity,"[55] some of which are too ingenious to be wholly wrong, suggests that Smart employed a series of overlapping local "unities" to imply the consummation of all such imperfect patterns in the reconciling spiritual unity of God.

Jubilate Agno is, of course, a song of praise—"Let Sia rejoice with Argemone Prickly Poppy" (C 114)—but it is also, in many of the antiphonal "For" sections, a song of prophecy—"For I prophecy that they will respect decency in all points." The overt introduction of a prophetic role probably accounts for the poem's initial strangeness. The construction of individual lines, for example, particularly the use of parallelism and repetition as a principle of composition, seems clearly indebted to Smart's reading of Lowth. "Lowth's insistence on parallelism as the basic factor in Hebrew poetry," Murray Roston explains, "led him to insist on literal prose translations [of the Bible] set out as poetry. . . . In the *Jubilate Agno*, Smart exploited biblical parallelism for original verse-writing. Here was a poem set out as verse as if it were metrical, but containing no trace of rhyme or metre other than the sense-rhythm by which it achieves its effect."[56] The structure of the lines, however, does not determine Smart's voice or vision but merely provides an appropriate vehicle for both:

> For I am the Lord's News-Writer—the scribe-evangelist—
> Widow Mitchel, Gun & Grange bless the Lord Jesus. (B₂ 327)

His study of Lowth may have suggested the form of the line and freed him from the necessity of producing a heightened poetic diction, but it was Smart himself who saw his role as that of "scribe-evangelist" and who alone knows why Widow Mitchel and Gun & Grange should be evoked in the same breath.

While *Jubilate Agno*, like *A Song to David*, expresses the world-view informing all of his verse, Smart's prophetic role requires a special twofold function which helps to create the uniqueness of *Jubilate*. The prophet traditionally relates individual and community experience to the thrust of divine history, and as interpreter Smart stresses in *Jubilate Agno* both his own individual role as speaker and the vision of a religious revival centered in England. Thus the impersonal (although highly distinctive) voice of *A Song to David* yields in the *Jubilate* to a style which forces us to consider the poet himself—an essential step if we are to acknowledge his role as interpreter:

> For I am come home again, but there is nobody to kill the calf or to pay the musick.
>
> For the hour of my felicity, like the womb of Sarah, shall come at the latter end.
>
> For I shou'd have avail'd myself of waggery, had not malice been multitudinous. (B_1 15–17)

In times less compelling, Smart implies, his prophetic impulse might have been diverted into the harmless folly of a jester. But although men interpret his strangeness as insanity, Smart insists that his apparent madness is divinest sense:

> For I bless the thirteenth of August, in which I was willing to be called a fool for the sake of Christ. (B_1 51)

Apparent madness is traditionally one of the credentials of the prophet, and Smart, by associating himself with "Christ's fools" and with a host of biblical figures, asks to be taken seriously as the interpreter of God's purposes. The uniqueness of his voice, including even the licensed obscurity of the prophet, emphasizes the uniqueness of his vision.

It is not Smart's prophecy of a religious revival which, at least in the general context of eighteenth-century poetry, comprises the uniqueness of *Jubilate Agno*: millennial schemes, if not commonplace, were certainly familiar to readers of religious literature. Rather, the uniqueness of *Jubilate Agno* derives from the particular means which Smart uses to impart a sense of inclusiveness. Language itself for Smart becomes the most fundamental means of expressing the spiritual unity underlying all things: his multilingual puns embody a principle of verbal interrelationship, just as the associations among animals, stones, plants, biblical characters, and contemporary Englishmen suggest a temporal and spatial web of connection. Thus supporting and justifying Smart's inclusion of the widest diversity of created things is the mystery of God's all-embracing power:

> Let Ethan praise with the Flea, his coat of mail, his piercer, and his vigour, which wisdom and providence have contrived to attract observation and to escape it. (A 36)

Unlike the physico-theologians, Smart implies that God's purposes are often paradoxical and inscrutable; the flea's vigor, a single quality, is "contrived" to achieve two different and opposite ends. Indeed, the flea, except as a figure of burlesque, is excluded from the world of neoclassical poetic conventions, but Smart ignores the rational conventions of mankind:

> For things that are not in the sight of men are thro' God of infinite concern. (B₂ 334)

With a voice and vision elevated by God—"For Christ Jesus has exalted my voice to his own glory" (C 151)—Smart refuses to mimic the "elevated" manner of most religious verse. Intent upon his mission as interpreter, he is willing to appear a Prodigal Son among poets:

> For it is the business of a man gifted in the word to prophecy good.
> For it will be better for England and all the world in a season, as I prophecy this day. (C 57–58)

It is characteristic that Smart's prophecy should be of goodness rather than of woe. He shows us no Pestilence stalking—and for some reason Pestilence always "stalks"—before the enraged Deity. His sublimity is quieter, based upon the conviction that every aspect of creation is "of infinite concern" to God.

Because *Jubilate Agno* and *A Song to David* are so different from standard exercises in the religious sublime, one is tempted to conclude that, after his Seatonian days, Smart lost all interest in the sublime. Yet "sublime" is one of the epithets which Smart applies to David in the *Song*, and it seems likely that he intentionally altered and refined (rather than rejected completely) standard ideas concerning the religious sublime. As the interpreter of a world of Christian unity, he attempts to infuse the sublime with his understanding that "The porches of the Christian school/ Are meekness, peace, and pray'r."[57] Instead of seeking the sublime in natural manifestations of power, he argues for a power of spirit which transcends any material force:

> Strong is the lion—like a coal
> His eye-ball—like a bastion's mole
>   His chest against the foes:
> Strong the gier-eagle on his sail,
> Strong against tide, th' enormous whale
>   Emerges, as he goes.
>
> But stronger still, in earth and air,
> And in the sea, the man of pray'r;
>   And far beneath the tide;
> And in the seat to faith assign'd,
> Where ask is have, where seek is find,
>   Where knock is open wide.[58]

For Smart, the Christian virtues replace whirlwinds, volcanos, and ghosts as sources of the sublime, and thus in the rapturous concluding passage of *A Song to David*, he climaxes the description of things beauteous, precious, and glorious with a stanza explicitly addressing David as the "father" of Christ:

> Glorious—more glorious, is the crown
> Of Him, that brought salvation down,

> By meekness, call'd thy Son;
> Thou at stupendous truth believ'd,
> And now the matchless deed's atchiev'd,
> Determin'd, dar'd, and done.

The heroism of Christ offers a "matchless" expression of power, but Smart prefers to emphasize the paradox of "meekness" as the ultimate expression of Christian strength. No passage in eighteenth-century poetry is more apparently sublime than the conclusion to *A Song of David*: paradoxically, no passage alters so completely the conventional paraphernalia of sublimity.

Allied to Smart's stress upon the spiritual power of Christianity is his rejection of terror as a source of the sublime. Perhaps the clearest expression of this attitude—which is embodied, not described, in the later poems—can be found in his Seatonian poem "On the Omniscience of the Supreme Being." The Fall, which many poets use as an excuse for imagining the grisly terrors of damnation, becomes for Smart an example of God's mercy and a cause for further adoration:

> Yet murmur not, but praise—for tho' we stand
> Of many a Godlike privilege amerc'd
> By Adam's dire transgression; tho' no more
> Is Paradise our home, but o'er the portal
> Hang in terrific pomp the burning blade;
> Still with ten thousand beauties blooms the Earth
> With pleasures populous, and with riches crown'd.
> Still is there scope for wonder and for love
> Ev'n to their last exertion.

Although Smart does not deny the terrors of the "burning blade," neither does he linger over them: instead, he directs us to a world still charged with the grandeur of God. In fact, by turning to his early Seatonian poem "On the Power of the Supreme Being," one can appreciate the quality which Smart consistently associated with sublimity and which in effect replaces terror: the experience of devout wonder. Personifying human reason in the figure of Philosophy, he brilliantly depicts reason's inability to fathom the ways of God:

> Baffled here
> By His Omnipotence, Philosophy
> Slowly her thoughts inadequate revolves,
> And stands, with all His circling wonders round her,
> Like heavy Saturn in th' etherial space
> Begirt with an inexplicable ring.

The use of scientific information—Huygens's explanation of the equatorial extension around Saturn as a "ring"—in order to suggest the inadequacy of science is typical of Smart's contemplative and tranquil celebration of the mysterious. His sublimity is characterized often by a gentle balking of the intellect, by an exploration of the limits of rationality beyond which praise is the only rational response.

In his mature poetry, then, the sublimity of Christopher Smart involves the celebration of Christian faith and the expression of suprarational praise. The sense of wonder, which is fundamental to his idea of the sublime, is not for Smart (as Dr. Johnson described it) the effect of novelty upon ignorance but rather a perception of divine mystery everywhere in creation, from the mighty to the meek, from the familiar to the strange. His sublimity is, further, almost always cumulative and stilling, not passionate and abrupt. In fact, this aspect of his poetry may reflect—and certainly supports—the view of some eighteenth-century critics who distinguished carefully, at a time when the distinction was breaking down under the assault of sentiment, between the sublime and the pathetic. Joseph Priestley, for example, argues that terror, by mixing sensations of fear with grandeur, cannot partake of what he calls the "pure sublime." "Moreover," he explains, "the pure sublime, by strongly engaging, tends to fix the attention, and to keep the mind in a kind of *awful stillness*; whereas it is the nature of every species of the pathetic to throw it into an *agitation*."[59] The emotion which Smart celebrates is usually the stilling power of love, extended through the whole scale of nature, and not the passions of agitation which pervade most of the poetry of the religious sublime. Indeed, his mastery is so complete that he can always reserve a certain amount of power for the proper moment—a skill lacked by most poets of the sublime, who spend themselves long before the moment of climax—as he proves in the magnificent final stanza of *A Song to David*. These distinctive qualities of Smart's use of the sublime, while they reveal him vastly more skillful and thoughtful than most religious poets of his day, represent in effect a refinement rather than a transformation of the religious sublime. Yet in one essential way his work does foreshadow the transformed sublimity of the age to come.

By assuming the role of interpreter, Smart implicitly asserted and explicitly demonstrated his confidence in the validity of an individual angle of vision. In rejecting the eyes of convention, he affirmed the right to see nature in his own way, a way consistent with his sense of a Christian aesthetic. Saint Augustine had discovered that, from a Christian point of view, the traditional rationale for the existence of high, middle, and low styles in writing was untenable: if all things are equal in God's eye, distinctions among styles cannot be based upon judgments concerning the importance of the subject.[60] Smart, in an analogous perception, understood that the neoclassical emphasis upon "general nature" conflicts fundamentally with the vision of Christianity. As he writes in the penultimate verse of *Jubilate Agno*,

> Let Odwell, house of Odwell rejoice with Lappago Maiden Lips. Blessed be the name of Jesus in singularities & singular mercies. (D 236)

The benediction upon apparent strangeness—mirrored in the punning name "odd-well"—is, of course, basic to the Christian outlook: "For thou bringest certain strange things to our ears," Paul was told by the philosophers of Athens, "we would know therefore what these things mean" (Acts 17:20). For Smart, strangeness is itself a form of meaning, evidence of a world not wholly explicable to human reason and illustration of God's active participation in even the "singularities" of existence. "For I have seen the White Raven & Thomas Hall of Willingham," Smart writes in perhaps the most strangely beautiful line from *Jubilate Agno*, "& am myself a greater curiosity than both" (B₁ 25). Any account of Smart's sublimity, then, has to recognize that he achieved it through a paradoxical emphasis upon the singular, the small, the meek, the odd, and the ridiculous. While his use of the sublime often looks to the past, his Christian joy in "singularities" anticipates a much different sublimity of the age to come.

'THE EGOTISTICAL SUBLIME': BLAKE, WORDSWORTH, AND COLERIDGE

One of the most amusing, revealing clashes between the old order and the new occurs in the margins of Blake's copy of Sir Joshua Reynolds's *Discourses on Art*. Although Reynolds must have partly redeemed himself in Blake's eyes by his final veneration of Michelangelo, much of the *Discourses* struck Blake as mischief and villainy. "This Man was Hired to Depress Art," he summarized.[61] One main issue on which they disagreed was the classical rule of generality. In describing his views on painting, Reynolds affirmed that "the whole beauty and grandeur of the art consists, in my opinion, in being able to get above all singular forms, local customs, particularities, and details of every kind." "A Folly!" Blake shot back in the margin. "Singular & Particular Detail is the Foundation of the Sublime."[62] This exchange is, of course, part of a larger battle between opposing conceptions of art which are traditionally called Classic and Romantic. But, for our purposes, it also reveals a fundamental change in attitudes toward the sublime.

The major shift in the analysis of sublimity appears in the work of a class of writers emerging around mid-century who were primarily concerned with understanding the psychological, physiological, and philosophical dimensions of the human response to aesthetic experience in general. Unlike earlier writers, who generally consider sublimity a quality inherent in things—in ideas, in objects, in words—the aestheticians sought to locate sublimity in the process of perception. The shift ought not to be construed too rigidly: Boileau and Dennis, for example, certainly acknowledged the role of the perceiving mind in their discussions of sublimity. But even Dennis, whose theory of Enthusiastic Passion reveals a more sensitive respect for the psychology of aesthetic experience than was shared by many of his contemporaries, tends to take for granted the relationship between mind and object: literary theory and applied criticism constitute his main areas of interest in the sublime. The aestheticians, however, make the process of interchange between mind and object the fundamental subject of their analysis, and they pursue the study of perceptual processes with a sophistication which leaves such forerunners as Hobbes and Dennis seeming merely crude pioneers. Perhaps the clearest illustration of this shift in viewpoint appears in associationalist theories of the sublime—for when associationalism (especially through the work of David Hartley, its most prominent eighteenth-century spokesman) began to influence contemporary ideas of the imagination, many Englishmen besides Tristram Shandy saw that external nature cannot be wholly understood without accounting for the mental processes by which it is perceived. Thus Dugald Stewart based his account of sublimity on what he called "the general laws of human thought"[63] —meaning associationalism—and argued that the mind, in perceiving any object of the imagination, habitually associates images of height and depth with religious ideas. Whatever their individual theories, most aestheticians, like Stewart, make the notion of human mental processes fundamental to their conception of the sublime. And, significantly, their work did not remain isolated from the literary concerns of eighteenth-century poets and critics.

Archibald Alison's *Essays on the Nature and Principles of Taste* (1790) illustrates the potentially close and fruitful relationship between literature and aesthetic analysis. Like Burke, he carefully distinguishes various qualities of external objects which contribute to the sublime: size, color, form, sound, and others. He does not, therefore, argue Kant's extreme position that sublimity "does not reside in anything of nature, but only in our mind."[64] He does, however, acknowledge an inevitable link between mind and nature. Indeed, he can investigate the sources of sublimity in nature only because they have previously evoked what he calls "the emotion of sublimity." Perhaps the most attractive aspect of his discussion is its supple allowance for human differences. He, like Burke, is searching for the "general laws" of taste which explain why different men agree that a particular poem, object, or quality strikes them as sublime. At the same time, however, he recognizes that differences in social class, age, cultural background, occupation, and general experience often create significant variations in the taste for sublimity. "The anecdote of a late celebrated Mathematician," he writes, "is well known, who read the Paradise Lost, without being able to discover in it, any thing that was sublime, but who said that he could never read the queries at the end of Newton's Optics, without feeling his hair stand on end, and his blood run cold."[65] If the mind and the human perceptual processes, then, are as essential to the sublime as are the qualities of external objects, two corollaries would seem to follow: first, that the taste for sublimity can be altered by changing men's patterns of association, and second, that the individual mind and emotions, however singular and particular, must be the poet's initial guide to an understanding of sublimity in nature and in art. Although Alison does not stress these corollaries, they are implicit in his analysis and, I believe, implicit in the attitudes toward the sublime shared by Wordsworth, Coleridge, and Blake. They imply what in fact occurred: a radical transformation of the religious sublime.

Blake's attitude toward the sublime, like his position on most other subjects, represents an extreme and profoundly personal formulation. He affirmed frequently and with passion that the perceiving mind, not external nature and not the world of general consensus, is the only source of great poetry and religious truth. Indeed, his conviction that he must create his own system or be ruled by another man's, while it may exaggerate the dangers of enslavement and the virtue of personal systems, suggests the fundamental subjectivity of his approach to life and art. He was a visionary, which for him meant that the external world was far less important than his ability to see, in or through nature, a supernatural reality. "I question not my Corporeal or Vegetative Eye any more than I would Question a Window concerning a Sight," he wrote, implying that he did not base his judgments solely upon the information supplied by his senses. "I look thro' it," he asserted of the sensual eye, "& not with it."[66]

In a famous passage, perhaps adapted from Dennis, he offers what amounts to a wholly visionary theory of the sublime in which the mind creates its own version of reality: "I assert for My Self that I do not behold the outward Creation & that to me it is hindrance & not Action; it is as the dirt upon my feet, No part of me. 'What,' it will be Question'd, 'When the Sun rises, do you not see a round disk of fire somewhat like a Guinea?' O no, no, I see an Innumerable company of the Heavenly host crying, 'Holy, Holy, Holy, is the Lord God Almighty.' "[67] The passage illustrates, as a similar one did for Dennis, the transforming perception which Blake thought to be the essence of sublimity. As he wrote in a letter to Thomas Butts concerning one of his own prophetic books, "I consider it as the Grandest Poem that this World Contains. Allegory addressed to the Intellectual powers, while it is altogether hidden from the Corporeal Understanding, is My Definition of the Most Sublime Poetry."[68]

Blake's definition of the most sublime poetry indicates how much he departed from conventional attitudes toward sublimity. Yet he drew his ideas concerning the sublime—with two vital exceptions—from the same sources which critics had cited for decades: the Bible, Dante, Michelangelo, Milton, and eighteenth-century religious poetry. These Blake adapted to his own visionary system, but only his praise of Dante and of Michelangelo would have startled some earlier writers.

Blake's view of the poet's office was essentially biblical.[69] At the end of his preface to Milton (1804–1808), he quoted a line from the book of Numbers (11:29) which reveals the impulse directing his own poetic activity: "Would to God that all the Lord's people were prophets." As the work of a self-proclaimed prophet, Blake's poetry in effect comprises the holy books of his own religious imagination. He was fond of quoting Milton's dictum that poetry is not created by the invocation of Dame Memory and her Siren daughters but is the direct gift of God. And, like many critics of the eighteenth century, he compared the Bible with the classics as a source of art and truth, complaining that "the Stolen and Perverted Writings of Homer & Ovid, of Plato & Cicero, which all men ought to contemn, are set up by artifice against the Sublime of the Bible."[70] In the Bible and in the biblical grandeur of Milton and Michelangelo, Blake discovered the models for his own kind of sublimity. His illustrations for *Paradise Lost*, for the *Night-Thoughts*, and for Robert Blair's lugubrious poem *The Grave* (which Blair published in 1743) show how his imagination habitually transformed materials associated with the eighteenth-century religious sublime into aspects of a personal visionary system.

A poet who can see the world in a grain of sand or a host of angels in the rising sun does not require the conventional props of sublime poetry. He can discover grandeur in or through the most ordinary aspects of human experience. This method, to anticipate, was Wordsworth's great contribution to the poetry of the religious sublime, although Blake too certainly at times cherishes in his poetry the small, the helpless, and the seemingly insignificant. Thus, a robin in a cage may suggest outrage as powerful and sublime as the war in Heaven. But Blake frequently chose to deal explicitly with the great, the vast, the overpowering, and the terrifying. In "The Tyger," for example, he deliberately intensifies the terror and sublimity normally associated with wild beasts, and he does so by creating a context of biblical and religious suggestiveness. Morton D. Paley, in a fine article entitled "Tyger of Wrath" (*PMLA* 81 [1966]: 540–51), explores in depth the effect of Blake's theme, imagery, and rhetoric in producing an unmistakable impression of awesome Hebrew sublimity, and there is no need to review his findings here. It is worth stressing, however, that unlike "The Lamb," which develops through a stanza of questions followed by a stanza of answers—as if the child were an infant catechist imitating the priest's role in her own religious education—"The Tyger" proceeds entirely through questions. And the questions, like those put to Job, defy the pat answers which the child has been forced to memorize in "The Lamb." Blake begins with the acknowledged fact that tigers are creatures of terror and mystery. (Dennis put them on his list of sublime ideas [1:361].) But he also makes us feel that the Being which could create the tiger is infinitely more terrible, mysterious, and sublime. Like Job, we are forced

to acknowledge a power which persuades us, despite our cate-
chisms, that the world contains mysteries which reason and mat-
ter cannot explain. As for Edward Young, sublimity for Blake is
itself a form of religious experience—jarring men not only out
of rational disbelief (as in the case of Young's Lorenzo) but out
of rational *belief* as well.

"The Tyger" works through indirection. While we concentrate
upon a vividly presented aspect of the material world, the poet's
manner of presentation encourages us to contemplate another
order of existence, one for which the material world provides
mere approximations. Blake does not describe directly the Power
which created the tiger; through his use of language and imagery,
he encourages us to pursue our own conceptions. The inevitable
obscurity of these conceptions becomes part of our experience of
the poem, while the poem itself never directly expresses obscurity.
The imagery of "The Tyger" may tease or puzzle our intellects,
but it is always vivid. We do not so often ask "What is Blake
saying?" as "What does he mean?" And Blake's intention is to
force us to experience the inadequacy of the rational processes
which conventionally direct our search for meaning. Like the
child in "The Lamb," we too often innocently accept the mean-
ing which aged men and wise guardians have taught us. "The
Tyger," then, attempts to free us from the mind-forged manacles
of reason, to make us experience a mystery and power which we
cannot easily explain. The indirect experience of mysterious
power is essential to Blake's idea of sublimity; he refuses to supply
us with direct answers.

But Blake did have answers. Some of them he presents in his
so-called prophetic books. The answers, however, are not those
of reason but of vision. In expressing his personal religious vision
—through a form of allegory addressed to faculties higher than
the "Corporeal Understanding"—Blake again turned to the sub-
lime. It was for him a vehicle for expressing ideas too vast or
complex for mere rational comprehension. It was a means of
embodying vision without explaining it away. "Fable or Allegory
[Blake insisted] are a totally distinct & inferior kind of Poetry.
Vision or Imagination is a Representation of what Eternally

Exists, Really & Unchangeably. Fable or Allegory is Form'd by the daughters of Memory. Imagination [or Vision] is surrounded by the daughters of Inspiration. . . . The Hebrew Bible & the Gospel of Jesus are not Allegory, but Eternal Vision or Imagination of All that Exists."[71] Vision of the kind Blake discovered in Milton and in the Bible became his model of the most sublime poetry. And yet, the sublimity of the "prophetic books" differs somewhat from the symbolic mode of "The Tyger." There Blake had approached the supernatural through indirection, making us experience the insufficiency of reason and nature alone in accounting for the awe inspired by a jungle animal. In the prophetic books we enter a land of supernatural vision, where the proportions are gigantic, the figures Michelangelesque, and the action a clash of elemental forces. The supernatural vastness, power, and machinery associated with the religious sublime, while adapted to Blake's own visionary system, are expressed directly. They create a world which is neither the material world of nature nor the spiritual otherworld of Christianity. It is a world of myth, in the sense that myth permits the direct expression of what the myth-maker understands to be true, without purporting to be a history of what actually happened.

The mythic vision of Blake's "prophetic books"—expressed in a verse-form and diction reminiscent of the Hebrew poets and accompanied by illustrations recalling the grandeur and power of Michelangelo—constitutes an inimitable, wholly personal, transformation of the religious sublime. He did not require the arguments of a theorist such as Alison to persuade him that his own emotions were an accurate guide to the sublime. "I know what is true by internal conviction," he said in conversation. "A doctrine is told me. My heart says it must be true."[72] His reliance upon the truth of his own feelings and vision, not upon a received set of ideas, parallels a similar confidence among poets of his age. As Wordsworth argued in the Preface (1800) to *Lyrical Ballads*, the poet's "own feelings are his stay and support, and if he sets them aside in one instance, he may be induced to repeat this act till his mind loses all confidence in itself and becomes utterly debilitated."[73] This faith in the validity of individual feeling, although it wavered drastically at times, underlies the development of a new kind of poetry in the Romantic era. For Wordsworth and Coleridge, the development of a new kind of poetry also involved the transformation of the religious sublime. Modern readers do not think of Wordsworth and Coleridge as religious poets, and in any conventional sense they are not. Yet they both saw the poet's office as a religious one. "Poetry," wrote Wordsworth, "is most just to its own divine origin when it administers the comforts and breathes the spirit of religion."[74] In an important passage from his "Essay, Supplementary to the Preface" (1815), he developed a series of parallels which explain his insistence on the fundamental relationship between poetry and religion:

> The concerns of religion refer to indefinite objects, and are too weighty for the mind to support them without relieving itself by resting a great part of the burthen upon words and symbols. The commerce between Man and his Maker cannot be carried on but by a process where much is represented in little, and the infinite Being accommodates himself to a finite capacity. In all this may be perceived the affinities between religion and poetry;—between religion—making up the deficiencies of reason by faith, and poetry—passionate for the instruction of reason; between religion—whose element is infinitude, and whose ultimate trust is the supreme of things, submitting herself to circumscription and reconciled to substitutions; and poetry—etherial [sic] and transcendant, yet incapable to sustain her existence without sensuous incarnation.[75]

Wordsworth here develops three main similarities between poetry and religion: 1) both rely upon suprarational conviction, 2) both deal with the realm of the transcendental and the infinite, and 3) both must use a system of "substitutions" to embody the transcendent and infinite in a manner accessible to the senses. But Wordsworth did not stop with an analysis of the similarities between poetry and religion. It was equally important to recognize their differences; thus he adds, "In this community of nature [between poetry and religion] may be perceived also the lurking incitements of kindred error;—so that we shall find that no poetry has been more subject to distortion, than that species the argument and scope of which is religious; and no lovers of the art have gone further astray than the pious and the devout."[76] Here Wordsworth clearly expresses his discontent with the explicitly religious poetry of the eighteenth century. The natural affinities between poetry and religion will not seduce him into writing poems on the Last Judgment or the Conflagration. The "substitutions" of religion, in other words, are not identical with the "substitutions" of poetry. But what then is the character of the substitutions by which a poet gives "sensuous incarnation" to his perception of the transcendental and the infinite? One important set of substitutions Wordsworth and Coleridge discovered in the sublime.

In discussing the attitudes of Wordsworth and of Coleridge toward the sublime, it is important to begin by dismissing one often-cited source of their ideas. Coleridge thought Burke's *Philosophical Enquiry* to be "a poor thing,"[77] and it seems likely that Wordsworth agreed. Their use of Burke's distinction between the sublime and the beautiful should not be construed as acceptance of his total system. Burke's mechanical explanations of how the mind and eye react in the perception of sublimity bear no relation to the ideas of Wordsworth and Coleridge, which center around their complex and un-Burkean theories of Imagination. James Scoggins, for example, argues that Wordsworth's comments on the sublime and on imagination "are almost always interchangeable, and the most important feature of all these comments is the religious associations of both concepts."[78] Similarly, in tracing Coleridge's attitudes toward sublimity, Clarence DeWitt Thorpe finds them most akin to "the English tradition of the religious sublime, exemplified in Dennis and James Usher, and to a less[er] extent in Addison."[79] Both scholars suggest that here the ideas of Wordsworth and of Coleridge are rooted in eighteenth-century attitudes toward the religious sublime. This view at first, however, may seem hard to reconcile with Wordsworth's rejection of explicitly religious verse.

The admiration of Wordsworth and Coleridge for the poetry

of the Hebrews offers one clue concerning their religious uses of sublimity. "Could you ever discover anything sublime, in our sense of the term," Coleridge once asked, "in the classic Greek literature? I never could. Sublimity is Hebrew by birth."[80] A passage from a letter he wrote to Josiah Wedgewood illuminates what Coleridge meant by Hebrew sublimity: "The more I think, the more I am convinced that the greatest of differences is produced when in the one case the feelings are worked upon thro' the Imagination and the Imagination thro' definite Forms (i.e. the Religion of Greece and Rome); and in the other cases where the Feelings are worked upon by Hopes and Fears purely individual, and the Imagination is kept barren in definite Forms and only in cooperation with the Understanding labours after an obscure and indefinite Vastness—this is Christianity."[81] Wordsworth makes an identical observation in the preface to his *Poems* (1815), where he argues that "the anthropomorphitism of the Pagan religion subjected the minds of the greatest poets in those countries too much to the bondage of definite form; from which the Hebrews were preserved by their abhorrence of idolatry."[82] For both Wordsworth and Coleridge, Hebrew poetry is more sublime than the poetry of Greece and Rome because it does not restrict the religious intuitions of its poets through the bondage of definite form. These religious intuitions were for Wordsworth and Coleridge the essence of the sublime. The problem of how best to express them in poetry, without writing explicitly religious verse, they solved in three ways.

The first and least successful way of giving "sensuous incarnation" to their religious intuitions was to describe them directly. In "Lines composed a few miles above Tintern Abbey" Wordsworth offers a literal description of a mind laboring after an obscure and indefinite vastness:

> And I have felt
> A presence that disturbs me with the joy
> Of elevated thoughts; a sense sublime
> Of something far more deeply interfused,
> Whose dwelling is the light of setting suns,
> And the round ocean and the living air,

> And the blue sky, and in the mind of man:
> A motion and a spirit, that impels
> All thinking things, all objects of all thought,
> And rolls through all things.[83]

"Does Mr. Wordsworth," asks Ezra Pound, "sometimes use words that express nothing in particular?"[84] The answer is that sometimes he does. Intentionally. In the passage from "Tintern Abbey" he is describing his own feelings, and neither his feelings nor the power which excites them are known precisely enough to receive "particular" expression. To give them a clarity and precision in art which they did not actually possess would be to falsify the experience. At any rate, Wordsworth composes in such a vein much less often than Pound's query might imply.

A second means of giving "sensuous incarnation" to their religious intuitions, and a better means of evoking strong feeling in the reader, was to describe the vast, the powerful, the terrible, and the grand in nature. Long eighteenth-century practice, stimulated by Thomson and developed in the landscape poem and Gothic novel, had associated the sublime scenes of nature with the experience of a religious awe in the beholder. This practice held certain advantages because the poet could be relatively certain of evoking strong feeling in the reader by describing the sources of his own. It also held certain disadvantages, for by the time Wordsworth and Coleridge were writing, such scenes had become rather hackneyed. By accuracy of observation and originality of imagery, however, a poet might still hope to give new excitement to old mountains. Further, unlike many of their predecessors, Wordsworth and Coleridge usually do not describe mountains in general: usually they describe their own reactions to particular mountain scenes, emphasizing the personalized transaction taking place between mind and nature. Their reactions to Mont Blanc, in fact, offer a fine illustration of the difference between neoclassical and Romantic ways of looking at sublimity in nature.

In "The Hymn before Sunrise in the Vale of Chamouni," Coleridge described an experience something like mystical ecstasy: his soul, as he gazed at Mont Blanc, left his body, and while the image of the mountain remained "still present to the bodily sense," "entranced in prayer/ I worshipped the Invisible alone."[85] With some irritation, Coleridge later wrote that Wordsworth condemned both that passage and the entire hymn "as a specimen of the Mock Sublime."[86] We can only conjecture why Wordsworth objected to the poem, and various conjectures are possible. Perhaps one reason for Wordsworth's disapproval can be discovered by considering his own reaction to Mont Blanc:

> That very day,
> From a bare ridge we also first beheld
> Unveiled the summit of Mont Blanc, and grieved
> To have a soulless image on the eye
> That had usurped upon a living thought
> That never more could be.[87]

In fantasy, in speculation, or beheld from a distance covered with clouds, the peak of Mont Blanc might suggest to the Imagination a remote, mysterious, indefinable transcendent Power. Viewed in person and with clarity, the peak no longer seemed to Wordsworth the material equivalent of the infinite. If Coleridge had seen Mont Blanc as it really is, Wordsworth may have felt, he would not have erred in confusing a "soulless image" with the revelation of a great and lofty but far from soulless Power. Despite Wordsworth's possible misgivings that Coleridge's imaginative religious experience of "the Invisible" had proceeded from an image inappropriately bounded and definite, both their reactions involve more than the experience of awe at the sight of mountain scenery. They emphasize a relationship between the poet seeing and the object seen, and their interest lies in the nature of the relationship. Few eighteenth-century enthusiasts for sublime scenery would have "grieved" at viewing the summit of Mont Blanc: shudders and gooseflesh are the standard response. Wordsworth's grieving, on the other hand, assures us that the individual consciousness, not nature alone, creates the sublime; and where guidebooks pointed out stretches of guaranteed sublime landscape, the mind of the poet might find only dreariness and grief.

Although what Ruskin called "mountain gloom" was an important part of Wordsworth's education in nature—witness the boat-stealing incident in *The Prelude*—he seldom in his poetry lingers over the merely great and powerful aspects of nature. Mountains, in effect, did not adequately convey the sense of a comprehensive "unity realized in and through the perception of multiplicity" which is, as James A. W. Heffernan has written, "fundamental to Wordsworth's use of the sublime."[88] Instead, he preferred to discover in nature's vastness and power images of permanence subsisting in the heart of flux:

> The immeasurable height
> Of woods decaying, never to be decayed,
> The stationary blasts of waterfalls. . . .[89]

These for Wordsworth are truly "types and symbols of Eternity"[90] because they convey in the processes of nature his own perception of unity in multiplicity. In fact, various images expressing the idea of a still point within a moving circle are Wordsworth's usual way of suggesting the notions of permanence in flux and of unity in multiplicity. The religious intuition of an abiding spirit or power in nature had for Wordsworth no necessary relationship with scenes conventionally considered to be sublime. Indeed, the most original and important aspect of his ideas regarding the sublime was his belief that the emotion of sublimity (to use Alison's term) did not depend upon the qualities of external nature but upon the transforming power of the Imagination and that, hence, even the most conventionally unsublime aspects of nature (a daisy, an odor, a girl singing) might be the stimulus for an experience which far transcended the sublimity of eighteenth-century "mountain gloom."

In one of his rare explicit discussions of the sublime and the pathetic, Wordsworth argued for a principle of subtlety and variety. The pathetic, he insisted, had mysterious as well as obvious sources, sources as "infinite as the combinations of circumstance and the constitutions of character."[91] Circumstance and character, matter and mind, provide in all their apparently infinite possibilities of combination a treasury of the pathetic which mocks the heavy-handed passion of the sentimentalists. What was true for the pathetic also held for the sublime. "And for the sublime," he continued, "—if we consider what are the cares that occupy the passing day, and how remote is the practice and the course of life from the sources of sublimity, in the soul of Man, can it be wondered that there is little existing preparation for a Poet charged with a new mission to extend its kingdom, and to augment and spread its enjoyments?"[92] We do not often think of Wordsworth as charged with a mission to extend the kingdom of the sublime, but that is how he thought of himself. He and Coleridge were, in Wordsworth's own phrase, "Prophets of Nature,"[93] and an essential part of their mission was to bring sublimity from the mountains to the valley, from the remote to the familiar—to augment and to spread its enjoyments by bringing it within the common experience of every reader. This intention helped to direct their poetic experiment in *Lyrical Ballads*, and it is a consistent concern in much of Wordsworth's verse. It represents the third way of giving "sensuous incarnation" to their religious intuitions.

A contemporary review of Coleridge's "Rime of the Ancient Mariner" suggests, unintentionally, the peculiar means which he and Wordsworth used to extend the kingdom of the sublime. Frankly puzzled by the poem, Robert Southey, writing for the *Critical Review*, wittily dismissed it as "a Dutch attempt at German sublimity."[94] The phrase *German sublimity* probably refers to the lofty religious sentiment which overflows in poems such as Klopstock's *Messiah*. The Dutch, however, were noted for the opposite of sublimity: a clear, precise, minute rendering of the surface of mundane life. Coleridge's poem, Southey implies, is paradoxical and therefore flawed. But Southey's perception of the apparent paradox has a significance which transcends his judgment of the poem. The plan of the *Lyrical Ballads* was indeed based on an apparent paradox: to reveal, by using clear, precise images drawn from common life, a grandeur abiding at the heart of things.

In *Lyrical Ballads* Wordsworth and Coleridge had attempted separate but related experiments. As everyone knows, Coleridge was to treat "persons and characters supernatural, or at least romantic," trying to make them seem natural enough to engage the "poetic faith" of the reader. Wordsworth, on the other hand, was to treat the familiar, trying to excite "a feeling analogous to the supernatural."[95] It is less commonly recognized, however, that underlying both experiments was the mutual intention to reveal an interpenetration of the natural and the supernatural, of the familiar and the strange. The ultimate aim of the volume, then, might be expressed in the words which Coleridge applied to Wordsworth's part in the experiment: to awaken men to the "wonders of the world before us; an inexhaustible treasure, but for which, in consequence of the film of familiarity and selfish solicitude we have eyes, yet see not, ears that hear not, and hearts that neither feel nor understand."[96] It is significant that Coleridge should describe the unawakened condition of mankind in the language which David used to condemn the gold and silver idols of the heathens: "They have mouths, but they speak not; eyes have they, but they see not; They have ears, but they hear not; neither is there any breath in their mouths" (Psalm 135: 16–17). The allusion suggests, indirectly but forcefully, that in their preoccupation with the world of matter, most men ignore the spiritual power which rolls through all things.

The process of awakening was to be twofold, identical with the twofold process of poetry which Coleridge describes in *Biographia Literaria*: "During the first year that Mr. Wordsworth and I were neighbours, our conversations turned frequently on the two cardinal points of poetry, the power of exciting the sympathy of the reader by a faithful adherence to the truth of nature, and the power of giving the interest of novelty by the modifying colors of imagination. The sudden charm, which accidents of light and shade, which moon-light or sun-set diffused over a known and familiar landscape, appeared to represent the practicability of combining both."[97] First, Coleridge argues, the poet must arouse feeling in the reader by causing him to discard the prejudices, artificial refinements, and false stimulations which prevent him from responding to nature and to his fellowman with uncorrupted sensibility. Thus the phrase "truth to nature" probably does not retain its eighteenth-century connotations of visual precision—although Wordsworth was to insist that the poet write as if he had his eye on the object—but instead implies the ability to recognize even in idiot boys, outcasts, and rustics a fundamental humanity which compels our sympathy. Second, by engaging the Imagination, the poet must cause the reader to modify or to transform the object of his perception. Just as moonlight reveals a new mystery, beauty, or grandeur in a familiar landscape, so the Imagination can discover undreamed of splendor in even the most common things. The world of man and of nature—not the realm of Revelation—offers Wordsworth an immense arena for pursuing his intimations of infinitude, and it is the transforming power of Imagination which allows him to extend the kingdom of the sublime into previously ignored or unperceived areas of poetic experience. As he insisted in the preface to *Lyrical Ballads*, "The feeling . . . gives importance to the action and the situation and not the action and situation to the feeling."[98]

Wordsworth's practical emphasis upon the role of the perceiving mind marks the ultimate transformation of the religious sublime. The poet's "sensuous incarnation" for his religious intuitions was no longer the images and symbols of Christian worship, as it had been in so many eighteenth-century poems of the religious sublime. Now the inexplicable clarities of a purely individual "spot of time" might convey a sense of the mind's mastery over external nature by virtue of its ability to endow the lifeless forms of memory or the inert materials of nature with the qualities of human feeling. Similarly, the ability of the mind to find intimations of an abiding spiritual power through its own recollections, as well as in the objects of nature, freed Wordsworth from adherence to a series of poetic props which Burke and others had classified as sublime. As he mused in the poem "Presentiments," to the man who has stripped the film of familiarity from his eyes nature offers a sense of being forever on the verge of new revelations:

> But who can fathom your intents,
> Number their signs or instruments?
> A rainbow, a sunbeam,

> A subtle smell that Spring unbinds,
> Dead pause abrupt of midnight winds,
> An echo, or a dream.[99]

By enlisting the modifying and creative powers of the Imagination in the perception of the most delicate or even commonplace aspects of nature, the poet in Wordsworth's view might inspire the same powerful emotions and elevated thought which eighteenth-century poets had sought in the pursuit of grandeur. To the poet who wrote that nature's "meanest flower" might touch him with thoughts too deep for tears, the still calm, instead of the storm, or an echo, rather than the Trump of Doom, create through their union with the perceiving mind a new and lasting poetry of the religious sublime.

This discussion of Romantic transformations of the religious sublime is not meant to be exhaustive. Byron, Keats, and Shelley all develop slightly different emphases in creating their own versions, but each can be understood as conforming to the general redirections of an "egotistical sublime." That phrase—which, of course, Keats used to describe the poetry of Wordsworth—provides a key to the basic shift implicit in most Romantic treatments of the sublime. The religious ideas which Dennis had recommended still remained a powerful source of poetic feeling but only when the traditional ideas and orthodox symbols had passed through the individual imagination, a process which inevitably transformed them. Macpherson's biblical ghosts, Smart's personal liturgy, Blake's invented myths, and Wordsworth's symbolic uses of the ordinary all represent new forms of the religious sublime, forms which correspond to changes in the principles of criticism and in the language of poetry. Change can be radical or slight; and some changes occur without apparent reason, either because the change is irrational or because the causes are hidden from us. But, while general explanations of changes in the nature of religious poetry must be approached in a spirit of speculation rather than of assertion, such explanations must be attempted if criticism is to transcend the simple perception of difference. This is the larger task immediately ahead.

Chapter Six

Literature and Religion:
A Speculative Conclusion

> Whatever is great, desirable, or tre-
> mendous, is comprised in the name of
> the Supreme Being. Omnipotence can-
> not be exalted; Infinity cannot be
> amplified; Perfection cannot be im-
> proved (Johnson, "Life of Waller").

To turn from the description of change to an analysis of its pos-
sible causes requires a willingness to answer large questions with
appropriately large generalizations, and in any operation so roomy
there is wide area for disagreement. Indeed, where definitive
proof would be a phantom of the designer's brain, the best pro-
cedure is to consider a limited range of representative evidence
and to speculate about its meaning. The tedium of reading any-
thing written entirely in the conditional or subjunctive will
necessitate the use of declarative statements in the following
pages, but the spirit of the inquiry is always tentative and hypo-
thetical. Nevertheless, the difficulty of establishing absolute
certainty should not deter us from considering the most funda-
mental issue underlying this study: the nature of the relationship
between literature and religion in eighteenth-century England.

If certainty in this matter is difficult, the difficulties in de-
ciding how to approach the question are equally imposing. A. R.
Humphreys's essay "Literature and Religion in Eighteenth-
Century England"[1] illustrates the hazards of attempting to inte-
grate studies of major trends in religion and of major literary
trends: often the effort becomes an exercise in parallelism yield-

ing insights as obvious and inadequate as they are bland. On the other hand, Donald Greene's discussion of the Augustinian tradition in eighteenth-century religious sensibility, although quite useful for an understanding of the age itself, fails to make convincing contact with the peculiarities of eighteenth-century literature.[2] The objection made by Vivian de Sola Pinto seems to me well taken:

> It is, doubtless, true that some, though by no means all the great English writers of this age believed in a type of Christianity that can be called "Augustinian," but the term is far too vague. Dante, Chaucer, Hooker, Donne, Newman, and Hopkins were all, I suppose, in different ways subscribers to "Augustinian" theology; but they can hardly be called writers of the same kind as Dryden, Swift, Pope, and Johnson, while to apply the same term to Rochester, Gay, Fielding, Thomson, Gibbon, and Hume is absurd. Moreover, Dryden, Swift, Pope, and Johnson are not primarily religious writers and to give them a theological label is misleading.[3]

Even when applied to poets of the religious sublime, the term *Augustinian* in many cases would be misleading. But that still misses the main question which needs to be asked. If, as William H. Halewood argues, Augustinian theology helps significantly to shape the poetry of Herbert, Marvell, Vaughan, and Milton,[4] why does eighteenth-century religious poetry (even granting that the writers share an "Augustinian" outlook) differ so markedly from that of the preceding century?

The most helpful studies of the relationship between religion and literature in the eighteenth century have not attempted to answer this question. They are generally either analyses of the religious thought of particular writers or investigations of how specific theological traditions affect the structure of essentially secular works.[5] Together these studies have provided strong confirmation of Alfred North Whitehead's view that the eighteenth century was an age of reason *based on faith*. Still, we are left at present knowing what we knew before: that religious literature in the eighteenth century is less passionate, less artful, and (to many readers) less interesting than that of the two periods which surround it. The explanation conventionally offered is that an age of reason constricts the expression of religious and poetic emotion. I would like to speculate about alternative causes.

RELIGION AND THE PRINTED WORD

The religious sublime, at least that aspect of it treated here, is a phenomenon primarily involving explicitly sacred writing. Perhaps the most disquieting observation which results from its study, however, is that for many poets spiritual experience does not seem to have been of primary importance. Interest in spiritual experience seems to have blended with a worldly literary impulse. This phenomenon of blending may not have been entirely deliberate, and a number of genuinely devout poets (Isaac Watts and Charles Wesley come immediately to mind) might challenge the observation. But even the apparently less devout could find themselves annoyed with the assertion of W. K. Wimsatt and Cleanth Brooks that the eighteenth century was an age "when in fact it was impossible for poetry and religion to come together without the dilution of one or the other."[6] The phrasing suggests, I think rightly, the operation of a historical force, as if individual writers were to some extent caught in an impersonal process which they could not entirely control or successfully oppose. The result, if not the cause, seems clear: secular literature was suffused with a pious religiosity, while explicitly sacred writing underwent a curious process of secularization.

The sermon reveals in miniature what happened to much eighteenth-century religious literature, nor should we forget that most eighteenth-century readers considered the sermon, like its cousin the essay, a recognized literary form. Johnson and Boswell could spend hours debating the prose styles of particular preachers with as much gusto as modern critics argue the virtues of their favorite poets. But the interest in sermons extended far beyond the learned circle of Dr. Johnson. The reason for such wide interest is not, apparently, because eighteenth-century congregations were necessarily less prone to sleeping in church than their modern successors. Here is James Downey's account of the reasons behind the popularity of the eighteenth-century sermon:

> The explanation of this seemingly insatiable demand for homiletic literature is to be found in an examination of the protean nature of the eighteenth-century sermon. Whereas the sermon today has a strictly religious character and is expected to do nothing more than provide a suitable concomitant to other aspects of public worship, two hundred years ago it had firm and conscious ties with secular society. Politics, education, philosophy, and literature all made demands upon, and in turn created demands for, sermons.[7]

Actually, the strong movement in American theology to make the church more immediately relevant to the needs of contemporary society may provide us with a means of understanding the particular kind of excitement offered by the eighteenth-century sermon. Religion is not necessarily moribund when it is not immediately involved with spiritual discovery.

The *Spectator*, Benjamin Franklin's Bible, reveals the same excitement offered by the de-etherealizing of religion which Downey finds characteristic of the eighteenth-century sermon. In fact, it is hardly a coincidence that one of the most popular features of the *Spectator* was Addison's Saturday "lay sermons." But in one sense the Saturday essays are simply an overt expression of the *Spectator*'s general tendency to blend homily with journalism, church with coffeehouse, divinity with diversion, Christianity with prudence. This blending, I would argue, represents a "dilution" of religion only if one accepts a rather exclusive definition of religious experience: Donne's Holy Sonnets, after all, represent one kind of religious literature which expresses one form of intensity. They are not necessarily the standard by which all other forms of religious experience are to be judged bogus, tepid, or second-rate. The modern composer John Cage's shrewd observation concerning contemporary life offers a perspective upon eighteenth-century literature when he notes that "boredom dropped when we dropped our interest in climaxes."[8] The curiously unclimactic quality of much eighteenth-century literature, including the sermon, is not necessarily a sign of weakness, and the same point could be made about its emphasis upon secular aspects of religious experience. Both, however, reflect a definite change of conception involving religion and literature, and the nature of this change and its causes are still widely misunderstood.

If the peculiar product which results from the eighteenth-century blend of secular and religious experience is rarely studied, we have not begun to ask how the process of mixture operates. The terms *blend* and *mixture* simply highlight the imprecision of our current understanding. What happens to the idea of the Fall, for example, when instead of understanding it directly as fact, or indirectly as myth or as allegory, eighteenth-century readers encounter it refracted and secularized in the worldly adventures of Robinson Crusoe? What happens to the idea of the marvellous, long associated with supernatural machinery, when Defoe boasts in his preface that *"the wonders of this man's life exceed all that . . . is to be found extant"*?[9] The importance of these questions is reflected by a split among modern critics of Defoe's novel: one group reading it as a study of economic man, another as a version of Puritan autobiography. The odd mixture of economics and religion which gives *Robinson Crusoe* its unique character is too often merely cited as evidence of its author's alleged hypocrisy, shallowness, and artistic confusion. We are rarely challenged to ask how the Addisonian mixture of secular and religious experience creates a work essentially different from *Pilgrim's Progress*, *Walden*, or *The Swiss Family Robinson*. Yet it is precisely this mixture which allies *Robinson Crusoe* with a whole class of eighteenth-century works.

The same basic issue can be approached profitably from a slightly more oblique perspective. Historians agree that religion in the eighteenth century loses much of the passionate intensity which characterizes the spiritual life of previous eras. One standard history of the English Church describes the period as one "of lethargy instead of activity, of worldliness instead of spirituality, of self-seeking instead of self-denial, of grossness instead of refinement."[10] The triumph of religious toleration forced the Anglican Church to intensify its attention to the worldly domain of politics and finance, where the survival of a strong national church (and, therefore, of religion itself in Swift's view) seemed truly at issue. Swift himself argued, as had others before him, that the failure of religion could often be traced directly to the ignorance and poverty of the clergy.[11] The *Guardian* seemed to share his concern. "How is it possible," Steele wondered, "for a Gentleman under the Income of fifty Pounds a Year, to be attentive to sublime things?" (No. 65) When not doing battle with the world and the flesh, where they often seemed content with a stalemate or compromise, numerous ecclesiastics took up the pen against the devils of free thought, whom they fought furiously. Thus, with the important exceptions of the Methodist and Evangelical movements, much of the vigor of eighteenth-century religious writing assumed the undeniably rationalistic form of polemics. "The enemies of the faith from all quarters were fairly grappled with and fairly vanquished by its defenders," write John H. Overton and Frederic Relton. "Never, perhaps, during the whole course of English Church history was the victory in such contests so obviously on the Christian side."[12] Such a climate does not sound friendly to Urania.

Few would wish to deny that the phenomenon called rationalism had much to do with the nature of eighteenth-century religious literature. (A writer in the *Gentleman's Magazine* could work out, with a wonderful show of reason, the exact floor plan of Noah's Ark.[13] Presumably he also believed that the question of how many angels could dance on the head of a pin was solvable by mathematics.) But medieval Christians also witnessed the victory of a rationalistic theology without therefore being prevented from composing a number of beautiful religious lyrics in Latin and in English. All I wish to contend is that rationalism alone is not responsible for the changes which characterize eighteenth-century religious literature and that, by itself, the phenomenon of rationalism cannot explain the particular kinds of poetry written during the century. Certainly the reactions against Puritan zeal account for some lowering of the temperature of religious literature. But the religious sublime, which appealed to readers of all persuasions, was designed in part to restore emotional intensity to literature *through* the use of religious ideas. In explaining the nature of eighteenth-century religious poetry, then, we must face apparent contradictions which cannot be resolved by the talisman of rationalism alone. Other explanations deserve to be explored.

One possible beginning is the work of Marshall McLuhan, whose investigations argue a point fundamental to literary analysis: that a close relationship exists between expression and the media of expression. "Societies," he maintains, "have always been shaped more by the nature of the media by which men communicate than by the content of the communication." [14] Here, as elsewhere, McLuhan is deliberately provocative. Yet, if his maxim is not universally true, it is true enough to deserve serious attention. Whether or not the technology of print "shaped" eighteenth-century society in general, it certainly influenced the form of such major works as *A Tale of a Tub*, the *Dunciad*, and *Tristram Shandy*, each of which plays with the idea that books are printed objects. They insist that literature, whatever it might have been in Homer's time, consists in the modern world of pieces of paper bound together and covered irregularly with black ink. As authors, Swift, Pope, and Sterne recognize the mysterious assumptions involved in reading books. They ask us to consider the puzzling fact that black ink on white paper can transmit thought or (what is stranger still) feeling from author to reader. The specific nature of their play with words does not concern us here. Their example does suggest, however, that the phenomenon of print seriously interested eighteenth-century writers, and it invites us to ask whether the medium of print might have had any effect upon the nature of eighteenth-century religious literature.

To take an extreme example, certain forms of sacred oratory seem almost incompatible with the printed word. Although they can be recorded in writing, they often appear cold, embarrassing, or tiresome on the printed page. Here, for instance, is part of a sermon by the great Methodist preacher George Whitefield:

Come, ye dead, Christless, unconverted sinners, come and see the place where they laid the body of the deceased Lazarus;

behold him laid out, bound hand and foot with grave-clothes, locked up and stinking in a dark cave, with a great stone placed on the top of it! View him again and again; go nearer to him; be not afraid; smell him, ah! how he stinks. Stop there now, pause awhile; and whilst thou art gazing upon the corpse of Lazarus, give me leave to tell thee with great plainness, but greater love, that this dead, bound, entombed, stinking carcase, is but a faint representation of thy poor soul in its natural state. . . . Perhaps thou hast lain in this state, not only four days, but many years, stinking in God's nostrils.[15]

This is not exactly the kind of reformed preaching Pope had in mind when he complained about the "soft Dean" who never mentioned Hell to ears polite. In fact, most cultured eighteenth-century readers would have responded to the printed sermon with deep discomfort. Whitefield's language represents an intrusion from another world: as in the *Dunciad*, a profoundly subversive form of speech emerges to threaten the literary conventions of polite society. "Me-thinks I see some of you affected at this part of my discourse," Whitefield continues, alerting us to the essentially oral and emotional character of his language. As Horton Davies explains, "Preaching is for Whitefield a reciprocal relationship between speaker and audience, a retroactivity, and he must respond to the impact he is making."[16] The fixed nature of print, then, necessarily alters the content of the communication: the distant, formal relationship between author and reader—a formality which Young, Richardson, and Sterne desperately attempt to shatter with their experiments in language, style, and form—impedes the retroactivity of Whitefield's sermon, transforming religious passion into literary bathos. The relatively uneducated character of Whitefield's audiences does not invalidate the basic contrast here between different media. Whereas the sweet rationalism of a sermon by Tillotson employs a language appropriate to the medium of print, evangelical fervor, even in a highly literate population, is always best conveyed through the spoken word.

The hymn offers another illustration of how the medium of print can eviscerate religious passion. Despite its simple power, the hymn often looks lifeless and clumsy on the printed page. Its spirit is freed only when the printed words, liberated by the emotional power of music, find their intended expression in song. It is easy to understand why one eighteenth-century reviewer, judging by criteria of polite literature developed for the medium of print, ridiculed Charles Wesley's hymns as "spiritual Billingsgate." Wesley, of course, addressed his hymns to an audience of unsophisticated literary taste. But, more importantly, he did not intend hymnody to be a form of written composition. For Wesley, print is only the temporary distillate of song. It is as if, for the necessary purposes of storage, a highly volatile gas were bottled as a liquid.

This much, because it deals with extreme instances, perhaps will be granted without major protest. I should like to speculate further, however, that print not only fails to represent adequately certain essentially oral forms of religious expression but also exerts a powerful, if indirect, influence over all literary treatments of religion in the eighteenth century. The immediate objection to this claim is that print offered the same difficulties and advantages to Donne as to Dryden and cannot therefore be isolated as a possible cause of the change in religious literature. Yet several points could be made in response. As McLuhan and others have shown, the sudden expansion of printing during the late seventeenth and early eighteenth centuries, reflected in the proliferation of journals, periodicals, pamphlets, broadsides, rejoinders, and pirated editions, created a situation without precedent. (The Battle of the Books, as a literary subject, almost requires the image of presses turning out vast squadrons of new works.) The trickle of books published during Donne's lifetime had swollen, in Pope's view, to a flood, and he carefully locates the *Dunciad* in the cluttered landscape of modern times "when (after providence had permitted the Invention of Printing as a scourge for the Sins of the learned) Paper also became so cheap, and printers so numerous that a deluge of authors cover'd the land."[17] Quantitative change, when it is great enough, often produces qualitative change, and between the reigns of Elizabeth and Anne, English writers exposed to a frighteningly vast quantity of new books experienced a radically altered consciousness of print. Further, print was closely associated in the eighteenth century with a theory of language fundamentally different from that of earlier ages. The sonorous language of much Renaissance poetry was written for the ear; the language of Pope and of Johnson, although still musical, was written primarily for the eye. Thus Pope carefully indexed his prized sound-sense patterns at the end of his Homer in order that the eye might appreciate what the ear had missed. The same implication follows from his "versifications" of Donne's satires: although Pope's version gains considerably in its visual aspects, he fails completely—in fact, does not try—to express Donne's sense of dramatic speech. These instances can serve only as illustrations, not proof, of McLuhan's view that the technology of print did indeed alter literary consciousness. They also call to mind a much maligned judgment of Matthew Arnold's which contains at least a germ of truth: that the so-called Age of Reason was also, inevitably, an age of prose.

Print is particularly suited to argument (and argument to prose) because the printed page offers the occasion, the distance, and the leisure required for detailed logical analysis. The appreciation of reasoned argument implies a slow, sequential, dispassionate process which oral delivery often prevents, and the lengthy controversies over the orthodoxy of Pope's *Essay on Man*, despite his claim that he could argue more concisely in poetry than in prose, suggest that prose is superior to verse in providing logical clarity. Significantly, Warburton's vindications of the *Essay*, for which Pope was inordinately grateful, were not made in verse. A similar point is made by Jean Le Clerc, who praised Archbishop Tillotson's sermons precisely because they were so well suited to logical analysis in their printed form. "Every Body knows," he wrote, "that Sermons are commonly fill'd with a flashy Rhetoric, which takes much better from the Pulpit than the Press; but Archbishop Tillotson's are for the most part exact Dissertations, which will bear being examin'd by the strictest Reasoners."[18] Prose and print, he implies, are the proper vehicles for argumentation: leisurely examination of Tillotson's logic will assure the "strictest Reasoners" that his sermons are sound at the core. Also implied is Le Clerc's opinion that the surest means of exposing religious charlatans is to submit their flashy rhetoric to the relentless hardening of print.

Although many Englishmen, Edward Young among them, shared the view that printed prose is the proper vehicle for argumentation, it is hard to know how many would have accepted Dryden's opinion that print not only expresses but in fact creates argument. The notion occurs in his attack upon the Dissenters' use of the Bible. The publication of English versions of the Bible, he implies, is a specific cause of controversy:

> *The Book thus put in every vulgar hand,*
> *Which each presum'd he best cou'd understand,*
> *The* Common Rule *was made the* common Prey;
> *And at the mercy of the Rabble lay.*
> *The tender Page with horney Fists was gaul'd;*
> *And he was gifted most that loudest baul'd:*
> *The Spirit gave the* Doctoral Degree:
> *And every member of a* Company
> *Was of his Trade, and of the Bible free.*[19]

Dryden's rhetoric here is not very admirable, but it is his logic which concerns us now. The new availability of the Bible, he says, permitted large numbers of common people, who had no training in divinity, to interpret its meaning for themselves. Thus the technology of print, by multiplying copies of scripture, indirectly created the "Thousand daily Sects" which troubled orthodox churchmen of the Restoration.

Swift, who shared Dryden's religious traditionalism although not his conversion to Rome, also shared his belief that the press itself was partly responsible for the creation of religious dissent. (The identical claim reappears today applied to political dissent.) With sacred polemics a form of Christian duty and with the itch for preferment encouraging superfluous conflict, at least among clerics lacking noble birth or noble patrons, Swift understandably longed for a period of enlightened censorship:

It cannot easily be answered to God or Man, why a Law is not made for limiting the Press; at least so far as to prevent the

publishing of such pernicious Books, as under Pretense of
Free-Thinking, endeavour to overthrow those Tenets in Re-
ligion, which have been held inviolable almost in all Ages by
every Sect that pretends to be Christian; and cannot therefore
with any Colour of Reason be called *Points in Controversy*, or
Matters of Speculation, as some would pretend. The Doctrine
of the *Trinity*, the *Divinity of Christ*, the *Immortality of the
Soul*, and even the Truth of all Revelation are daily exploded,
and denied in Books openly printed.[20]

Swift does not criticize individual Free-Thinkers in this passage
but the books themselves, almost as independent objects, and he
clearly attributes an active role to the press. Print is not, in
Swift's eyes, merely a vehicle; nor is it merely a convenient
synecdoche for the ideas which books convey. Instead, he thinks
of it as an active, potentially subversive force which encourages
and even creates religious controversy. Both he and Dryden agree
on one fundamental point: the publication of books is directly
related to the creation of arguments about religion.

No period of history has been free from religious arguments,
and inevitably some of the controversy will take the form of
books. But the late seventeenth and early eighteenth centuries
saw books published in a quantity never witnessed before. The
Grub Street subculture produced in Swift's Hack a man who was
little more than a pen, "worn to the Pith in the Service of the
State, in *Pro's* and *Con's* upon *Popish Plots*, and *Meal-Tubs*,
and *Exclusion Bills*, and *Passive Obedience*, and *Addresses of
Lives and Fortunes*; and *Prerogative*, and *Property*, and *Liberty
of Conscience*, and *Letters to a Friend*." His life has been noth-
ing but books and controversy: "Fourscore and eleven Pam-
phlets have I written under three Reigns, and for the Service of
six and thirty Factions."[21] He is, in the most horribly surreal
sense of the phrase, a mere man-of-letters, the most lasting contri-
bution of the eighteenth century to modern culture. To imagine a
small army of such creatures all churning out fat pamphlets on re-
ligion is to allow that it was perhaps not reason but the "print
explosion" (to use McLuhan's phrase) which helped to alter
the nature of religious writing. Reason and prose together can,

in the presence of genius, produce Richard Hooker's *Ecclesiastical Polity*. Reason, prose, and the print explosion, in the absence of genius, produce Parson Adams on the road to London with his saddlebag full of sermons.

In a roundabout way, we have discussed the possibility that the nature of eighteenth-century religious literature—its controversial, argumentative, prosaical qualities—may be related to the massive changes in the quantity of printed matter: to the creation, in short, of the popular press. No other age has had to adjust to the same phenomenon. Its impact is comparable only to that created upon contemporary literature by the advent of radio, television, and the cinema. But surely the general mixture of secular and religious experience in the eighteenth century, even when combined with an enormous increase in the number of books, cannot wholly account for the changes in religious literature. We still have not considered the mass of sacred poetry, most of which is neither argumentative nor essentially oral in nature, and which therefore is not necessarily subject to the same changes (or, at least, to the same degree of change) which affected the sermon, the essay, and even the novel. To explore the possible causes of change in sacred poetry, then, will require introducing an additional line of argument, one involving a particular theory of poetic language which underlies much eighteenth-century verse. For such a purpose, it will be useful to consider Samuel Johnson's objections to religious poetry, for his objections arise directly from his understanding that a fundamental conflict exists between the language of neoclassical poetry and the nature of religious ideas.

WORDS AND THINGS: JOHNSON AND THE LANGUAGE OF POETRY

Johnson distinguished among various kinds of religious verse: pious poetry, devotional poetry, divine poetry, as well as different genres adapted to religious subjects. There would certainly be merit in lingering over these distinctions, for Johnson's evaluations of religious poetry vary with the kind of verse considered. But while such distinctions are important for a full knowledge of Johnson's criticism, our main concern is with the grounds for his generally consistent objection to most religious poetry. These objections are perhaps best introduced and illustrated in his well-known "Life of Cowley."

Johnson's "Life of Cowley" is read today mainly for the famous discussion of "metaphysical" poetry, but it offers an equally fine treatment of Cowley's unfinished biblical poem, the *Davideis*. As one might suspect, Johnson was not pleased with Cowley's attempt to improve upon scripture: "Sacred History has been always read with submissive reverence, and an imagination over-awed and controlled. We have been accustomed to acquiesce in the nakedness and simplicity of the authentick narrative, and to repose on its veracity with such humble confidence as suppresses curiosity. We go with the historian as he goes, and stop with him when he stops. All amplification is frivolous and vain: all addition to that which is already sufficient for the purposes of religion seems not only useless, but in some degree profane."[22] The passage offers two intertwined objections to Cowley's poem, one moral, the other pragmatic. The moral argument stresses simply the fact of sacrilege: religious poetry, paradoxically, profanes the mystery which it serves, like the Old Testament figure who foolishly touched the ark of Jehovah. Yet Johnson seldom employs this argument alone. Usually he reserves it as a weapon to be hurled only in moments of Olympian exasperation. "With these trifling fictions," he thunders at the pastoralisms and mythology of "Lycidas," "are mingled the most awful and sacred truths, such as ought never to be polluted with such irreverent combinations" (1:65). What such moments reveal, through language as intemperate as that of Stephen Gosson or Jeremy Collier, is not the penetration of Johnson's critical insight but the strength of his religious convictions; and, unfortunately, to many modern readers judgments based solely upon Johnsonian piety often seem narrow-minded and irrelevant. Generally, however, Johnson does not merely denounce the profaneness of religious poetry. He instead insinuates a moral judgment through reliance upon pragmatic considerations which he believed account for the consistent failure of religious verse.

Johnson's pragmatic objections to religious poetry are based ultimately on his idea of poetry itself. Poetry in its very nature, he believed, was wholly unsuited to the treatment of religious subjects. Thus in his "Life of Denham" he dismissed that poet's version of the Psalms with magnificent disdain. "In this attempt he has failed," Johnson pronounced, "but in sacred poetry who has succeeded?" (1:75) This view has been the despair of at least one recent admirer of Johnson who finds Johnson's rhetorical question readily answerable and hence attempts to excuse its inadequacy: "Had Johnson enjoyed a cultural and religious climate more open to the sacramental view of the universe, as did Dante, Donne, Hopkins, and Eliot; had his personal religious attitude held more familiarity and less anxiety; and had he thought of religious poetry—as he surely proportionately did of other kinds—as revealing human experience of the divine rather than idealizing it; his judgment would surely have been other than it was."[23] I am not sure that, even had those conditions been fulfilled, Johnson would have altered his views of religious poetry, for to alter his judgment would have necessarily required changing his entire understanding of how poetic language affects the mind. It would also have meant denying insights which are particularly valid within the context of eighteenth-century poetic practice.

Johnson held firmly to his view of the moral efficacy of poetry because he believed that the poet's special power consisted in his ability to create a link between fiction and reality. "Poetry," he wrote, "is the art of uniting pleasure with truth, by calling imagination to the help of reason" (1:170). It is the particular pleasure inspired by imaginative perception which distinguishes poetry from philosophy or science, where truth is equally the object of contemplation, and in the *Dictionary* Johnson was helpfully specific in defining imagination as "the power of forming ideal pictures." The idealizing function of poetry, as John D. Boyd has pointed out, thus accounts for part of Johnson's objection to religious verse. Poetry pleases by exhibiting "an idea more grateful to the mind than things themselves afford," he insisted, while religion, by contrast, "must be shewn as it is; suppression and addition equally corrupt it" (1:292). But the process

of idealization does not explain the main objection which John-
son raised concerning religious verse. The idealizing process it-
self depends upon the pictorial quality of imaginative perception,
and it was the imagination's necessary creation of visual pictures
or images which in Johnson's view especially hampered religious
poets. Because poetry pleases essentially through its descriptive
powers—through its ability to convey "pictures to the mind"
$(1:51)^{24}$—the poet requires a subject capable of graphic repre-
sentation and illustration. Thus the bliss of Heaven lies outside
the sphere of poetic representation, Johnson argued, because
"poetical pleasure must be such as human imagination can at
least conceive" (1:182). The thought of the Last Day, similarly,
makes every reader "*more than poetical* by spreading over his
mind a general obscurity of sacred horror, that oppresses dis-
tinction and disdains expression" (3:393–94, italics mine). In
its resistance to the visualizing powers of the imagination, then,
religion effectively thwarts the language of poetry. The printed
word fails to evoke a pictorial image in the mind.

In defining *word* in the *Dictionary*, Johnson cited an illustra-
tion from the sermons of Robert South, the learned Restoration
churchman, which applies directly to his own theory of poetic
language. "As conceptions are the images of things to the mind
within itself," he quotes South as writing, "so are *words* or names
the marks of those conceptions to the minds of them we con-
verse with." Words, in representing conceptions, thus also
represent the "images of things" which are identical with our
ideas. Although the link between words and things is arbitrary—
for custom alone dictates that the letters s-u-n should signify a
particular natural object—many eighteenth-century readers be-
lieved that a direct and automatic connection existed in the mind
between the perception of the letters and the imaginative
beholding of the thing signified. This theory of language was con-
veniently summarized in 1792 by a writer for the *Monthly Maga-
zine*: "when, therefore, we use words," he explains, "we revive in
the minds of those that understand our language, the pictures of
the objects of which we speak." This, he concludes, is "the sum-
mit" of the poet's art.[25] Whether this theory is in fact true is

less important than the fact many thought it true: like the theory of bodily humours or the psychology of fancy and judgment, it inevitably affected the literary work of those who believed it. Probably it is even reflected in the typography of eighteenth-century poems. In folio or quarto volumes, the individual words stand out in bold relief, defined against the expanse of white paper which surrounds them, suggesting a process of reading which emphasized the visual aspects of language. While modern editions of Pope, for example, jam hundreds of tiny words onto a single page, the original eighteenth-century texts tend to isolate not only individual lines but also individual words within the lines. The modern version invites us to skim rapidly over the verses, getting the sense or meaning of the passage; the eighteenth-century page achieves an almost tactile reality, urging us to linger over the images evoked by the printed characters. To readers accustomed to such a process of reading, which directly linked the word on the page with an image in the reader's mind, the language of religious poetry might well thwart their normal modes of perception. Like a television picture suddenly scrambled by interference, the words would yield only an incomprehensible blur.

Such an explanation may help to account for Johnson's pragmatic objections to religious verse. Poetry of personal devotion, the heart's cry to God, he rejected out of hand: "Man admitted to implore the mercy of his Creator and plead the merits of his Redeemer," he declared, "is already in a higher state than poetry can confer" (1:291). But most other forms of religious poetry were equally flawed for practical reasons. Religion, in Johnson's view, was a topic which yielded relatively few images. He thought of it, Jean Hagstrum observes, as "colorless, general, austere, and inscrutable."[26] It requires the commitment of faith, not the experience of imaginative pleasure. The words of the religious poet thus could be classified with the most hollow of eighteenth-century vacancies: mere signs unattached to things. As an account of all religious language, of course, Johnson's position is easily dismantled. But it is particularly relevant to the work of eighteenth-century poets in illuminating the difficulties they labored to overcome. Before we examine its relationship to the changes in religious poetry, however, it is necessary to confront what seems at first a glaring inconsistency in Johnson's criticism: his contention that *Paradise Lost* is the greatest poem written in English.

In discussing Johnson's views on *Paradise Lost*, I should like to advance a speculation which his remarks partly support and which helps to explain the particular qualities of eighteenth-century religious verse. The study of the religious sublime supports the view that religious poetry is not simply distinguished from other poems by its subject but comprises a special subclass of poetry which requires adherence to informal "laws" of its own. And the fundamental law seems to be that religious poetry has the best chance to succeed if it is either personal or dramatic; its failure most often accompanies use of an impersonal or descriptive approach. Some would reply that, as a special subclass of poetry, religious verse establishes its own standards of success or failure which are not necessarily those of other forms, and such an argument is valid for those who read or write religious poetry for the exclusive purposes of devotion. But most eighteenth-century religious poets, especially poets of the religious sublime, intended their works to succeed by the standards applied to other poems, and it seems fair to ask whether they do indeed possess the power to please by virtue of qualities which are not strictly devotional.

The main advantage of personal religious poetry is that passion and apparent conviction in the poet, not theological doctrine, provide a source of pleasure shared by wide classes of readers, most of whom today would affirm Wordsworth's conviction that the "appropriate business of poetry . . . is to treat of things not as they are, but as they *appear*; not as they exist in themselves, but as they *seem* to exist to the *senses* and to the *passions*."[27] This is one main strength of seventeenth-century religious poetry. In the great majority of seventeenth-century religious lyrics, Helen Gardner writes, "the centre is man, shown in prayer, or meditation, or wrestling with temptation."[28] We read Herbert's "The Collar" not for theological illumination but for the vivid, personal rendering of a human dilemma: the relationship of the individual will to God. Our attention is drawn to the drama of human emotion, and the final victory of the divine will is shown through its effects upon the speaker:

> But as I rav'd and grew more fierce and wilde
>   At every word,
> Me thoughts I heard one calling, Child!
>   And I reply'd, My Lord.[29]

Certainly it is one of the deficiencies of eighteenth-century religious poetry that few poems adequately explore the personal aspects of religious experience, except perhaps through the generalized language of the hymn, which subsumes individual religious emotion to the voice of the entire congregation. The shades of feeling too subtle or too personal for the hymn, emotions which Johnson said are "to be felt rather than expressed" (1:292), remain outside the range of eighteenth-century religious poetry. Only perhaps in Smart's *Jubilate Agno* does the voice of personal religious experience find expression in poetry of power and originality. Significantly, the *Jubilate* was unknown in its own time, and it draws much of its uniqueness from a theory of language which few of Smart's contemporaries were prepared to accept or even to understand.

Johnson had little use for public poetry which expressed private and personal religious feeling. His interest in learning the peculiar angle of genius in individual poets did not extend to an appreciation of their poetical devotion. One mark of his extraordinary respect for *Paradise Lost*, however, was his willingness to exempt from censure—on the grounds that we gladly learn whatever we can about truly great poets—Milton's personal digressions at the beginning of the third, seventh, and ninth Books. "Perhaps no passages," he wrote, "are more frequently or more attentively read than those extrinsick paragraphs; and, since the end of poetry is pleasure, that cannot be unpoetical with which all are pleased" (1:175). The judgment illustrates the flexibility of Johnson's pragmatic approach. In the experience of the common reader, Johnson's ultimate arbiter of poetic pleasure, he finds a reaction which implicitly challenges his general objections to devotional poetry. Much in the digressions, of course, is personal without being explicitly devotional; but the sublime prayer which begins Book Three ("Hail holy Light") certainly combines devotion with personal revelation in a way Johnson might be expected to disapprove, as do parts of the other passages. His willingness to praise them is virtually a paradigm of his general reading of Milton's poem. Without surrendering his basic objections to religious poetry, he undertook a process of careful discrimination in criticizing *Paradise Lost* in order to explain how Milton, facing an apparently impossible task, managed to transform normally "unpoetical" materials into poetry of unparalleled sublimity.

One explanation of Johnson's praise involves Milton's use of a dramatic mode. Although the form of the poem is not dramatic but narrative, Milton had originally considered treating the story of man's Fall as a formal drama, and he skillfully varied his narrative in *Paradise Lost* with extensive passages of dialogue. Longinus had praised the *Iliad* above the *Odyssey* because its greater reliance upon dramatic presentation permitted greater opportunity for the vividness and passion which contribute to the sublime (sect. 9). But Johnson's approval of the dramatic qualities of *Paradise Lost* emphasizes rather the Aristotelian virtues of design which drama shares with even those narratives least characterized by dramatic techniques. Thus, although Johnson praised Milton's abilities to express through action the motives of both human and supernatural characters, he reserved stronger commendation for the intricacy and coherence of the plot: "To the compleatness or *integrity* of the design nothing can be objected; it has distinctly and clearly what Aristotle requires, a beginning, a middle, and an end. [*Samson Agonistes*, although dramatic in form, had failed in Johnson's view for its want of a middle.] There is perhaps no poem of the same length from which so little can be taken without apparent mutilation" (1:175). Whereas he illustrated, to the chagrin of one admirer of Thomson, that *The Seasons* lost little if one read aloud only every other line, Milton's careful attention to structure, even in a poem which Johnson believed no man ever wished longer, made any subtraction of parts a genuine source of deficiency. This judgment of *Paradise Lost* is not simply a curiosity reflecting Johnson's classical regard for design. It can also remind us that structural precision is a quality generally absent from most long poems (and most long religious poems) of the eighteenth century. Edward Young's "bursts of sublimity" in the *Night-Thoughts* are, like the sublimity of many other religious poems, almost necessarily the consequence of a poetic which locates drama in the shifts in intensity manipulated within a loosely connected descriptive verse, not within the logical sequences of an Aristotelian probable action.

Since I have maintained that dramatic as well as personal poetry is most successful for treating religious subjects, I should like to discuss one further aspect of dramatic presentation which seems to have been ignored by eighteenth-century religious poets. Probably the most important advantage of dramatic presentation, in addition to its opportunity for Longinian vividness and passion, is its almost inherent necessity of conflict. The opposition in Herbert's "The Collar" between man's will and God's creates, even in a poem utilizing a single speaker, a drama of conflicting demands. A need for resolution grows directly from the clash of opposites, so that many seventeenth-century religious works—as Stanley Fish has argued concerning *Paradise Lost*[30]—establish a pattern of development which involves the reader directly in making the choices which are an almost unavoidable response to conflict. The poetry of the religious sublime, on the other hand, often lacks any pattern of conflict. The reader observes, perhaps feels a sense of excitement at what he sees, but the poem rarely aspires to do more than compel awed attention. It may be, in fact, that the sublime poem, despite its apparent lack of overt didacticism, is really a variant of the Augustan didactic poem: instead of being asked to regard a particular intellectual proposition, as in *An Essay on Criticism*, the reader is simply asked to regard a nonintellectual proposition which takes the form of a description. Regardless of whether the poem shows him a sublime landscape fading away into an impression of eternity or an awesome scene of the Last Day, the reader is not involved in the choices and in the drama of choice essential to the success of religious verse.

The failure of impersonal and descriptive religious poetry to please many readers over long periods of time seems due to the poet's necessity of overcoming major difficulties which seem peculiar to religious subjects. The sententious impersonality of *An Essay on Man* (and even his friends were unable to detect Pope's authorship when the individual epistles first appeared anonymously) implies a standard of exact truth and common consent which is not likely to extend beyond the limits of a particular period. Johnson believed that the poet "who has the happy power of arguing in verse will not lose it [simply] because his subject is sacred" (1:291), but the ability to argue does not necessarily imply that readers other than the poet's contemporaries will accept the reasoning. Young's vast tracts of religious argument in the *Night-Thoughts* are, to modern readers, a wasteland of intolerable bleakness. But even when impersonality avoids the perils of the didactic mode it still remains a serious obstacle to the enjoyment of religious poetry. The divine abstractions versified by the Seatonian poets illustrate the soundness of Johnson's belief that, where human actions and manners are absent, the reader "finds no transaction in which he can be engaged, beholds no condition in which he can by any effort of imagination place himself; he has, therefore, little natural curiosity or sympathy" (1:181). The Thomsonesque poem of natural description offers an exception to this generalization which I will discuss later. At the moment, however, it is worth observing that Johnson's statement, although he intended it to explain some of the defects of *Paradise Lost*, applies particularly to the host of explicitly religious eighteenth-century poets who resemble the Seatonians. For many, the religious sublime became synonymous with descriptions of the supernatural. And without the personal voice of the poet to guide us (as Virgil guided Dante) through scenes of awesome or hellish grandeur, even the passion evoked by sublimity can have the unpleasant aftereffect of those emotions which we feel in the presence of cheaply sentimental or blatantly sensationalistic contrivances. The sublimity of Klopstock's *Messiah* is achieved at some cost to the stern dignity of his subject. Although an impersonal descriptive poetry, divorced from a context of human emotion and personal perception, is likely to fail whatever its subject, it is mainly the choice of a religious subject which could lure a poet so far away from what Johnson called "the real state of sublunary nature." Even *Paradise Lost*, in Johnson's view, suffered from its lack of human actors, although he admitted that Milton had skillfully compensated for this deficiency through his characterizations of the various supernatural beings. At one point he remarked that because all mankind is implicated in Adam's Fall the subject of Milton's poem is therefore "universally and perpetually interesting" (1:174). Later, however, he appeared to reverse himself by declaring that the very familiarity of the subject undercuts its poetic value: "what we knew before we cannot learn; what is not unexpected, cannot surprise" (1:182). The charge that *Paradise Lost* conveys neither the pleasure of novelty nor the usefulness of instruction, especially when added to Johnson's usual moral and pragmatic objections to religious poetry, ought to have dictated a judgment of strong censure. Yet Johnson qualified his objection to Milton's subject. In a passage crucial to an understanding of his attitude toward *Paradise Lost*, he expressed his qualification through a discussion of Milton's descriptive imagery, a subject which returns us to Johnson's theory of poetic language.

The passage discussing Milton's imagery reveals, I think, a certain amount of straining on Johnson's part which seems to result from his desire to recognize the source of Milton's success without simultaneously relinquishing his objections to the language of most religious poetry:

> Pleasure and terrour are indeed the genuine sources of poetry; but poetical pleasure must be such as human imagination can at least conceive, and poetical terrour such as human strength and fortitude may combat. The good and evil of Eternity are too ponderous for the wings of wit; the mind sinks under them in passive helplessness, content with calm belief and humble adoration.

Known truths however may take a different appearance, and be conveyed to the mind by a new train of intermediate images. This Milton has undertaken, and performed with pregnancy and vigour of mind peculiar to himself. Whoever considers the few radical positions which the Scriptures afforded him will wonder by what energetick operations he expanded them to such extent and ramified them to so much variety, restrained as he was by religious reverence from licentiousness of fiction (1:182–83).

The passage deserves to be quoted fully because the first paragraph repeats Johnson's view that religious subjects are too mighty and unimaginable for poetic treatment, while the second paragraph explains the grounds of Milton's success. The discovery of "a new train of intermediate images" both satisfies the requirement of novelty and avoids the failure which in Johnson's view necessarily accompanies the immediate and direct description of rel'gious truth. Whereas Cowley in the *Davideis* merely appropriated his plot from scriptural history, Milton had demonstrated the primary poetic talent of invention by creating a fully coherent and elaborately developed dramatic action from the "few radical positions" provided in the Bible. But the novelty of his action could please only if Milton was also able to engage the imaginations of his readers, and in this, Johnson believed, he succeeded equally well. The description of the War in Heaven struck him as perhaps the major failure in Milton's attempt to clothe the pictureless realm of religious truth in concrete imagery, but this one major lapse simply emphasized the consistent brilliance of the rest. "Whatever be his subject," Johnson concluded, "he never fails to fill the imagination" (1:178). In giving pictorial expression to the abstract and familiar truths of religion, Milton had triumphed where Johnson believed no poet before him had found a way.

Johnson's generous praise of Milton's achievement in poetry, even though he despised his politics, contains nevertheless a note of caution in its emphasis upon the uniqueness of his genius. Usually in the *Lives*, Johnson attempts to discover the peculiar mental powers and biographical accidents which create the characteristic individuality of particular poets. In arguing that Milton's pregnancy and vigor of mind are "peculiar to himself," however, Johnson also tacitly warned lesser poets concerning the dangers of imitation. "He seems to have been well acquainted with his own genius," Johnson repeats, "and to know what it was that Nature had bestowed upon him more bountifully than upon others" (1:177). If Milton's imitators understood their own powers as well as Milton knew his, Johnson may be implying, they would cease imitating a poet whom they could not equal. The powers which Milton possessed by nature, which he subsequently developed and controlled through practice, might in fact prove dangerous in imitators without his force of mind; and the man who had seen both Smart and William Collins collapse in madness, who himself experienced fearful premonitions of insanity, and who warned in *Rasselas* against the dangerous prevalence of imagination, might indeed feel wary about encouraging more of his contemporaries to follow Milton into the endlessly wide regions of possibility. "He had accustomed his imagination to *unrestrained indulgence*," Johnson said of Milton, in language which ordinarily might have implied extremest censure, "and his conceptions therefore were extensive. The characteristick quality of his poem is sublimity" (1:177, italics mine). Although the last sentence simply repeats a formula of criticism almost a century old, in the context of Johnson's thought it seems hard won and meaningful. For Johnson, Milton was sublime in spite of, not because of, his religious subject, and that difference transforms a literary cliché into an insight of considerable value.

UT PICTURA POESIS: IMAGINARY SISTERS

The flexibility which Johnson achieves by stressing his pragmatic rather than moral objections to religious poetry, while admirable, is achieved within a rather narrow range. One of the main limitations of his theory of poetic language, for example, is that its emphasis upon the pictorial aspects of poetry inevitably slights other possibilities of poetic expression. Thus his criticism of the *Davideis* seems curiously blind to the merits of Cowley's un-Johnsonian uses of language. "Cowley," he objects, "gives inferences instead of images, and shews not what may be supposed to have been seen, but what thoughts the sight might have suggested" (1:51). What Johnson criticizes is a theory of poetic language which might be called "impressionistic" rather than "pictorial," and the difference can serve to remind us that Johnson tends to ignore or to censure all those aspects of Milton's diction which do not fit his own theory of imagistic language. It can also remind us that Johnson's view of poetic language was not shared by all his contemporaries.

In Johnson's day, one of the most thorough challenges to the neoclassical theory of pictorial language appeared in Section V of Edmund Burke's *Philosophical Enquiry*. Perhaps the best way to measure the originality and boldness of Burke's discussion is to compare his idea of obscurity with that of Hugh Blair, who as the champion of Ossian found himself in direct opposition to Johnson. In praising Ossian's sublimity, Blair deliberately departed from the prevailing neoclassical belief, which Dennis had insisted upon in his criticism of Pope's Homer, that poetic imagery must be clear and distinct. Yet Blair's break with the past is not as thorough as it seems at first because his praise of obscurity still implies a framework of literary pictorialism. The poet, for Blair, continues to paint pictures with words, and although the pictures are now dim and misty, they remain pictures nonetheless. Burke's radical break with the past lies in divorcing the notion of obscurity from any necessary pictorial context. When Burke praises obscurity, he includes more than the creation of Ossian's misty landscapes: he recommends the manipulation of words in order to release the connotative, musical, and suggestive powers of language. For Burke, the Miltonic phrase *darkness visible* does not evoke a pictorial image of the gloomy interior of Hell; rather, through the logical paradox of oxymoron, it baffles the visual imagination and confounds the reason, achieving its power through thematic relevance and an awesome suggestiveness. "In reality," Burke claimed, "poetry and rhetoric do not succeed in exact description so well as painting does; their business is to affect rather by sympathy than imitation; to display rather the effect of things on the mind of the speaker, or of others, than to present a clear idea of the things themselves. This is their most extensive province, and that in which they succeed the best."[31] One implication of Burke's argument is that the inability of eighteenth-century religious poets to match the sublimity of Raphael, Michelangelo, and Handel may not be due entirely to lack of genius. Instead, it is possible to speculate that a main cause of their failure was adherence to a pictorial theory of poetic language, a theory supported by the prevalence of a dubious simile misappropriated from Horace: that poetry is like painting.

To many eighteenth-century writers, especially in the first half of the century, the differences between poetry and painting seemed superficial rather than essential. The two appeared so closely related in their aims and methods that they were spoken of as "sister arts." Thus the claim that poetry is a speaking picture (and painting, inarticulate poetry) passed into ready currency among critics and poets alike, and the idea quickly created its own truth when poets began to write as if it were true. One modern scholar describes the situation as follows:

> Because painting, of all the arts, most clearly illustrates the doctrine that the arts are imitative, and because psychological analysis of the imagination took its pattern, after Hobbes, from the sense of sight, painting was invoked again and again in the early years of the eighteenth century as the model and test for all works of art. *Ut pictura poesis*, whatever it had once meant, exhorted poets to think of themselves as the wielders of a phantom brush; and poets like Pope . . . were prepared to criticize poems as so many pictures, and to defend their own practice with paintings wielded like a shield of Achilles.[32]

The analogy between poetry and painting was so pervasive that the German philosopher, dramatist, and critic Gotthold Lessing could seem almost revolutionary in pointing out essentially irreconcilable differences that separated the sisters. But even well after the publication of Lessing's *Laokoon* in 1766, a number of English writers remained convinced that the poet simply performs with language the same act the artist performs with paint.

The analogy between poetry and painting certainly had some beneficial effects upon the work of eighteenth-century poets.[33] From the satiric portrait to the georgic descriptive poem, many of the familiar techniques (even stock phrases of poetic diction, such as the *enamel'd ground*) are borrowed from the artist's studio. But it is also certain that general acceptance of the analogy prevented many poets from understanding the unique potential of their own medium. Archibald Alison at the end of the century offered the Age of Johnson a cogent analysis of the differences between poetry and painting, emphasizing the special powers which belong to language alone:

> The Painter addresses himself to the Eye. The Poet speaks to the Imagination. The Painter can represent no other qualities of Nature, but those which we discern by the sense of sight. The Poet can blend with those, all the qualities which we perceive by means of our other senses. The Painter can seize only one moment of existence, and can represent no other qualities of objects than what this single moment affords. The whole history of Nature is within the reach of the Poet . . . . The Painter can give to the objects of his scenery, only the visible and material qualities which are discerned by the eye, and must leave the interpretation of their expression to the imagination of the spectator; but the Poet can give animation to whatever he describes. All the sublimity and beauty of the moral and intellectual world are at his disposal; and by bestowing on the inanimate objects of his scenery the characters and affections of the mind, he can produce at once an expression which every capacity may understand, and every heart may feel. Whatever may be the advantage which painting enjoys, from the greater clearness and precision of its images, it is much more than balanced by the unbounded powers which the instrument of language affords to the Poet.[34]

There is no need to accept Alison's verdict in favor of poetry. What matters is that he understands some of the unique powers which poetry does not share with painting, and his analysis suggests that eighteenth-century poets seriously diminished the possibilities of their art when they insisted upon seeing themselves primarily as verbal painters. Not everyone who practiced painterly techniques, of course, ignored other uses of language: Thomson's poetry of natural description employs many of the animating devices which Alison found appropriate to the poet. But in the area of religious poetry the analogy between poet and painter proved especially dominant and debilitating. By blurring the distinctions between the sister arts, eighteenth-century religious poets almost inevitably doomed their own efforts.

The doctrine of *ut pictura poesis*, particularly when supported by a theory of poetic language which emphasized the use of visual images, necessarily handicapped poets of the religious sublime by encouraging the use of impersonal and descriptive techniques better suited, when the subject is religious, to painting than to poetry. The desire to be verbal painters not only helped to exclude them from the more fruitful provinces of personal and dramatic poetry but it also blinded them to various nonvisual uses of language such as Burke and Alison had described. It seems pertinent that Wordsworth, Blake, and Coleridge managed to transform the religious sublime with some success only by working within an entirely different conception of poetic language and only after a basic shift had occurred in the analogies for poetry. In the Romantic period, as M. H. Abrams has shown, music replaced painting as the sister art of poetry, and the replacement signaled an essential change in ideas about poetic language.[35] Rejecting the older mimetic and pictorial theory of poetic language, in which words "mirror" things, the Romantics espouse an "expressive" poetic, in which the language of the poet operates with musical and symbolical powers to evoke and communicate feeling. For most eighteenth-century poets, whose language remained primarily visual, objective, mimetic, and painterly, their efforts to express the unimaginable resulted only in the circumscription of mystery within the inadequate flesh and forms of the merely imaginable. In this respect Johnson is right: Omnipotence cannot be exalted. And the attempt to do so among eighteenth-century religious poets met with a predictable fate. Quite literally, words failed them.

Eighteenth-century religious poets, in effect, forced themselves into a competition with painters which they could not win. Even worse, by abandoning their own inherent powers in order to become like painters they made themselves less than poets. Addison's Latin poem *The Resurrection*, in its translation by Nicholas Amhurst, offers a convenient opportunity to compare the religious sublime in poetry and in painting because the poem is ostensibly a description of the altarpiece at Magdalen College, a copy of which appears opposite the title page.[36] The reproduction conveys its power immediately by creating an impression of massive space. In the lower half, the dead arise from their graves for Judgment, while to one side an Avenging Angel herds sinners into the flames of Hell. In the top half, Christ sits in glory surrounded by multitudes of the saved. The altarpiece, without being a distinguished work of art, nevertheless succeeds through a careful exploitation of spatial grandeur and visual detail. Although the painter invites us to linger over particular details, minute inspection comes only after the initial overwhelming experience of viewing the whole. Instead of witnessing a series of discrete actions occurring at different places, we feel an awesome sense of simultaneity. In fact, the impression of so much happening at once reinforces the spatial impact of the scene. The expansiveness and power of the altarpiece might well produce, as the poem certainly does not, the stunning effect of a Longinian thunderbolt.

The poem, by a use of maddeningly miscellaneous similies, allusions, and digressions, manages to include a range of subjects and ideas which do not appear in the altarpiece. This diffuse temporal and intellectual expansion, however, distracts rather than fixes the attention and seems intended mainly as learned decoration. The particular aptness of poetry for exploring thoughts, sentiments, and emotions is never utilized to advantage. The poet's power of placing himself inside the experience of another person yields only the most generalized and grotesquely unpsychological insights. How does it feel to awaken after centuries in the grave to face the prospect of eternal Damnation? Donne or Milton would have improved upon Addison's answer:

> *Slow to new Life the thawing Fluids creep,*
> *And the stiff Joints wake heavily from Sleep.*
> *Here on the guilty Brow pale Horrors glare,*
> *And all the Figure labours with Despair.*

This much the painter himself shows us through the immediacy, clarity, and dignity of external representation. The poet, in trying to express in the two couplets both inner and outer, fails to accomplish either. For practical purposes, his imagination stops with the eye of the painter.

Perhaps the main failure of the poem, symptomatic of many smaller lapses and representing a general failure of the religious sublime, comes with the climactic description of Christ. The history of art offers numerous beautifully expressive portraits of Christ, and the altarpiece provides a worthy imitation suggesting a calm, manly, wise, forgiving Redeemer, who is clearly the center of the work. The poet—despite his commands "Look!" and "See!"—presents only a series of verbal abstractions which aspire to painting:

> *Look! where thy Saviour fills the middle Space,*
> *The Son of God, true Image of his Face,*
> *Himself eternal God, e'er Time began her Race.*
> *See! what mild Beams their gracious Influence shed,*
> *And how the pointed Radiance crowns his Head!*
> *Around his Temples lambent Glories shine,*
> *And on his Brow sits Majesty Divine;*
> *His Eye-balls lighten with Celestial Fires,*
> *And ev'ry Grace to speak the God conspires.*

It is not unfair to use a minor poem as our example here, because anyone who reads the religious poetry of the eighteenth century will encounter hundreds of passages which are almost identical to it. Its poverty is representative, and my intention is not simply to expose a representative example of bad religious poetry but to ask why it fails. And the answer, I believe, involves the attempt to use a language which aims at visual portrayal, which fails to achieve its aim, and which provides no other complexity or resource of language beyond the pictorial. The failure of Amhurst's translation occurs not simply because he is a poor poet. Its failure involves his inability to surmount the general difficulties which faced eighteenth-century poets in attempting to reconcile religious subjects with a language of literary pictorialism.

There is no need to prolong an analysis of *The Resurrection* because the poem's failure can be mirrored in any number of similar experiments. Perhaps the best illustration is provided by eighteenth-century imitators of Milton. The graphic imitations by Henri Fuseli, as well as those by William Blake and by John Martin in the next century, demonstrate that painters have consistently excelled poets in imitating Miltonic sublimity. And one sure source of their success is their use of visual techniques appropriate to painting: significantly, they do not labor to make their illustrations resemble poems. Thus Hogarth's "Satan, Sin, and Death"—a departure from the "readable" engravings of his satiric mode—creates a pictorial sublimity which far exceeds the range of Milton's shadowy descriptions. Milton, on the other hand, engages his infernal trinity in a coherent dramatic action, describes them in language rich with thematic resonance, and suggests a dimension of psychic disorder which Hogarth never approaches through external representation alone. We need not ask whether Hogarth is better than Milton, although the question is appropriate if we are comparing *Paradise Lost* with Richard Cumberland's Miltonic poem *Calvary*. Milton and Hogarth, each in pursuing the unique potential of his own art, succeed equally well in different ways.

Thomson's success in attaining sublimity through the poetry of natural description can offer another test case. For Thomson, sublime landscape becomes a means for man, in this world rather than in the otherworld of conventional sublime religious poetry, to experience an approximation of the infinite through a visual process which exploits, while it simultaneously affirms, the inherent limitations of human perception. A cloud-capped mountain or a prospect which at last fades away into apparent nothingness are, of course, not infinite. They simply *appear* infinite because, as Burke pointed out, the absence of definite boundary creates in the mind an impression of endlessness. There is no threat of sacrilege or diminishment of Omnipotence in such scenes, for they make no attempt at the direct treatment of religious truth, while they may in fact become positive stimulants to worship. The sight of a storm-tossed sea, Addison wrote, naturally created in his mind the idea of an "Almighty Being" and, as thoroughly as a "Metaphisical Demonstration," persuaded him that such a Being exists (*Spec.* 489). It is in this sense that the poetry of natural description employs a somewhat distinctive use of the sublime. Whereas the explicitly religious poet attempted to express directly the realm of Revelation and of mystery, the poet whose subject is the appearances of nature can approach the infinite from an oblique and indirect angle. Further, the religious poet always implicitly runs the danger of seeming to deny his own limitations by writing about a subject which lies beyond human powers; the soul's conscious pride in its own exertions, which Longinus had declared to be one of the pleasures produced by the sublime, involves a dangerous brush with the solipsistic vanity which Pope attacks in *An Essay on Man*. In many respects the poetry of natural description was much better suited than explicitly religious poetry to achieving sublimity within the contexts of a pictorial theory of language and of an ethics of limitation.

The relationship of language to religious poetry is a subject which I cannot hope to settle here, and I mean this discussion to retain a high degree of tentativeness. But there seems no better way of providing a final illustration of the issue which I have been raising than to quote two passages dealing with the nature of poetic language which emphasize the shift which occurred over the hundred years which separate Pope's *An Essay on Criticism* (1711) from Wordsworth's *Prelude* (1805).

> No longer now that Golden Age appears,
> When Patriarch-Wits surviv'd a thousand Years;
> Now Length of Fame (our second Life) is lost,
> And bare Threescore is all ev'n That can boast:
> Our Sons their Fathers' failing Language see,
> And such as Chaucer is, shall Dryden be.
> So when the faithful Pencil has design'd

> Some bright Idea of the Master's Mind,
> Where a new World leaps out at his command,
> And ready Nature waits upon his Hand;
> When the ripe Colours soften and unite,
> And sweetly melt into just Shade and Light,
> When mellowing Years their full Perfection give,
> And each Bold Figure just begins to Live;
> The treach'rous Colours the fair Art betray,
> And all the bright Creation fades away![37]

> Visionary power
> Attends the motions of the viewless winds,
> Embodied in the mystery of words:
> There, darkness makes abode, and all the host
> Of shadowy things work endless changes,—there,
> As in a mansion like their proper home,
> Even forms and substances are circumfused
> By that transparent veil with light divine,
> And, through the turnings intricate of verse,
> Present themselves as objects recognised,
> In flashes, and with glory not their own.[38]

Pope views language as a fading canvas which inevitably betrays the conceptions of the poet; for Wordsworth language is a transparent veil providing access to a world of shadowy forms which our normal perception often misses altogether. To compare the passages is to sense why Pope would be hesitant to submit the highest mysteries of Christian truth to a medium of circumscription and betrayal; it is also to sense why Wordsworth would consider language an essential means to break through the dullness of our ordinary perceptions into a world of religious mystery and intuition. The comparison further suggests that the difference between language used for painterly purposes and language which veils (rather than expresses directly) its object is a difference crucial to the creation of good religious poetry. It is one means of explaining why most eighteenth-century poets when they turned to religious subjects so often met with the fate of Milo: "Wedg'd in that timber which he strove to rend."[39]

An attempt to explain some of the failures of the religious sub-

lime should not obscure its successes nor its strong appeal to
eighteenth-century poets and critics. Poets who succeeded in
writing descriptive religious verse, as Pope did in his "Messiah,"
deserve special credit for having solved or avoided the technical
difficulties which blocked most other writers. Further, although
the century cannot boast religious poets of the stature of Donne
and of Herbert, Isaac Watts and Christopher Smart show that
eighteenth-century ideas concerning biblical sublimity could
inspire some unique and valuable writing. Young's *Night-
Thoughts*, although a difficult work to enjoy, deserves to be read
today with some appreciation of its originality in employing
the sublime: "with all his defects," Johnson concluded, "he was
a man of genius and a poet" (3:399). Surely, too, there is room
for serious study of the Ossian poems, despite the judgments of
Johnson and of Wordsworth, especially in considering the rela-
tionship of Ossian's "Gothic machinery" to the uses of religious
sublimity in the eighteenth-century novel. Finally, although
Wordsworth certainly was justified in rejecting much of the ex-
plicitly religious poetry of the eighteenth century, it is quite
possible that his recognition of earlier failure partly accounts for
his development of a symbolic mode. He and Coleridge, in bring-
ing the sublime from the mountains to the valley, from the
grandly and explicitly religious subjects of eighteenth-century
poetry to the everyday world of the common man, discovered a
new and successful way of uniting religion with sublimity. Their
language, which is fundamentally different from the pictorial
language of eighteenth-century religious poets, represents a sig-
nificant breakthrough in shifting the locus of sublimity from ex-
ternal grandeur to the relationship between mind and object.
Their development of what Earl Wasserman (quoting Shelley)
calls a "subtler language"[40] was the prerequisite of a revitalized
religious poetry, one able to reject the exaltation of Omnipotence
in favor of expressing the personal, halting, half-understood inti-
mations of a power beyond nature and the self—a poetry able
to render in language those blessed moods and spots of time in
which the imagination sees into the life of things. But a study
of the changes in religious poetry is useful beyond stressing the

experimental alternatives developed by poets who recognized the failures and rigidity of previous forms. It also instructs us about a too frequently neglected aspect of eighteenth-century culture. The religious sublime, even in its least successful appearances, testifies to the power of a single idea to interest serious writers for more than a century, and their struggle to make the concept useful to their own immediate poetic concerns provides in itself a significant drama of literary change.

Notes

INTRODUCTION

¹ "Space, Deity, and the 'Natural Sublime,' " *Modern Language Quarterly* 12 (1951): 20–38; and *The Imagination as a Means of Grace: Locke and the Aesthetics of Romanticism* (Berkeley, Calif., 1960). For a very different kind of study, see Walter John Hipple, Jr., *The Beautiful, the Sublime, & the Picturesque in Eighteenth-Century British Aesthetic Theory* (Carbondale, Ill., 1957).

² *Mountain Gloom and Mountain Glory: The Development of the Aesthetics of the Infinite* (1959; rpt. New York, 1963).

³ *Eras & Modes in English Poetry*, 2d ed. (Berkeley, Calif., 1964), pp. 48–77.

⁴ "The Sublime Poem: Pictures and Powers," *Yale Review* 58 (1968–1969): 194–213.

⁵ *The Imagination as a Means of Grace*, p. 68. For a good example of this process, see Mrs. Radcliffe's description of Emily St. Aubert's travels in the mountains of southern France: "From the consideration of His works, her mind arose to the adoration of the Deity, in His goodness and power; wherever she turned her view, whether on the sleeping earth, or to the vast regions of space, glowing with worlds beyond the reach of human thought, the sublimity of God, and the majesty of His presence appeared" (*The Mysteries of Udolpho* [1794], ed Bonamy Dobrée [Oxford, 1966], pp. 47–48).

⁶ *Philological Quarterly* 15 (1936): 166.

⁷ "Préface" to the *Traité du Sublime* (1674), in *Oeuvres complètes*, ed. Françoise Escal (Paris, 1966), p. 338. Translation mine.

⁸ *Mountain Gloom and Mountain Glory*, p. 30, n. 39. See, however, the objections of John Arthos in his review of Miss Nicolson's book: "I find a more general difficulty in this kind of thinking where it excludes Dante, Ariosto and Tasso from a sense of the sublime in nature. Miss Nicolson says that men had no true idea of this until science developed its particular notions of the infinite. The vast reaches of the *Paradiso* and of the heavens through which journey the angels of Ariosto and Tasso, and the great stage of *Lear* do not, apparently, share in this conception" (*Philological Quarterly* 39 [1960]: 303).

⁹ *Spectator* No. 489. All quotations are from *The Spectator*, ed. Donald F. Bond, 5 vols. (Oxford, 1965). Addison's view is supported by Archibald Alison in his *Essay on the Nature and Principles of Taste* (Edinburgh, 1790): "The generality of mankind live in the world, without receiving any kind of delight, from the various scenes of beauty which its order displays. . . . We may all remember a period in our lives, when this was the state of our own minds; and it is probable most men will recollect, that the time when nature began to appear to them in another view, was, when they were engaged in the study of classical literature. In most men, at least, the first appearance of poetical imagination is at school, when their imaginations begin to be warmed by the descriptions of ancient poetry, and when they

have acquired a new sense as it were, with which they can behold the face of nature" (pp. 44–45).

¹⁰ For one indication of its continuous spell, see a volume by Ferdinand Tugnot de Lanoye entitled *The Sublime in Nature*, tr. anon. (New York, 1870).

¹¹ The anecdote appears in James Beattie's "Illustrations on Sublimity" (in *Dissertations Moral and Critical* [London, 1783], p. 617).

¹² *The Correspondence of Thomas Gray*, ed. Paget Toynbee and Leonard Whibley (Oxford, 1935), 1:128.

¹³ If Ralph Cohen is correct that "common poetic assumptions and practices" ally sublime verse with a general Augustan mode, we should expect to find no essential differences between sublime poems ostensibly dealing with nature and those explicitly religious ("The Augustan Mode in English Poetry," *Eighteenth-Century Studies* 1 [1967–1968]: 17, n. 6). Except for Thomson's *The Seasons*, the poetry of natural description lies outside the focus of this study.

¹⁴ *A Course of Lectures on Oratory and Criticism* (London, 1777), p. 160.

¹⁵ *Religion and Literature* (London, 1971), p. 135.

¹⁶ *Rambler* No. 125 (1751), in *The Yale Edition of the Works of Samuel Johnson*, ed. Allen T. Hazen and John H. Middendorf (New Haven, Conn., 1958–   ), 4:300. The *Rambler* is edited in the Yale series by W. J. Bate and Albrecht B. Strauss.

¹⁷ See René Wellek, "The Concept of Evolution in Literary History," in *Concepts of Criticism*, ed. Stephen G. Nichols, Jr. (New Haven, Conn., 1963), pp. 37–53. (Wellek's essay was first published in a collection entitled *For Roman Jakobson* [The Hague, 1956].) See also Louis O. Mink, "Change and Causality in the History of Ideas," *Eighteenth-Century Studies* 2 (1968–1969): 7–25; and Robert Nisbet, "Genealogy, Growth, and Other Metaphors," *New Literary History* 1 (1969–1970): 351–63.

¹⁸ *Eighteenth-Century Studies* 2 (1968–1969): 24. Forster's well-known distinction between story and plot appears in his *Aspects of the Novel* (1927).

¹⁹ "The Life and Death of Literary Forms," *New Literary History* 2 (1970–1971): 199–216.

CHAPTER ONE

¹ In *The Critical Works of John Dennis*, ed. Edward Niles Hooker (Baltimore, Md., 1939–1943), 1:358.

² Bernard Weinberg, "Translations and Commentaries of Longinus, On the Sublime, to 1600: A Bibliography," *Modern Philology* 47 (1949–1950): 145–51.

³ In *Critical Essays of the Seventeenth Century*, ed. J. E. Spingarn (Oxford, 1908–1909), 1:41 (hereafter cited as Spingarn).

⁴ *Institutio Oratorio*, tr. H.E. Butler, Loeb Classical Library (Cambridge, Mass., 1921–1922), 12. 10. 58.

⁵ *The Sublime*, p. 14.

⁶ *Institutio Oratorio*, tr. Butler, 12. 10. 65.

[7] See Israel Baroway, "The Bible as Poetry in the English Renaissance: An Introduction," *Journal of English and Germanic Philology* 32 (1933): 447–80.

[8] (London, 1657), sig. A5^r–A5^v.

[9] *Timber, or Discoveries* (1641), in Spingarn, 1:51. For a repetition of this view in the Augustan age, see Samuel Cobb's *Discourse on Criticism and of Poetry* (1707), Augustan Reprint Society, Ser. 2, no. 1 (Ann Arbor, Mich., 1946), pp. 179–84.

[10] *An Apologie for Poetrie* (1595), in *Elizabethan Critical Essays*, ed. G. Gregory Smith (Oxford, 1904), 1:158 (hereafter cited as Smith).

[11] *An Apologie for Poetrie*, in Smith, 1:158.

[12] *Timber*, in Spingarn, 1:29.

[13] See John Donne, "Vpon the translation of the Psalmes by Sir Philip Sydney, and the Countess of Pembroke his Sister"; and Edmund Waller, "To Mr. George Sandys."

[14] *A Preparation to the Psalter* (London, 1619), p. 72.

[15] Preface to *Poems* (1656), in Spingarn, 2:90.

[16] Hugh Blair in 1783 simply repeated what had long been common knowledge when he asserted that sacred odes "ought to have sublimity and elevation, for their reigning character" (*Lectures on Rhetoric and Belles Lettres* [London, 1783], 2:355).

[17] "From Action to Image: Theories of the Lyric in the Eighteenth Century," in *Critics and Criticism: Ancient and Modern*, ed R. S. Crane (Chicago, 1952), p. 419.

[18] Preface to *Poems*, in Spingarn, 2:90. For a good idea of the vast literature included in Cowley's dismissal, see Lily B. Campbell, *Divine Poetry and Drama in Sixteenth-Century England* (Berkeley, Calif., 1961).

[19] See Samuel Holt Monk, " 'A Grace Beyond the Reach of Art,' " *Journal of the History of Ideas* 5 (1944): 131–50.

[20] *A Preparation to the Psalter*, p. 75.

[21] *The Compleat Gentleman* (1622), in Spingarn, 1:117–18.

[22] Preface to *Theophilia* (1652), in *Minor Poets of the Caroline Period*, ed. George Saintsbury (Oxford, 1905–1921), 1:319.

[23] Preface to *Theophilia*, in *Minor Poets of the Caroline Period*, ed. Saintsbury, 1:319.

[24] "Urania," in *Bartas His Devine Weekes and Works*, tr. Joshua Sylvester (1605), Scholars' Facsimiles & Reprints (Gainesville, Fla., 1965), p. 531. See also Lily B. Campbell, "The Christian Muse," *Huntington Library Bulletin* 8 (1935): 29–70.

[25] "Urania," in *Bartas*, tr. Sylvester, p. 538.

[26] In Spingarn, 1:199. See also Milton's "Ode on the Morning of Christ's Nativity," ll. 27–28.

[27] In Spingarn, 2:59.

[28] In Spingarn, 2:59.

[29] "Urania," in *Bartas*, tr. Sylvester, p. 533.

[30] In Spingarn, 2:59.

[31] *An Essay on Translated Verse* (1684), in Spingarn, 2:306.

[32] *An Historical Account of the Lives and Writings of our Most Considerable English Poets* (London, 1720), p. xix.

[33] *An Essay upon Poetry* (1682), in Spingarn, 2:286–87.

[34] Quoted by Monk, *The Sublime*, p. 21.

[35] "The Author's Apology for Heroic Poetry and Poetic Licence" (1677), in *Essays of John Dryden*, ed. W. P. Ker (1900; rpt. New York, 1961), 1:179 (hereafter cited as Ker).

[36] *On Great Writing (On the Sublime)*, tr. G. M. A. Grube (New York, 1957), p. 48 (sect. 36).

[37] *On Great Writing*, tr. Grube, pp. 56–58 (sect. 44).

[38] *On Great Writing*, tr. Grube, pp. 47–48 (sect. 35). Mark Akenside in *The Pleasures of Imagination* (London, 1744) offers a Christianized version of the famous thirty-fifth chapter of Longinus in which he associates man's admiration for the sublime works of creation with the soul's ultimate approach toward God: "Thro' all th' ascent of things [to] inlarge her view, / Till every bound at length should disappear, / And infinite perfection close the scene" (1.219–21).

[39] Dryden, "Heroic Poetry and Poetic Licence," in Ker, 1:179; Swift *The Battle of the Books* (1704), in *Prose Works*, ed. Davis et al., 1:153.

[40] Ll. 677–78. All quotations from Pope's poetry refer to the eleven-volume Twickenham edition of *The Poems of Alexander Pope* (New Haven, Conn., 1939–1969), under the general editorship of John Butt.

[41] *Dionysius Longinus On the Sublime* (1739), 4th ed., Corrected and Improved (London, 1777), p. 96.

[42] "Of Simplicity and Refinement" (1741), in *Essays and Treatises on Several Subjects* (London, 1767), 1:220.

[43] "Illustrations on Sublimity," in *Dissertations Moral and Critical*, p. 612.

[44] *Traité du Sublime*, in *Oeuvres*, ed. Escal, p. 363 (sect. 15 in standard translations of Longinus).

[45] "Heroic Poetry and Poetic Licence," in Ker, 1:186. In the lines immediately following, Dryden quotes a long passage from the "Des Images" section of Longinus. His stress upon the value of "imaging," however, appears as early as 1667 in the Preface to *Annus Mirabilis* (in Ker, 1:14–15), so that it is likely Longinus confirmed rather than inspired Dryden's views on the subject. Warton's opinions are studied extensively by Hoyt Trowbridge, "Joseph Warton on the Imagination," *Modern Philology* 35 (1937): 73–87.

[46] *An Apologie for Poetrie*, in Smith, 1:155.

[47] See *The Conversations of Aristo and Eugene* (1671), in *The Continental Model*, ed. Scott Elledge and Donald Schier (Minneapolis, Minn., 1960), p. 237.

[48] *The Art of Criticism* (1687), tr. "a person of quality" (1705), in *The Continental Model*, ed. Elledge and Schier, p. 266. Italics mine.

[49] "Préface" to the *Traité du Sublime*, in *Oeuvres*, ed. Escal, p. 338. Translation mine.

[50] See Richard F. Jones, "The Attack on Pulpit Eloquence in the Restoration: An Episode in the Development of the Neo-Classical Standard for Prose," *Journal of English and Germanic Philology* 30 (1931): 188–217.

[51] *The History of the Royal-Society of London* (London, 1667), p. 113.

[52] *An Essay concerning Preaching* (1678), in Spingarn, 2:277.

[53] *An Essay on Criticism* (1711), ll. 311–17.

54 See E. B. O. Borgerhoff, *The Freedom of French Classicism* (Princeton, N.J., 1950), pp. 226–27.

55 "Essay Second. On the Sublime," in *Philosophical Essays* (Edinburgh, 1810), p. 366.

56 See Monk, *The Sublime*, pp. 33–35; and A. F. B. Clark, *Boileau and the French Classical Critics in England* (Paris, 1925), pp. 377–79. A similar controversy flared in the eighteenth century over the question whether biblical sublimity represented an absolute or variable standard. William Warburton in his *Doctrine of Grace* (1762) objected to Conyers Middleton's "An Essay on the Gift of Tongues" (first published in Middleton's *Miscellaneous Works* [1752]) and asserted that sublimity depends upon "the application of such images, as arbitrary or casual connexions, rather than their own native grandeur, have dignified and ennobled." Warburton's position was attacked by Thomas Leland in *A Dissertation on the Principles of Human Eloquence* (1764), and Leland in turn was refuted by Richard Hurd in his *Letter to the Rev. Dr. Thomas Leland* (1764), to which Leland replied in the second edition (1765) of his *Dissertation*.

57 *Windsor-Forest* (1713), ll. 327–28; *The Rape of the Lock* (1714), 3. 46.

58 "Préface" to *Traité du Sublime*, in *Oeuvres*, ed. Escal, p. 338. Translation mine. For a thorough study of Boileau's interpretation of Longinus, see Jules Brody, *Boileau and Longinus* (Geneva, 1958).

59 "Préface" to *Traité du Sublime*, in *Oeuvres*, ed. Escal, p. 338. Translation mine.

60 See R. A. Sayce, *The French Biblical Epic in the Seventeenth Century* (Oxford, 1955).

61 *La formation de la doctrine classique en France*, 2d ed. (Paris, 1931), p. 295. Translation mine.

62 *Réflexions sur la poétique (en général)* (1674), in *Oeuvres de R. Rapin* (La Haye, 1725), 2:131. Translation mine.

63 "Heroic Poetry and Poetic Licence," in Ker, 1:187.

64 *History of the Royal-Society*, p. 340.

65 Ibid.

66 "Of Heroic Plays" (1672), in Ker, 1:152–53. On the Italian background of the Christian marvellous, see Baxter Hathaway, *Marvels and Commonplaces: Renaissance Literary Criticism* (New York, 1968), pp. 133–51.

67 Preface to *Albion and Albanius, An Opera* (1685), in Ker, 1:270.

68 "Dedication of the Aeneis" (1697), in Ker, 2:210.

69 "A Discourse concerning the Original and Progress of Satire" (1693), in Ker, 2:34.

70 "Original and Progress of Satire," in Ker, 2:36.

71 *Essay on Heroic Poetry*, 2d ed. (1697), Augustan Reprint Society, Ser. 2, no. 2 (Ann Arbor, Mich., 1947), pp. 7–13. Dr. Johnson called Dryden's version of the Christian marvellous the "most reasonable scheme of celestial interposition that ever was formed" (*Lives of the English Poets*, ed. George Birkbeck Hill [Oxford, 1905], 1:385).

72 *Art poétique*, in *Oeuvres*, ed. Escal, p. 173.

73 *Lives of the English Poets*, ed. Hill, 1:292–93.

74 *Art poétique*, in *Oeuvres*, ed. Escal, p. 174. Translation mine.

[75] Quoted by Bray, *La doctrine classique*, p. 337. Translation mine.
[76] *Boileau and the French Classical Critics in England*, p. 324.
[77] *Essay on Heroic Poetry*, p. 23.
[78] Ibid. See Dryden's "Lines Printed under the Engraved Portrait of Milton" (1688) where he asserts that Milton surpasses Virgil in majesty and Homer in loftiness of thought.
[79] *The Correspondence of Thomas Gray*, ed. Toynbee and Whibley, 1:128.

CHAPTER TWO

[1] *An Historical Account of the Lives and Writings of Our Most Considerable English Poets* (London, 1720), p. 257. For some modern comment on Dennis, see Monk, *The Sublime*, pp. 45–54; Clarence DeWitt Thorpe, *The Aesthetic Theory of Thomas Hobbes*, University of Michigan Publications in Language and Literature, Vol. 18 (Ann Arbor, Mich., 1940), pp. 221–59; Nicolson, *Mountain Gloom and Mountain Glory*, pp. 276–89; James A. W. Heffernan, "Wordsworth and Dennis: The Discrimination of Feelings," *PMLA* 82 (1967): 430–36. The ultimate authority on Dennis is Edward Niles Hooker in the notes and introduction to his fine edition of Dennis's critical works.
[2] *The Aesthetic Theory of Thomas Hobbes*, p. 258.
[3] *The Critical Works of John Dennis*, ed. Hooker, 1:336. All subsequent quotations will be documented within the text.
[4] See H. G. Paul, *John Dennis: His Life and Criticism* (New York, 1911), p. 136. In the discussion which follows concerning Enthusiastic and Ordinary passion, I have summarized Dennis's main points in two passages (1:216 and 338), keeping as close to the original language as possible.
[5] See Hooker, ed., *The Critical Works of John Dennis*, 1:452.
[6] *De Rerum Natura*, tr. W. H. D. Rouse, Loeb Classical Library (New York, 1928), 5. 564–65.
[7] See Thomas De Quincey's letter dated 30 August 1842 in which he notes that Wordsworth and Coleridge went through a "craze" for Dennis's works (Hooker, ed., *Critical Works*, 2:lxxiii).
[8] Charles Edward Mallet, *A History of the University of Oxford* (New York, 1924), 2:321. For a discussion of Hermogenes' views, see Annabel M. Patterson, *Hermogenes and the Renaissance: Seven Ideas of Style* (Princeton, N.J., 1970).
[9] "I will not determine whether the *hupsous* of Longinus, and the *megathous* of Hermogenes, are the same, as many have thought; or whether there is a Difference between them, as Tanaquil Faber was of Opinion, and the ingenious Translator of Longinus in French, Monsieur Boileau" (Samuel Warenfelsius, *A Discourse of Logomachys, . . . to which is Added, A Dissertation concerning Meteors of Stile, or False Sublimity*, tr. anon. [London, 1711], p. 188).
[10] *The Narrative of Dr. Robert Norris* (1713), in *The Prose Works of Alexander Pope*, ed. Norman Ault (Oxford, 1936), p. 164.
[11] *Mountain Gloom and Mountain Glory*, p. 279.

¹² Dryden wrote to Dennis, "Your own Poetry is a more Powerful Example, to prove that the Modern Writers may enter into comparison with the Ancients, than any which Perrault could produce in France" (Letters upon several Occasions . . . [London, 1696], p. 53). In A Tale of a Tub, Swift includes Dennis among a number of other Moderns. Even the title Advancement and Reformation of Modern Poetry allies Dennis with the Baconian notion of progress (see Richard Foster Jones, Ancients and Moderns: A Study of the Rise of the Scientific Movement in Seventeenth-Century England, 2d ed. [St. Louis, Mo., 1961], p. 42).

¹³ The Critical Specimen (1711), in Prose Works, ed. Ault, p. 7. Dryden, of course, had also emphasized the usefulness of Christianity to modern poets; see especially his letter to Dennis on the subject (Letters upon several Occasions, p. 54).

¹⁴ See George Herbert's poem "Jordan." Cowley vowed to recover poetry "out of the Tyrants hands, and to restore it to the Kingdom of God, who is the Father of it" (Preface to Poems, in Spingarn, 2:88). An anonymous contemporary introduced an edition of Crashaw's poems, saying, "Here's Herbert's second, but equall, who hath retriv'd Poetry of late, and return'd it up to its Primitive use; Let it bound back to heaven gates, whence it came" (The Poems of Richard Crashaw, ed. L. C. Martin [Oxford, 1927], p. 75).

¹⁵ Charles Rollin (1661–1741), a French writer popular in England, reflects the merging of the two terms when he notes, "The sublime, or marvellous, is that which constitutes the grand and true eloquence" (The Method of Teaching and Studying the Belles Lettres, tr. anon. [London, 1734], 2:64).

¹⁶ Quoted by H. T. Swedenberg, Jr., The Theory of the Epic in England, 1650–1800, University of California Publications in English, Vol. 15 (Berkeley, Calif., 1944), p. 133. Ogilvie's "Dissertation" was published in 1801; but, as Swedenberg has noted, "Much of what Ogilvie said might well suggest that the essay was written in 1701 rather than 1801, for he used materials a hundred years old and more" (p. 133).

¹⁷ In translating, Dennis changed Horace's famous passage (Car. 4.2. 2) describing Pindar to state that as a mountain stream is raised above its ordinary level by an "influx of celestial waters" (for Horace's simple imbres = rain), so Pindar is "rais'd by influence divine" (1:43). The idea of divine influence is Dennis's own addition to the poem.

¹⁸ Preface to The Iliad (1715), in Prose Works, ed. Ault, p. 229.

¹⁹ See, for example, James Beattie's "Illustrations on Sublimity," in Dissertations Moral and Critical, pp. 621–22.

²⁰ France never seemed to escape from Boileau's influence in this matter. Charles Rollin reports in the 1730s that a recent French translation of Paradise Lost "gave a general offence by the . . . intermixture of things sacred and profane, and the more so as the subject treated of contains the most sublime and sacred truths of religion" (The Method of Teaching and Studying the Belles Lettres, tr. anon., 1:285).

²¹ The Influence of Milton on English Poetry (Cambridge, Mass., 1922), p. 93. Dennis claimed that Paradise Lost had been neglected for thirty (2:170) or forty (2:32) years after its publication.

[22] Havens, *Influence of Milton*, p. 95. For a specimen of Dennis's blank verse, these lines from *Britannia Triumphans* (1704) will do:

> BEGIN my Soul, and strike the living Lyre,
> O raise thy self! O rouze thy utmost Pow'rs!
> Contemn the World, and ev'ry thing below,
> And soaring tow'r above Mortality,
> To meet and welcome thy descending God.
> 'Tis done! O Raptures never felt before!
> Tempestuous Whirlwind of transporting Flame!
> O whither am I caught! O whither rapt!
> To what immense unutterable Heights?

(in *The Select Works of Mr. John Dennis* [London, 1721], 1:153–54). Dennis had announced in the preface that "the Consideration of reducing some former critical Speculations into Practice, made me resolve as far as I was able to make the following Verses turn upon Religion" (*Critical Works*, ed. Hooker, 1:374). The poem thus puts into practice Dennis's "critical Speculations" concerning the religious sublime.

[23] See Vincent Freimarck, "The Bible and Neo-Classical Views of Style," *Journal of English and Germanic Philology* 51 (1952): 509.

[24] *A Further Account of the most Deplorable Condition of Mr. Edmund Curll* (1716), in *Prose Works*, ed. Ault, p. 281.

[25] *The Sublime*, p. 54. For a study of the cult of terror and related subjects, see Patricia Meyer Spacks, *The Insistence of Horror: Aspects of the Supernatural in Eighteenth-Century Poetry* (Cambridge, Mass., 1962).

[26] 1:53 and 252.

[27] See Hooker, ed., *Critical Works*, 1:463.

[28] Monk, *The Sublime*, pp. 31–36: "Simplicity is the narrow gate through which the sublime enters into Boileau's system of thought" (p. 36).

[29] The periodical, written by Aaron Hill, was collected in two volumes in 1730.

[30] Quoted by Hooker, ed., *Critical Works*, 2:lxv.

CHAPTER THREE

[1] *A Preface to Eighteenth Century Poetry* (Oxford, 1948), p. 2.

[2] "Secular Masque," ll. 96–97. All quotations from Dryden's poetry refer to *The Poems of John Dryden*, ed. James Kinsley, 4 vols. (Oxford, 1958).

[3] *The Eighteenth Century Background: Studies on the Idea of Nature in the Thought of the Period* (1940; rpt. Boston, Mass., 1961), p. 101.

[4] See Raymond D. Havens, "Changing Taste in the Eighteenth Century: A Study of Dryden's and Dodsley's Miscellanies," *PMLA* 44 (1929): 515, 534.

[5] *A Letter of Advice to a Young Poet* (1721), in *Prose Works*, ed. Davis et al., 9:331. For present purposes, the question of authorship is not essential.

[6] 16 (1763): 417.

[7] *Lives of the English Poets*, ed. Hill, 1:291.

8 Preface to *A Paraphrase on the Book of Job* (London, 1700), sig. b1ᵛ. Printing regularized.

9 *The Lives of the Poets* (London, 1753), 5:180. Although the younger Cibber, for a fee, contributed his name to this collection, much of the writing was done by Robert Shiels, one of the amanuenses who worked on Johnson's *Dictionary*.

10 Preface to *Horae Lyricae*, 2d ed. (London, 1709), pp. xii-xiii.

11 "David's Lamentation over *Saul* and *Jonathan*," in *Reliquiae Juveniles: Miscellaneous Thoughts in Prose and Verse* (London, 1734), p. 96.

12 Preface to *Horae Lyricae*, pp. xv-xvi.

13 Preface to *The Creation*, Augustan Reprint Society, Ser. 4, no. 2 (Ann Arbor, Mich., 1949), p. 5.

14 *Plain Dealer* Nos. 54, 57, and 82.

15 Preface to *The Creation*, p. 12.

16 *The Correspondence of Alexander Pope*, ed. George Sherburn (Oxford, 1956), 2:37.

17 Preface to *The Last Judgment of Men and Angels* (London, 1723), sig C1ᵛ.

18 Preface to *A Miscellany of Poems by several Hands* (Oxford, 1731), sig. a4ᵛ.

19 *Conjectures on Original Composition* (London, 1759), p. 72.

20 When Charles Gildon in *The Complete Art of Poetry* ([London, 1718], 1:51–52) repeated this idea, he did so in a shameless plagiarism of Sidney. Of course, contemporary views concerning the chronology of the world and the descent of all languages from the original Hebrew also supported the view that the Bible contains the most ancient of all poetry.

21 Preface to *The Creation*, p. 4.

22 *Gentleman's Magazine* 3 (1733): 40.

23 Gildon, *The Laws of Poetry* (London, 1721), p. 115; Hill, *Plain Dealer* No. 95; [John Newbery], *The Art of Poetry on a New Plan* (London, 1762), 2:72; Aulay Macaulay, *Essays on various subjects of Taste and Criticism* (London, 1780), p. 15—to cite just a few. Charles Rollin's *The Method of Teaching and Studying the Belles Lettres* contains a long explication of the song of Moses (2:397–424).

24 *The Art of Poetry on a New Plan*, 1:ii.

25 Preface to *Horae Lyricae*, p. iii.

26 43 (1777): 252.

27 *The Sublime*, p. 79.

28 In *Prose Works*, ed. Ault, p. 246.

29 Preface to *A Miscellany of Poems by several Hands*, sig. g4ʳ.

30 (London, 1725), pp. 222–23.

31 *Dionysius Longinus On the Sublime*, p. 42. Smith's edition, published in 1739, became the standard eighteenth-century text (see Monk, *The Sublime*, p. 10).

32 *Lectures on Rhetoric and Belles Lettres*, 2:399–400.

33 See Freimarck, "The Bible and Neo-Classical Views of Style," pp. 507–26.

34 Preface to *Horae Lyricae*, pp. vii-viii.

35 *The Sacred Classics Defended and Illustrated*, p. 279.

[36] Dionysius Longinus On the Sublime, p. 38.

[37] Explanatory Notes and Remarks on Milton's "Paradise Lost" (1734), in The Early Lives of Milton, ed. Helen Darbishire (London, 1932), p. 290. The title page indicates that both Richardsons, father and son, collaborated on the essay.

[38] Lectures on Rhetoric and Belles Lettres, 1:61.

[39] Steele, Guardian No. 86; and Husbands, Preface to A Miscellany of Poems by several Hands, sig. o3^r.

[40] Lives of the English Poets, ed. Hill, 1:177.

[41] Lectures on Rhetoric and Belles Lettres, 2:471.

[42] Coleridge's Miscellaneous Criticism, ed. Thomas Middleton Raysor (Cambridge, Mass., 1936), p. 164.

[43] See Richardson, Explanatory Notes and Remarks on Milton's "Paradise Lost," in Early Lives of Milton, ed. Darbishire, p. 317; [Newbery], The Art of Poetry on a New Plan, 2:326; Macaulay, Essays on Taste and Criticism, p. 46. Probably Philip Neve best expressed the prevailing view: "Others rise to sublimity, when they succeed; Milton's institution, his quality, his element is sublimity" (Cursory Remarks on some of the Ancient English Poets, particularly Milton [London, 1789], p. 142).

[44] Influence of Milton, p. 404.

[45] Wesley, Essay on Heroic Poetry, p. 23; Spectator No. 267; Gildon, The Laws of Poetry, p. 259; Richardson, Explanatory Notes and Remarks on Milton's "Paradise Lost," in Early Lives of Milton, ed. Darbishire, p. 316; Blair, Lectures on Rhetoric and Belles Lettres, 2:471.

[46] Watts, Preface to Horae Lyricae, pp. xx–xxi; Spectator No. 285; Pope (see Joseph Spence, Observations, Anecdotes, and Characters of Books and Men, ed. James M. Osborn [Oxford, 1966], 2:637).

[47] Lectures on the Sacred Poetry of the Hebrews, tr. G. Gregory (London, 1787), 2:191. The Lectures were first published in Latin in 1753.

[48] Dissertation on Reading the Classics, and Forming a Just Style (London, 1713), pp. 131–32.

[49] Lives of the English Poets, ed. Hill, 1:174.

[50] Observations on Poetry, Especially the Epic . . . (London, 1738), p. 155.

[51] Lectures on Rhetoric and Belles Lettres, 1:50.

[52] A Philosophical Enquiry into the Origin of Our Ideas of the Sublime and Beautiful (2d ed., 1759), ed. James T. Boulton (New York, 1958), p. 59.

[53] Philosophical Enquiry, ed. Boulton, p. 61; Smith, Dionysius Longinus On the Sublime, pp. 44–45.

[54] "Illustrations on Sublimity," in Dissertations Moral and Critical, p. 612.

[55] Literary Hours: or Sketches Critical and Narrative (London, 1798), p. 270. See also Arthur Barker, " '. . . And on His Crest Sat Horror': Eighteenth-Century Interpretations of Milton's Sublimity and his Satan," University of Toronto Quarterly 11 (1941–1942): 421–36.

[56] Characteristics of Men, Manners, Opinions, Times (1711), ed. John M. Robertson (1900; rpt. 2 vols. in 1, Indianapolis, Ind., 1964), 1:189.

[57] See Crane's review of Monk's The Sublime (Philological Quarterly 15 [1936]: 165–67).

[58] An Historical Account of Our Most Considerable English Poets, p. xviii.
[59] 5 (1735): 462.
[60] Clio: or a Discourse on Taste, 2d ed. (London, 1769), p. 132.
[61] Essays, Moral and Literary (1778–1779), in The Works of Vicesimus Knox (London, 1824), 1:84.
[62] Clio, p. 102.
[63] Clio, p. 242.
[64] Literary Hours, p. 261.
[65] The Sublime Puritan: Milton and the Victorians (Madison, Wis., 1963), pp. 39–73.
[66] An Essay on Taste, 2d ed. (Edinburgh, 1764), p. 23. The first edition appeared in 1759.
[67] "On the Sublime," in Philosophical Works, p. 362.
[68] "On the Sublime," in Philosophical Works, p. 370.
[69] "On the Sublime," in Philosophical Works, p. 369.

CHAPTER FOUR

[1] Ed. Selma L. Bishop (London, 1962), pp. liii-liv.
[2] In Hymns and Spiritual Songs, ed. Bishop, p. 227.
[3] Preface to Hymns and Spiritual Songs, ed. Bishop, p. liv.
[4] Preface to Hymns and Spiritual Songs, ed. Bishop, p. liv.
[5] Preface to Hymns and Spiritual Songs, ed. Bishop, p. liv.
[6] "The Law given at Sinai," in Horae Lyricae.
[7] 11:465.
[8] In Poems on Several Occasions (London, 1748).
[9] "Psalm CIV. God the Creator, and Preserver," in A Miscellany of Poems by several Hands (Oxford, 1731).
[10] [James Arbuckle], A Collection of Letters and Essays (Hibnericus's Letters) on several subjects, lately publish'd in the Dublin Journal, 2 vols. (London, 1729).
[11] Preface to A Paraphrase on the Book of Job, sig. i2ʳ.
[12] Lives of the English Poets, ed. Hill, 2:17.
[13] See Hill, Plain Dealer No. 54; and James Beattie, "Illustrations on Sublimity," in Dissertations Moral and Critical, p. 647.
[14] Peri Bathous: or . . . The Art of Sinking in Poetry (1728), ed. Edna Leake Steeves (New York, 1952), p. 6.
[15] Peri Bathous, ed. Steeves, p. 25.
[16] 15:156.
[17] See The Correspondence of Alexander Pope, ed. Sherburn, 1:136.
[18] New Series, 15 (1795): 32.
[19] Essays, Moral and Literary, in The Works of Vicesimus Knox, 2:210.
[20] An Essay on the Genius and Writings of Pope, 3d ed. (London, 1772–1782), 1:11. Volume one was first published in 1756; volume two in 1782.
[21] Appendix to the Preface to Lyrical Ballads, in Literary Criticism of William Wordsworth, ed. Paul M. Zall (Lincoln, Nebr., 1966), p. 65.
[22] See The Correspondence of Alexander Pope, ed. Sherburn, 1:146.
[23] (London, 1705), p. 14.
[24] Lives of the English Poets, ed. Hill, 2:129.

25 *Lectures on Rhetoric and Belles Lettres*, 1:78.

26 Joseph Priestley discussed the image at length in his *Lectures on Oratory and Criticism* (pp. 167–68), and Pope introduced Addison's last line verbatim in *The Dunciad* (1729 ed. [3.260]), in a context satirizing the supernatural marvels which filled the theatrical farces of the period. Dr. Johnson's dislike of the image hardly affected either its success or notoriety.

27 51 (1781): 185, 188.

28 *The Life of Samuel Johnson, LL.D.*, ed. George Birkbeck Hill, rev. by L. F. Powell (Oxford, 1934–1950), 2:359.

29 *The Background of Gray's Elegy: A Study in the Taste for Melancholy Poetry, 1700–1751* (New York, 1924), p. 29. See also William Powell Jones, *The Rhetoric of Science: A Study of Scientific Ideas and Imagery in Eighteenth-Century English Poetry* (Berkeley, Calif., 1966), pp. 47–54.

30 (London, 1721), p. 101.

31 (Rpt. London, 1965), p. 305 (3. 12). The Latin version first appeared in 1681, followed in 1684 by Burnet's own English translation.

32 From a letter dated 2 August 1726 (quoted by Monk, *The Sublime*, p. 90).

33 (Oxford, 1713), sig. A3v.

34 (Oxford, 1720), sig. A2v.

35 *A Dissertation on the Principles of Human Eloquence* (London, 1764), p. 52.

36 In *Horae Lyricae*.

37 *The Correspondence of William Cowper*, ed. Thomas Wright (1904; rpt. New York, 1968), 1:356.

38 *Lives of the English Poets*, ed. Hill, 3:393–94.

39 *Philosophical Enquiry*, ed. Boulton, p. 172.

40 Hoxie Neale Fairchild, *Religious Trends in English Poetry* (New York, 1939–1968), 1:450.

41 (London, 1721), p. iii. Although Hill can be said to have identified the problem, Mrs. Radcliffe seems much closer to an adequate solution in distinguishing between obscurity and confusion as sources of the sublime: "Obscurity leaves something for the imagination to exaggerate; confusion, by blurring one image into another, leaves only a chaos in which the mind can find nothing to be magnificent, nothing to nourish its fears or doubts, or to act upon in any way" ("On the Supernatural in Poetry," *New Monthly Magazine* 7 [1826]: 150).

42 *The Poems of Jonathan Swift*, ed. Harold Williams, 2d ed. (Oxford, 1958), 2:579.

43 (London, 1723), sig. C1v.

44 Cibber, *Lives of the Poets*, 5:150.

45 4 (1734): 382. Printing regularized.

46 Quoted by Arthur Paul Davis, *Isaac Watts: His Life and Works* (New York, 1943), p. 226.

47 5 (1735): 413.

48 5 (1735): 410.

49 4. 636, 640, 655–56.

50 *On the Poetry of Pope*, 2d ed. (Oxford, 1950), p. 27.

51 *Leviathan* . . . (London, 1651), p. 11 (1. 3).

[52] See Monk, *The Sublime*, p. 24.

[53] *An Essay on the Sublime* (London, 1747), p. 21.

[54] *The Sacred Classics Defended and Illustrated*, p. 5.

[55] 7:241–42 and 305–7.

[56] See E. Hudson Long, "Notes on Sir Richard Blackmore," *Modern Language Notes* 58 (1943): 589.

[57] The relevant portion of the will is printed in the *Monthly Review*, 4 (1751): 508.

[58] See Gerard, *An Essay on Taste*, p. 14.

[59] In *Musae Seatonianae: A Complete Collection of the Cambridge Prize Poems . . .*, 2 vols. (London, 1808). All quotations from Smart's Seatonian poems refer to this edition.

[60] Quoted by Edward G. Ainsworth and Charles E. Noyes, *Christopher Smart: A Biographical and Critical Study*, University of Missouri Studies, Vol. 18, no. 4 (Columbia, Mo., 1943): p. 46.

[61] *Philosophical Enquiry*, ed. Boulton, p. 69.

[62] *Winter Evenings; or, Lucubrations on Life and Letters* (1788), in *Works*, 3:176.

[63] *Winter Evenings*, in *Works*, 3:176.

[64] 19:74.

[65] 34:82.

[66] New Series, 3 (1790): 218.

[67] *Peri Bathous*, ed. Steeves, p. 27.

[68] New Series, 3 (1790): 217.

[69] *Winter Evenings*, in *Works*, 3:175.

[70] *An Essay on the Sublime*, p. 5.

[71] *The Correspondence of Thomas Gray*, ed. Toynbee and Whibley, 1:128.

[72] Translator's preface to *The Resurrection: A Poem*. The poem is included in a volume of Addison's works entitled *Poems on Several Occasions* (London, 1719), published without permission by Edmund Curll.

[73] See Donald F. Bond., ed., *The Spectator*, 1:lxvii–lxix.

[74] In Houyhnhnm land, Gulliver reports, reason strikes with "immediate Conviction" (Swift, *Gulliver's Travels*, in *Prose Works*, ed. Davis et al., 11:267).

[75] See Frederick Staver, " 'Sublime' as Applied to Nature," *Modern Language Notes* 70 (1955): 484–87.

[76] *Philosophical Enquiry*, ed. Boulton, p. 107. The imagination not only "prevents" the reason; it provides a psychic reassurance which reason could not entirely supply. As Tuveson writes, "The imagination, for Addison, serves as a means of reconciling man, with his spiritual needs and his desire to belong to a living universe of purpose and values, with a cosmos that begins to appear alien, impersonal, remote, and menacing" (*The Imagination as a Means of Grace*, p. 97).

[77] *The Background of Thomson's "Seasons"* (Minneapolis, Minn., 1942), p. 7. Ralph Cohen's rigorous study *The Unfolding of "The Seasons"* (Baltimore, Md., 1970) helps to correct the overemphasis upon science.

[78] Ll. 468–69. All quotations from Thomson's poems refer to *The Complete Poetical Works of James Thomson*, ed. J. Logie Robertson (1908; rpt.

Oxford, 1951). All quotations from *The Seasons* refer to the 1746 version. The relationship between the poet's imitative art and God's creative art is discussed by Ralph Cohen in "The Augustan Mode in English Poetry" (pp. 24–25).

79 Preface to *Winter*, in *Eighteenth-Century Critical Essays*, ed. Scott Elledge (Ithaca, N.Y., 1961), 1:406 (hereafter cited as Elledge).

80 Preface to *Winter*, in Elledge, 1:407.

81 "An Account of the Life and Writings of Mr. James Thomson," in *The Works of James Thomson* (London, 1762), 1:iv.

82 "A Paraphrase of Psalm CIV."

83 Ll. 195–201.

84 *Lives of the English Poets*, ed. Hill, 3:299.

85 *The Sublime*, p. 88.

86 C. A. Moore, "Shaftesbury and the Ethical Poets in England, 1700–1760," *PMLA* 31 (1916): 268.

87 Ll. 959–65.

88 *Dionysius Longinus On the Sublime*, p. 56.

89 In Elledge, 1:408.

90 Ll. 897–903.

91 See Louis L. Martz, *The Poetry of Meditation: A Study in English Religious Literature* (1954; rpt. New Haven, Conn., 1965), pp. 25–70.

92 Ll. 904–5.

93 5:203.

94 See John More, *Strictures, Critical and Sentimental, on Thomson's Seasons* (London, 1777), pp. 247–79.

95 In *Dissertations Moral and Critical*, p. 626.

96 In *Dissertations Moral and Critical*, p. 633.

97 *The Art of Discrimination: Thomson's "The Seasons" and the Language of Criticism* (Berkeley, Calif., 1964), pp. 274–75.

98 *Coleridge's Miscellaneous Criticism*, ed. Raysor, p. 438.

99 *An Essay on the Genius and Writings of Pope*, 2:205.

100 Preface to *Poems* (1815), in *Literary Criticism of Wordsworth*, ed. Zall, p. 142.

101 (London, 1767), p. 69.

102 *Literary Hours*, p. 263. See also [Samuel Jackson Pratt], *Observations on the Night Thoughts of Dr. Young* (London, 1776), p. 55.

103 See Isabel St. John Bliss, "Young's *Night Thoughts* in Relation to Contemporary Christian Apologetics," *PMLA* 49 (1934): 37–70; and Phillip Harth, *The Contexts of Dryden's Thought* (Chicago, 1968), pp. 56–94.

104 *Eighteenth Century Background*, p. 108.

105 "Night Sixth," l. 427, in *The Complaint: or Night-Thoughts on Life, Death, & Immortality* (London, 1747), 1:261. This edition of the complete poem does not supply line numbers. These are added from a modern edition, with the original volume and page number noted in parentheses.

106 "Night Fourth," ll. 628–31 (1:155).

107 "Night Fourth," ll. 199–200 (1:130).

108 Ll. 164–68 (2:178).

109 "Illustrations on Sublimity," in *Dissertations Moral and Critical*, p. 638.

110 L. 190 (2:180).

111 Ll. 262–67 (2:184).
112 Ll. 837–39 (2:216).
113 (London, 1759), p. 28.
114 "Night Ninth," l. 1861 (2:272).
115 "Night Seventh," l. 389 (2:23).
116 Form and Frenzy in Swift's "Tale of a Tub" (Ithaca, N.Y., 1970), Chapter Two.
117 An Essay on Man, 2. 19–30.
118 "A Satyr against Mankind," ll. 96–97 (in Poems by John Wilmot, Earl of Rochester, ed. Vivian de Sola Pinto, 2d ed. [Cambridge, Mass., 1964]).
119 Spence, Observations, ed. Osborn, 1:135–36.
120 "Night First," l. 452 (1:31).
121 Guide to Kulcher (1938; rpt. New York, 1968), p. 135.
122 An Essay on the Genius and Writings of Pope, 2:481.

CHAPTER FIVE

1 Essays, Moral and Literary, in Works, 1:147.
2 In Mr. Hervey's Meditations and Contemplations (London, 1764), 2:v.
3 46:467. For a general account of German interest in issues related to the religious sublime, see J. H. Tisch, "Milton and the German Mind in the Eighteenth Century," in Studies in the Eighteenth Century: Papers Presented at the David Nichol Smith Memorial Seminar, ed. R. F. Brissenden (Toronto, 1968), pp. 205–29.
4 Translator's Preface to The Messiah, tr. Joseph Collyer (London, 1763–1769), 1:xii.
5 Translator's Preface to The Messiah, 1:xiii–xiv.
6 "Of Divine Poetry," in The Messiah, tr. Collyer, 1:xxx.
7 "Of Divine Poetry," in The Messiah, tr. Collyer, 1:xxxi, xlvii.
8 "Of Divine Poetry," in The Messiah, tr. Collyer, 1:xxxi, xlvii.
9 Literary Hours, p. 263.
10 The Messiah, tr. Collyer, 2:188.
11 Quoted by the Critical Review 32 (1771): 393.
12 New Series, 9 (1792): 1.
13 New Series, 9 (1792): 2.
14 Calvary (London, 1792), 4. 766–71.
15 Johnsonian Miscellanies, ed. George Birkbeck Hill (Oxford, 1897), 1:284.
16 64 (1787): 321 and 78 (1788): 311.
17 Lectures on the Sacred Poetry of the Hebrews, tr. G. Gregory (London, 1787), 1:348 (hereafter cited as Lectures).
18 Lectures, tr. Gregory, 1:372–74.
19 Lectures, tr. Gregory, 1:376–77.
20 Lectures, tr. Gregory, 1:36. Italics mine.
21 Lectures, tr. Gregory, 1:113.
22 Lectures, tr. Gregory, 1:155.
23 Lectures, tr. Gregory, 1:309.

24 For a discussion of Hebrew poetry and of Lowth's contributions, see Murray Roston, *Prophet and Poet: The Bible and the Growth of Romanticism* (Evanston, Ill., 1965).

25 *Lectures on Rhetoric and Belles Lettres*, 2:385. Although first published in 1783, Blair's lectures had reached final form some twenty years before.

26 *Lectures on Rhetoric and Belles Lettres*, 2:397.

27 *Lectures on Rhetoric and Belles Lettres*, 2:392.

28 *Lectures on Rhetoric and Belles Lettres*, 1:61.

29 *Lectures on Rhetoric and Belles Lettres*, 1:60–61.

30 [Samuel Jackson Pratt], *The Sublime and Beautiful of Scripture* (London, 1777), 2:160.

31 *Lectures on Rhetoric and Belles Lettres*, 1:65.

32 (London, 1763), p. 47 (hereafter cited as *Critical Dissertation*).

33 *Critical Dissertation*, p. 49.

34 *Critical Dissertation*, p. 63.

35 *Philosophical Enquiry*, ed. Boulton, p. 63.

36 *Philosophical Enquiry*, ed. Boulton, p. 60.

37 *Philosophical Enquiry*, ed. Boulton, p. 58.

38 *Lectures on Rhetoric and Belles Lettres*, 1:50.

39 "A Dissertation concerning the Antiquity, &c. of the Poems of Ossian," in *Fingal . . . Together with several other Poems* (London, 1762), p. v.

40 *Critical Dissertation*, p. 36.

41 *Critical Dissertation*, p. 34.

42 *Critical Dissertation*, p. 39.

43 In *Fingal*, p. 199.

44 "Essay, Supplementary to the Preface" (1815), in *Literary Criticism of Wordsworth*, ed. Zall, p. 178.

45 *Critical Dissertation*, p. 40.

46 In *The Oxford English Prize Essays* (Oxford, 1836), 1:269.

47 *Letters on Chivalry and Romance* (London, 1762), p. 60.

48 Quoted by Murray Roston, *Prophet and Poet*, p. 148.

49 "Reason in Madness: Christopher Smart's Poetic Development," *Southern Humanities Review* 4 (1970): 60.

50 From Smart's advertisement of the first edition of *A Song to David*, quoted by Robert Brittain, ed., *Poems by Christopher Smart* (Princeton, N.J., 1950), p. 294. All quotations from *A Song to David* refer to this edition.

51 Stanza 50.

52 15 (1763): 324.

53 Quoted by Sophia B. Blaydes, *Christopher Smart as a Poet of His Time: A Re-Appraisal*, Studies in English Literature, Vol. 28 (The Hague, 1966), p. 21.

54 *Jubilate Agno*, ed. W. H. Bond (London, 1954), B1 30. All quotations from *Jubilate Agno* refer to this edition and are identified by Bond's notation of fragment and line number.

55 Robert Browning in his *Parleyings with Certain People of Importance in Their Day* (1887) suggests that the poem has a cathedral-like structure; Raymond D. Havens ("The Structure of Smart's Song to David," *Review of English Studies* 14 [1938]: 178–82) proposed a numerical structure based

upon units of three and seven; and, in a paper delivered at the SAMLA Conference (Washington, D.C., 1970), Robert D. Saltz proposed a bi-partite structure stressing David's role as "type" of Christ. These strike me as the most rational accounts, and I see no reason why all three structures cannot be mutually reinforcing.

56 *Prophet and Poet,* p. 148.

57 *A Song to David,* stanza 41, lines 5–6.

58 *A Song to David,* stanzas 76–77.

59 *Lectures on Oratory and Criticism,* p. 159.

60 *On Christian Doctrine,* tr. D. W. Robertson, Jr. (Indianapolis, Ind., 1958), pp. 143–44 (4. 18. 35). The justification for different styles, Augustine insists, depends not on the magnitude of the subject but upon the purpose of the oration: thus the plain style is for teaching, the middle for praise, the great for persuasion.

61 [Annotations to Sir Joshua Reynolds's Discourses], in *Poetry and Prose of William Blake,* ed. Geoffrey Keynes (New York, 1927), p. 970. This edition, while not the most recent or textually the most accurate, is the most convenient for general purposes. Blake's annotations appear in the first volume of the three-volume *Works of Sir Joshua Reynolds* (1798), edited by Edmond Malone.

62 *Discourses on Art,* ed. Stephen O. Mitchell (Indianapolis, Ind., 1965), p. 29; [Annotations to Reynolds's Discourses], in *Poetry and Prose,* ed. Keynes, p. 988.

63 "On the Sublime," in *Philosophical Works,* p. 346.

64 *The Critique of Judgment* (1790), tr. J. H. Bernard, 2d ed. (London, 1914), p. 29 (1. 1. 28).

65 (Edinburgh, 1790), p. 62.

66 [A Vision of the Last Judgment], in *Poetry and Prose,* ed. Keynes, p. 844.

67 [A Vision of the Last Judgment], in *Poetry and Prose,* ed. Keynes, p. 844.

68 In *Poetry and Prose,* ed. Keynes, p. 1076.

69 "The Old & New Testaments," he wrote, "are the Great Code of Art" ([The Laocoon Group], in *Poetry and Prose,* ed. Keynes, p. 766).

70 Preface to *Milton,* in *Poetry and Prose,* ed. Keynes, p. 464.

71 [A Vision of the Last Judgment], in *Poetry and Prose,* ed. Keynes, pp. 828–29.

72 In *The Diary of Henry Crabb Robinson: An Abridgement,* ed. Derek Hudson (New York, 1967), p. 87.

73 In *Literary Criticism of Wordsworth,* ed. Zall, p. 29.

74 "Essay, Supplementary to the Preface," in *Literary Criticism of Wordsworth,* ed. Zall, p. 162.

75 "Essay, Supplementary to the Preface," in *Literary Criticism of Wordsworth,* ed. Zall, p. 163.

76 "Essay, Supplementary to the Preface," in *Literary Criticism of Wordsworth,* ed. Zall, pp. 163–64.

77 *Coleridge's Miscellaneous Criticism,* ed. Raysor, p. 403.

78 *Imagination and Fancy: Complementary Modes in the Poetry of Wordsworth* (Lincoln, Nebr., 1966), p. 147.

79 "Coleridge on the Sublime," in *Wordsworth and Coleridge: Studies*

in Honor of George McLean Harper, ed. Earl Leslie Griggs (Princeton, N.J., 1939), p. 206.

80 Coleridge's Miscellaneous Criticism, ed. Raysor, p. 412.

81 Unpublished Letters of Samuel Taylor Coleridge, ed. Earl Leslie Griggs (New Haven, Conn., 1933), 1:117.

82 In Literary Criticism of Wordsworth, ed. Zall, p. 150.

83 Ll. 93–102. Except where noted, all quotations from Wordsworth's verse refer to The Poetical Works of Wordsworth, ed. E. de Selincourt, 5 vols. (Oxford, 1940–1949).

84 ABC of Reading (New York, 1960), p. 77.

85 Ll. 14–16, in The Complete Poetical Works of Samuel Taylor Coleridge, ed. Ernest Hartley Coleridge, 2 vols. (Oxford, 1912).

86 Unpublished Letters of Coleridge, ed. Griggs, 2:261.

87 The Prelude (1850 ed.), 6. 523–28. All quotations are from The Prelude, ed. Ernest de Selincourt and Helen Darbishire, 2d ed. (Oxford, 1959).

88 "Wordsworth on the Sublime: The Quest for Interfusion," Studies in English Literature 7 (1967): 612.

89 The Prelude, 6. 624–26.

90 The Prelude, 6. 639.

91 "Essay, Supplementary to the Preface," in Literary Criticism of Wordsworth, ed. Zall, p. 185.

92 "Essay, Supplementary to the Preface," in Literary Criticism of Wordsworth, ed. Zall, p. 185.

93 The Prelude, 14. 444.

94 New Series, 24 (1798): 201.

95 Biographia Literaria, ed. J. Shawcross (1907; rpt. Oxford, 1954), 2:6.

96 Biographia Literaria, ed. Shawcross, 2:6.

97 Ed. Shawcross, 2:5.

98 In Literary Criticism of Wordsworth, ed. Zall, p. 20.

99 Ll. 37–42.

CHAPTER SIX

1 Journal of Ecclesiastical History 3 (1952): 159–90.

2 "Augustinianism and Empiricism: A Note on Eighteenth-Century English Intellectual History," Eighteenth-Century Studies 1 (1967–1968): 33–68.

3 "Augustan or Augustinian? More Demythologizing Needed?" Eighteenth-Century Studies 2 (1968–1969): 291–92. Punctuation altered slightly.

4 Poetry of Grace: Reformation Themes and Structures in English Seventeenth-Century Poetry (New Haven, Conn., 1970).

5 A brief list of studies would include Martin C. Battestin, The Moral Basis of Fielding's Art (Middletown, Conn., 1959); Phillip Harth, Swift and Anglican Rationalism (Chicago, 1961); Maurice Quinlan, Samuel Johnson: A Layman's Religion (Madison, Wis., 1964); J. Paul Hunter, The Reluctant Pilgrim: Defoe's Emblematic Method and Quest for Form (Baltimore, Md., 1966); Thomas E. Maresca, Pope's Horatian Poems (Columbus, Ohio, 1966); Phillip Harth, The Contexts of Dryden's Thought

(Chicago, 1968); Aubrey Williams, "Poetical Justice, The Contrivances of Fortune, and the Works of William Congreve," *English Literary History* 35 (1968): 540–65; Ralph Cohen, *The Unfolding of "The Seasons"* (Baltimore, Md., 1970). Various articles and studies by Earl Wasserman might be added to those above; in fact, the relevance of Christianity to an interpretation of eighteenth-century literature has been widely recognized by scholars in the last decade.

6 *Literary Criticism: A Short History* (New York, 1957), p. 323.

7 *The Eighteenth-Century Pulpit: A Study of the Sermons of Butler, Berkeley, Secker, Sterne, Whitefield and Wesley* (Oxford, 1969), p. 10.

8 "Diary: How to Improve the World (You Will Only Make Matters Worse) Continued 1970–71," *New Literary History* 3 (1971–1972): 210.

9 Preface to *Robinson Crusoe* (1719), ed. James Sutherland (Boston, Mass., 1968), p. 3.

10 John H. Overton and Frederic Relton, *The English Church from the Accession of George I. to the End of the Eighteenth Century* (1906; rpt. New York, 1967), p. 1. See also G.R. Cragg's discussion of "rationalism" and "stability" (*The Church and the Age of Reason, 1648–1798* [1960; rpt. Baltimore, Md., 1966], pp. 11–14).

11 Swift's career and opinions as a churchman are discussed by Louis A. Landa, *Swift and the Church of Ireland* (Oxford, 1954).

12 *The English Church*, p. 1. "Between the primacies of Sheldon and Secker . . . the church had to face the full and multifarious assault of a theological revolution, comprising the impact of science and philosophy, the vogue of Deism and natural religion and the revival of Arianism and Socinianism" (Norman Sykes, *From Sheldon to Secker: Aspects of English Church History, 1660–1768* [Cambridge, Eng., 1959], pp. 218–19). Like many revolutions in theology, this one was fought mainly with the pen.

13 19 (1749): 70–74.

14 *The Medium Is the Massage: An Inventory of Effects* (New York, 1967), p. 8. See also McLuhan's *The Gutenberg Galaxy: The Making of Typographic Man* (Toronto, 1962).

15 Quoted by Horton Davies, *Worship and Theology in England from Watts and Wesley to Maurice, 1690–1850* (Princeton, N.J., 1961), p. 171.

16 *Worship and Theology*, p. 171.

17 "Martinus Scriblerus, of the Poem," in *The Dunciad* (1729 ed.). In commenting upon some of the poems contained in *Letters between the Honorable Andrew Erskin and James Boswell, Esq.* (1763) the *Critical Review* called them "the cheapest and most nauseous drugs of this press-surfeited age and country" (quoted by Frederick A. Pottle, ed., *Boswell's London Journal, 1762–1763* [New Haven, Conn., 1950], p. 271, n. 2).

18 Le Clerc's defense of Tillotson's writings is appended to Francis Hutchinson's *The Life of the Most Reverend Father in God John Tillotson, Archbishop of Canterbury* (London, 1717), p. 3.

19 *Religio Laici* (1682), ll 400–408.

20 *A Project for the Advancement of Religion* (1709), in *Prose Works*, ed. Davis et al., 2:60–61.

21 *A Tale of a Tub*, ed. A. C. Guthkelch and D. Nichol Smith, 2d ed. (Oxford, 1958), p. 70.

²² *Lives of the English Poets*, ed. Hill, 1:49–50. Although many readers would prefer that citations mention the particular "Life" being quoted, I have decided to omit such information in the interests of reducing the number of footnotes and will hereafter provide volume and page references in parentheses within the text. The "Lives" cited in this section are those of Cowley, Denham, Milton, Waller, and Young.

²³ John D. Boyd, S.J., *The Function of Mimesis and Its Decline* (Cambridge, Mass., 1968), p. 295.

²⁴ Donald Greene has demonstrated that pictorialism also plays a distinctive role in Johnson's prose style (" 'Pictures to the Mind': Johnson and Imagery," in *Johnson, Boswell and Their Circle: Essays Presented to Lawrence Fitzroy Powell* [Oxford, 1965], pp. 137–58).

²⁵ Quoted by Ralph Cohen, *The Art of Discrimination*, pp. 160–61.

²⁶ *Samuel Johnson's Literary Criticism* (1952; rpt. Chicago, 1967), p. 68.

²⁷ "Essay, Supplementary to the Preface," in *Literary Criticism of Wordsworth*, ed. Zall, p. 160.

²⁸ *Religion and Literature*, p. 186.

²⁹ In *The Works of George Herbert*, ed. F. E. Hutchinson (Oxford, 1941).

³⁰ See Stanley Eugene Fish, *Surprised by Sin: The Reader in Paradise Lost* (New York, 1967).

³¹ Ed. Boulton, p. 172.

³² Lawrence Lipking, *The Ordering of the Arts in Eighteenth-Century England* (Princeton, N.J., 1970), p. 116. See also Jean H. Hagstrum, *The Sister Arts: The Tradition of Literary Pictorialism and English Poetry from Dryden to Gray* (Chicago, 1958).

³³ William H. Halewood, " 'The Reach of Art' in Augustan Poetic Theory," in *Studies in Criticism and Aesthetics, 1660–1800: Essays in Honor of Samuel Holt Monk*, ed. Howard Anderson and John S. Shea (Minneapolis, Minn., 1967), pp. 192–212. Halewood explains that his essay attempts to show "that the analogy with painting had a clandestine usefulness to poetry in resisting its danger from a too narrowly understood mimetic purpose, in revising its conception of its nature and function, and, incidentally, in raising its self-esteem" (p. 194).

³⁴ *Essays on the Nature and Principles of Taste*, pp. 91–92. James Harris in his *Three Treatises* (1744) argues Alison's position some fifty years earlier, asserting that poetry can combine both the visual appeal of painting and the affective power of music (see Robert Marsh, *Four Dialectical Theories of Poetry: An Aspect of English Neoclassical Criticism* [Chicago, 1965], pp. 139–43).

³⁵ *The Mirror and the Lamp: Romantic Theory and the Critical Tradition* (1953; rpt. New York, 1958), pp. 50–51 and 91–94.

³⁶ I have seen only the second and fourth editions of the translation, and the frontispiece to which I refer in the following analysis appears in the fourth edition; the second edition contains an entirely different illustration. The copy of the fourth edition which I have used appears in Addison's *Poems on Several Occasions* (London, 1719), an unauthorized collection published by Curll.

³⁷ *An Essay on Criticism*, ll. 478–93. It is pertinent that Pope should couch his discussion of language in the metaphor of painting.

[38] *The Prelude*, 5. 595–605. I quote from the standard version of 1850.

[39] The line, from Roscommon's *Essay on Translated Verse* (1684), is quoted by Pope in a note the 1729 edition of *The Dunciad* (2. 278), where he applies it directly to Dennis.

[40] *The Subtler Language: Critical Readings of Neoclassic and Romantic Poems* (Baltimore, Md., 1959). Wasserman's thesis, much oversimplified, is that Romantic poets developed a language of personal symbolism in response to the collapse of a public language based upon general consensus.

Index

Abrams, M. H., 225
Addison, Joseph, 188, 229;
comments on *Robinson Crusoe*,
131–32; confusion on simplicity,
89–90; on connection of nature
and art, 6; criticism of, by
Tuveson, 245n; criticism of
Milton, 97; criticism of
Paradise Lost, 66–67; discusses
greatness, 134–35; effect of
Longinus on his criticism of
Paradise Lost, 32; interpreting
Locke, 123, 124; lay sermons, 200;
links reason and imagination to
the sublime, 131–38; on Milton's
sublimity, 95; on passion and
aesthetics, 35. Works: *Campaign,
The*, 113; *Resurrection, The*,
226–28; "The Spacious
Firmament on High," 135–36,
137
Akenside, Mark, 236n
Alison, Archibald, 224–25, 233n;
*Essays on the Nature and
Principles of Taste*, 181–82
Ancients and Moderns, 58–59
Arianism, 251n
Aristotle, 133
Arthos, John, 233n
Art poetique (Boileau), 43
Associationalism, 181
Augustinian Christianity, 198

Baillie, John, 125, 130
Bard, The (Gray), 7
Beattie, James, 33–34, 97, 148;
"Illustrations on Sublimity," 144
Benlowes, Edward, 22
Biographia Literaria (Coleridge),
194
Blackmore, Sir Richard, 48, 82–84,
85, 110–11; *Creation, The*, 83

Blackwall, Anthony, 90, 125
Blair, Hugh, 91–92, 93; on the
casting of *Paradise Lost*, 96;
champion of Ossian, 222;
criticism of Milton, 93; praise of
Addison, 113; sacred odes, 235n.
Works: *Critical Dissertation on
the Poems of Ossian*, 164–69;
*Lectures on Rhetoric and Belles
Lettres*, 164–66
Blair, Robert, *Grave, The*, 184
Blake, William, 182, 196; on detail
in the sublime, 180; graphics, 228;
note on the text, 249n; "prophetic
books," 186. Works: "The
Lamb," 184, 185; *Tyger, The*,
184–86
Blank verse. See Dennis, John
Bodmer, Johann, 157
Boileau-Despreaux, Nicolas, 27, 74,
76, 156; citing Hermogenes, 54;
limiting use of the term sublime,
36–37; his preface to Longinus,
36–39; stressing perception in the
sublime, 180; his translation of
Longinus, 28–39; on transport,
127
Boswell, James, 199n
Bouhours, Father, 35
Boyse, Samuel, 125, 126
Bray, René, 39
Brooks, Cleanth, 199
Buckingham, George Villiers, 41
Burke, Edmund, 74, 188;
characterizing Death in *Paradise
Lost*, 97; discussing sublimity and
power, 127; influence on Blair,
165, 166; links imagination and
reason to sublime, 136;
Philosophical Enquiry, 188, 222;
poetic obscurity, 222; terror and
the sublime, 102–3

Dryden, John, 40, 45, 58, 205;
criticism of, by Johnson, 237n;
criticism of Longinus, 28–29;
favorably compares Milton to
Virgil, 238n; on images, 35,
236n; concerning the marvelous,
41–42; print creating Dissenters,
207; praises Dennis, 239n
Du Bartas, Guillaume de Salluste,
22–24, 39
Dunciad, The (Pope), 111, 122,
128, 203-5
Duff, William, 145

"Essay, Supplementary to the
Preface" (Wordsworth), 187
Essay of Dramatic Poesy (Dryden),
42
Essay on Criticism, An (Pope),
111, 217, 229
Essay on Man, An (Pope), 31, 151,
152, 206, 218, 229
Essay on Original Genius (Duff),
145
Essay on the Conflagration
(Catherall), 117
Essays on the Nature and Principles
of Taste (Alison), 181–82

Farrer, John, 114
Felton, Henry, 94
Fiat lux (Genesis 1:3), 37–38
Fowler, Alastair, 13
Foxton, James, 115
Fuseli, Henri, 228

Gardner, Helen, 214
Gentleman's Magazine, 99, 121,
125, 202
Gerard, Alexander, 99, 101
German religious sublimity, 247n
Gessner, Salomon, 157
Gothic machinery, 169–70
Gothic novel, 190
Grave, The (Blair), 184
Gray, Thomas, 45, 131; Bard, The,
7
Greene, Donald, 198

Grounds of Criticism in Poetry
(Dennis), 14
Guardian, 117, 202

Halewood, William H., 198
Hartley, David, 181
Herbert, George, 214
Hermogenes. See Dennis, John
Hervey, James, 156
Hibernicus's Letters, 110
Hill, Aaron, 84–85, 87–88, 119, 148
Hobbes, Thomas, 22, 24–26, 123,
181
Hogarth, William, 228
Homer, 183
Hooker, Edward Niles, 238n
Hooker, Richard, 209
Horace, 34, 40, 222
Horae Lyricae (Watts), 106-7
Hume, David, 31
Humphrey, A. R., 197
Husbands, John, 86, 90, 109–10
"Hymn." See Seasons, The
"The Hymn before Sunrise in the
Vale of Chamouni" (Coleridge),
190
Hymns and Spiritual Songs
(Watts), 105-7

"Illustrations on Sublimity"
(Beattie), 144

Jacob, Giles, 25, 47, 99
Je ne sais quoi. See Bouhours, Father
Johnson, Samuel, 92, 118, 199, 225;
comments on infidels, 114; criti-
cism of Longinus, 28; criticism of
Milton, 93, 95; criticism of
religious poetry, 159, 209–21;
criticism of Thomson, 140; on
definitions, 9–10; "Life of Addi-
son," 108; "Life of Cowley," 210;
"Life of Denham," 211; opposi-
tion to le merveilleux chrétien,
43, 237n; praise of Addison, 113.
Works: Dictionary of the English
Language, 107–8, 211, 212; Lives
of the English Poets, The, 220;
Rasselas, 221

This book has been set in
W. A. Dwiggins' Electra with Electra Oblique.
The display is Hermann Zapf's Palatino.

Composition & printing by
Heritage Printers, Inc. Binding by
The C. J. Krehbiel Co.

Design by Jonathan Greene